Everybody Knew

Everybody Knew

A Boy. Two Brothers.
A Stolen Childhood.

MICHAEL CLEMENGER

EBURY
PRESS

5 7 9 10 8 6

Published in 2012 by Ebury Press, an imprint of Ebury Publishing
A Random House Group company
First published in Ireland by O'Brien Press with the title
Holy Terrors in 2009

The Random House Group Limited Reg. No. 954009

Addresses for companies within the Random House Group can be
found at www.randomhouse.co.uk

A CIP catalogue record for this book is available from
the British Library

ISBN 9780091946692

To buy books by your favourite authors and register for offers visit
www.randomhouse.co.uk

The Random House Group Limited supports The Forest Stewardship
Council (FSC®), the leading international forest certification organisation.
Our books carrying the FSC label are printed on FSC® certified paper.
FSC is the only forest certification scheme endorsed by the leading
environmental organisations, including Greenpeace. Our
paper procurement policy can be found at
www.randomhouse.co.uk/environment

Printed and bound in Great Britain by Clays Ltd, St Ives PLC

This book is dedicated to all children who were incarcerated during the period 1871 to 1970 at St Joseph's Industrial School, Tralee, Co. Kerry

Contents

Author's Note

The names of certain people mentioned in the book, including those of some family members, have been changed for the privacy and protection of the individuals concerned. The names of people quoted in published documents remain unchanged, as do those with public responsibility for aspects covered by the book. Some people were advised that they were named in the book at the draft stage and given the opportunity to comment on this before publication.

PART ONE

'Monoboy'

Earliest Memories

I WAS BORN on 1 November 1950, All Saints Day. It's generally considered a lucky day to be born, but an exception must have been made in my case. Soon after my birth I was baptised in a nearby parish to avoid embarrassing the neighbours and then quickly passed on to the Sisters of Charity, St Philomena's Home in Stillorgan, Co. Dublin

My earliest memory is of being locked in a big room with pictures of Jesus and His mother Mary hanging on the walls. I was afraid because they kept looking at me. As soon as the door opened I bolted out and ran down a long corridor. From other rooms nuns, in various stages of dress, came running out to try and catch me. Eventually I was caught at the end of the corridor and safely returned to my room where the door was locked once more.

I have vague memories of being toilet trained, sitting on a yellow potty and looking up at a clear blue sky. I played with the occasional passing white cloud, turning them into animals in my mind's eye.

Jimmy was my best friend. He was a lovely, fair-haired boy. We did everything together. By day we couldn't be parted in the playground, classroom, refectory or chapel, while at night he slept in the bed next to mine. I remember learning our letters and multiplication tables side by side. One time, when we were about four years old, all the windows were covered with blankets after Jimmy and I, along with some other boys, came down with the mumps.

My surname fascinated the nuns because they had great difficulty pronouncing it in class. To this day I cannot recall the name of a single nun who cared for me in St Philomena's. Collectively they treated me in a very impersonal way with little outward signs of love, tenderness or kindness. I found them to be very strict and distant. They certainly talked a lot about the love of Jesus and His mother Mary, but that's about it. They endeavoured more in spiritual things, particularly in the chapel. I often noticed that their countenances only lit up when they were praying. Only then could you be assured of a half smile if you caught their eye. Prayer for them was the essence of their being, and they saw it as their sacred duty to ensure that I learned my prayers with similar enthusiasm. Accordingly, they pinned pictures of Jesus and Mary at the top of my bed and encouraged me to kiss them before I went to sleep. For me, however, a warm smile from Jimmy would suffice to put me to sleep at night.

I have no memory of the nuns ever reading me a bedtime story, tucking me into bed or giving me a hug.

There was no physical contact, save in punishment. To me, they seemed always too busy praying to bother with my emotional development in those early years. Anyway I had Jimmy who I loved more than Jesus and Mary together, whatever that meant.

One evening, as I was leaving the chapel after benediction, I asked the Reverend Mother what a mother was. My question seemed to cause her some anxiety and she quickly brushed me along the corridor to supper. Indignantly I promised myself that I would never ask her another question again. A few days later a priest came into the classroom and we all stood up. He announced to us with great solemnity that we would soon be making our First Holy Communion. It meant nothing to me except that the image of Jesus hanging on the wall would soon be living in my belly.

He, Jesus, would be coming into us, the priest said, because He loved us madly unto death. I wanted to ask him what death was, but the class Sister glared at me so I thought better of it. I always wanted to ask questions even at that age. Furthermore, the priest told us, children – yes, even us – were very special in the eyes of God and his son, Jesus, pointing to the crucifix hanging on the wall. The interchange between the words Jesus and God confused me and that was before I'd heard, or understood, the idea of the Holy Ghost. *Surely*, I thought, *Jesus couldn't love Jimmy more than I did?* That love was a very strong and intense one and not even

Jesus could get between us. Sometimes I felt Jimmy staring at me when I was not looking. This made me feel very good.

On Visit Days, when Jimmy had a visitor, I always went along with him. I never had visitors of my own, and Jimmy refused to see his by himself. Despite this he was always upset when his visitors had left. His most frequent one was a beautiful, tall woman with a bun in her hair and white beads hanging from her neck. I never understood her relationship to Jimmy and he was quite hesitant with her. She always brought sweets. I would play with some of them on the floor as Jimmy sat uncomfortably, in a tight embrace, on her lap. He remained calm as long as he could see me.

One evening, in the yard, the Reverend Mother called Jimmy to her. The yard sister gave me some sweets, which had never happened before, and told me to stay beside her. Jimmy was going on a visit, so I put some of the sweets into my pocket to give him later. He smiled and waved to me as he walked off with the head nun. In the meantime I settled down to eat my few sweets. At supper time I waited for Jimmy to give him his small share of the toffees. To my surprise there were three sisters and the Reverend Mother on duty that evening. With no sign of Jimmy I looked at the Reverend Mother for answers. She approached; her cold eyes fixed on me while she told me abruptly that Jimmy was gone away and wouldn't be coming back ever again.

The other sisters hovered nearby ready to grab me should I react badly to the news. My initial reaction was shock. For a few minutes I couldn't breathe, nor move. Then I began to cry.

The suddenness of Jimmy's loss and the cold, callous indifference adopted by the Reverend Mother engendered in me such a rage that it frightened even me. I lunged at her, throwing Jimmy's sweets at her, kicking and scratching at her hands and face. Nuns tried to grab me, but I ran under a table. One of the sisters tried to get me out using a sweeping brush. She landed a blow on the top of my head, which started to bleed slightly. Eventually I was unceremoniously dragged out from under the table and carried to a side room, the door was closed and the key turned in the lock. Even here there were pictures of Jesus and Mary, still looking down on me. I glanced up at them with equal bouts of anger, rage and despair in turn.

As I sat on the floor a thousand questions filled my mind. Chiefly I wanted to know why Jimmy was taken away while I had been left behind. Could we not have gone together? I fretted about how scared Jimmy would be without me, and imagined him crying too. Jesus and Mary failed to comfort me and I placed little store in what the nuns had told us, that Jesus had a special love for little children. To me it was no more than a nursery rhyme. (Perhaps my doubts about Jesus were sown then; they continue to plague me even now.) Finally I thought to myself that perhaps it was something I did that caused Jimmy to be sent away. I never got over his loss and cried for weeks after he left, but mostly inside.

The Reverend Mother said that in time I would forget about Jimmy, but she was wrong. While I became bitterly resigned to the fact that he was gone, the hurt I felt inside changed me forever. I was never so innocent again and became circumspect in my feelings. Other friends came into my life, but it was never the same. I resolved never to let anybody get so emotionally close to me again.

The tears still flow as I write, fifty years later. I never did forget Jimmy and I sincerely hope that life was good to him.

With the loss of Jimmy I also lost a lot of my innocence and sense of security. I withdrew into myself, feeling confused and frightened. The nuns were cold and insensitive, showing little understanding or concern about the emotional impact the separation from Jimmy would have on me. Therefore, I was left to cope alone as best I could. Their prayers continued around me happily, oblivious to how I was dealing with my grief.

Fortunately for me I discovered books, and they became my new best friends. I cradled them in my arms, carefully studying the pictures to help me understand the words. Books provided me with the consolation that the nuns failed to. I became totally preoccupied with them and escaped between their covers whenever I could.

Books offered me the possibility of a new and better tomorrow.

*

My First Holy Communion day was fast approaching, but my heart wasn't really in it. For weeks beforehand the Reverend Mother worked hard to ensure that I knew the thin, green catechism book inside out. I learned all the answers without any understanding. She seemed to know this, but didn't care as long as I didn't let her down while being questioned by the priest: Who is God? Who made the world? Who was Our Blessed Lady? What is sin? Why is confession important before receiving a good Communion? I fed him all the right answers. The Reverend Mother looked mighty relieved when the priest was finished with me.

All the boys passed and the Reverend Mother informed us that we would be making our First Holy Communion in the month of May 1958. May, she added, with a sweet smile, was a special month devoted to our Blessed Lady. As if I cared. I must have looked unimpressed, because she suddenly shouted across the room.

'Clemenger, don't give me the dirty eye!'

We both agreed to go back to our respective corners for the moment, but neither of us gave an inch. There were to be no more tears shed in front of her, rather a mask of defiance and loathing. I was disinclined to let her forget how I felt over the loss of Jimmy. I was beginning to grow a steel spine, which would help me survive the much worse that was to come.

To make a good Holy Communion we had to be in a state of grace, and that meant making a good confession. As far as I was concerned the experience of the confession was all a game. I loved to run in and out of the confessional when I was in the chapel. The black box had a sense of danger and intrigue about it. In addition my bold behaviour annoyed the Reverend Mother, which is why I persisted in this habit. It was worth the slaps on the back of my legs to see the Reverend Mother lose her temper. Afterwards I would have to confess to the sin of wilful disobedience to the priest. Sometimes I made up sins and exaggerated the severity to try to shock the priest. I don't think he was very amused and would give me one of his glances of disapproval. The idea of confessing to a priest in a dark box, with a tiny light shining on his face, amused me. I never gave much thought to how Jesus was feeling about me at the time.

When the day finally arrived I was woken early to be washed and scrubbed by the sisters. Next I was lined up and inspected for cleanliness by the Reverend Mother before being introduced to my new suit for the great event: completely white with matching ankle socks, and black shoes that were a little too small for me. With my hair combed and a badge pinned to my jacket lapel I was ready for the chapel. I complained that I was hungry, but the Reverend Mother told me that I had to be

fasting from the midnight before and would get breakfast after Mass.

'Besides, you'll be full up after receiving Baby Jesus.'

I wondered about this, but thought better of asking
any dangerous questions. There were about a dozen of
us making our First Holy Communion on that day.

Just before the Mass I was given a new prayer book –
white cover with beautiful coloured pictures, coupled
with a sparkling set of blue rosary beads. The priest
came over and wished us the best of luck, reminding us
to show respect for Holy Jesus, who would soon be
living within us. Mass commenced with the singing of
hymns by the nuns' choir. After the consecration the
Reverend Mother ushered us up to the altar rails. For
some reason Jimmy came into my mind and I became
preoccupied. So much so, I didn't fully notice the priest
coming towards me with the outstretched host to be
placed on my tongue. To my horror I pulled my tongue
in at the wrong moment and watched the Sacred Host
fall to the floor. Fear gripped me. I dreaded to think of
what the Reverend Mother was thinking – all her good
work had gone up in smoke.

I imagined Jesus lying in a pool of blood on the floor
and everyone looking at me in horror. Perhaps the most
embarrassed of all was the altar boy who was holding the
paten under my chin. He had failed to catch the host as
it fell. I just wanted the ground to open up and swallow
me. *Oh, that Clemenger boy*, I could hear the Reverend

Mother say in my mind. The priest walked slowly back up the steps to the altar and fetched a small bowl of water and a towel. Returning, he reverently knelt down to retrieve the fallen Jesus, whereupon he kissed the host and swallowed it. Then he washed the spot where Jesus fell, and kissed it. When he made a second attempt to give me Holy Communion he was much more careful. I didn't think he would offer it to me again after what had happened. I opened my mouth and he placed the host right onto the back of my tongue, closing my lower jaw quickly with his hand. The host attached itself firmly to the roof of my thoroughly dry mouth. I tried to chew it but it broke into pieces.

My First Holy Communion had been a disaster and I didn't think that Jesus would be very pleased with me. Nothing was said to me by the Reverend Mother, though she studiously avoided me for the remainder of the day. In the evening my white suit was taken off me and placed neatly in a brown box. I hoped that the next wearer would have better luck.

St Joseph's Industrial School,
Tralee, Co. Kerry, 18 August 1959

WE WERE ASSEMBLED in the refectory after breakfast and told that the Reverend Mother wanted to talk to each of us individually. By the time it was my turn to be brought into her office I had watched a stream of boys come out crying and distressed. Gazing coldly at me, the Reverend Mother informed me that, because I had no parents and was an orphan, I was to be transferred to St Joseph's Industrial School in Tralee, County Kerry.

I made no response, determined to show her no tears nor signs of weakness, and left her office pondering what the word 'parents' meant, along with my new official label of 'orphan'. The Reverend Mother showed us on a map where Kerry was in relation to Dublin. It seemed a long way away and we would have to get there by train, which delighted some of the boys.

On the appointed day of departure we were lined up in the driveway of St Philomena's for an inspection by our new minders. I was shocked when I saw two big men dressed in black, walking towards us. They looked like priests, but the Reverend Mother introduced them as Christian Brothers. They differed only in the size of their dog collars, which were half the size of a priest's collar. The lead Brother appeared very businesslike and confident as he stood next to the Reverend Mother. They looked like giants to me and immediately struck terror into the hearts of us boys. The lead Brother introduced himself as Brother Price, telling us we were to call him 'sir' at all times.

He was a big man with piercing eyes who was obviously used to giving orders and having them obeyed instantly. Passing up and down the two rows of boys he peered at us in quite a menacing fashion. If it was his intention to frighten and instil the fear of God in all assembled, he achieved his goal. When he passed me I diverted my eyes towards my shoes. After a few words with the Reverend Mother he approached me and asked my name.

'Michael Clemenger,' I replied nervously without daring to look up.

'Very well, Michael, I am Brother Price. Can you repeat it for me, Michael?'

'Brother Price, sir.'

With that he touched my face with his fingers and half smiled as I recoiled from him. I was filled with fear and felt distinctly uncomfortable especially as he had not asked any other boy a single question.

With a wave of his hand a large bus drove up the

avenue and Brother Price told us to say our goodbyes. Most of the boys were crying; some were hugged by the nuns who did their best to reassure them. For myself I made no attempt to show any emotion. I did notice, however, Brother Price talking very intently to the Reverend Mother and looking directly at me. A large brown envelope and some letters were handed over to him, which he passed on to the other Brother. As our names were called we got on the bus. Mine was called out last. The Reverend Mother ran her fingers through my hair as I made my way up the steps. I ignored her and refused to look back. On the way to the station, Brother Price, in a loud voice, warned us against running up and down the train or talking to strangers. We were to be quiet and behave ourselves. Throughout the commotion the other Brother said nothing.

At the platform a conductor showed us onto the train. We had a carriage to ourselves. Brother Price pulled me aside and told me to wait. When everybody else was seated he sat down and placed me firmly on his knee, holding me very close to him, in a way that I had never experienced before. Nervously I looked out of the carriage window. He never let go of me once throughout the entire journey. His preoccupation with me, which made me a little uncomfortable, caused him to ignore the other boys tearing up and down the train, shouting at the tops of their voices and throwing pennies out of the windows. They had a great time all the way to Kerry while I sat on Brother Price's knee feeling miserable. Occasionally the other Brother would reprimand the other boys but they paid no attention.

Eventually, in the late afternoon, the train arrived in Tralee. The other passengers hurried off the train in different directions. Taxis brought us from the railway station to St Joseph's. Nothing could have prepared me for the shock and panic I felt when I first laid eyes on the school. It was a grim sight. The building looked like a castle with a million windows, and was surrounded by a very high wall and lots of trees. I thought to myself that I must have done something very bad to end up here. You could almost smell the fear in the boys when the taxis pulled up outside the door. Nobody was laughing now as we nervously got out of the cars. My feet didn't touch the ground, however, as I found myself suddenly sitting on the shoulders of Brother Price.

We were met by an older Brother who was the superior of the school. He was smiling and spoke pleasantly to us. On seeing him, Brother Price took me off his shoulders and let me stand on my own two feet. It was good to be free of him, if only for a while. We were brought to the refectory, a large, spacious room with lots of tables and chairs, where tea and bread was served to us. I ate mine very quickly and was surprised to be given a second portion from Brother Price. There was no such thing as seconds in St Philomena's, or at St Joseph's either as it transpired.

During the tea, four or five other Brothers came past, eyeing us up. One Brother in particular seemed to cause a stir in Brother Price. I sensed hostility between them. This Brother introduced himself to me as Brother Roberts. He was older than Brother Price, walked slowly, was slightly bent over, but he had a winning smile. I didn't feel afraid of him at that moment. He asked me my name.

'Michael Clemenger, sir.'

'That's a lovely name.'

I don't remember what else he said, but his being near me made Brother Price very uncomfortable indeed, which pleased me. They did not speak to one another, but both sat close to me. I alternated between smiling at Brother Roberts and looking anxiously at Brother Price.

When tea was finished Brother Roberts gently brushed my face with his hands and said that he would see me later. We were lined up again and led out to the playground, where a blast of noise overwhelmed me. Its force was such that I instinctively clung to Brother Price's knee. This seemed to please him and he rubbed the back of my neck. Silencing the noise immediately with a click of his fingers, he called one of the bigger boys. The boy, who was about fifteen years old, looked frightened. It seemed that Brother Price was charging him to take very good care of me or he would beat the bejasus out of him. Before leaving the yard Brother Price lifted me off my feet, swinging me around for a few giddy seconds. Then he handed me over to this boy and was gone.

Sitting on the steps in the playground my minder asked me my name.

'Michael Clemenger.'

'That's a long name. The Brothers will have trouble trying to call out that name in class.'

He told me that Brother Price mainly ran the school and was in charge of discipline. He also told me that all the boys were afraid of him.

'Brother Price would skin you alive if you got on the wrong side of him. You're lucky that he likes you. No one will dare touch you when he's around.'

'What do you mean?'

'Don't worry, you'll find out soon enough.'

I asked him how many boys were in St Joseph's.

'Hundreds! We have to stay here until we are sixteen years old, then we can leave and the Brothers can't stop us. I'm nearly sixteen so I'll be leaving soon meself. Boys here are called "Monoboys". "Mono" is short for "monastery", and that's what you'll be known as.'

I asked him what an orphan was and why orphans only came to St Joseph's.

'An orphan is a boy who has no parents. I have parents though, with lots of brothers and sisters. It's just that my mam and dad couldn't manage us all. Have you brothers or sisters?'

'I don't know.'

'That's all right; you must be an orphan then. How old are you?'

'I think I'm nearly nine, but I'm not sure.'

'Well you'll be here until you are sixteen anyway. So you'll have plenty of time to get to know what Brother Price is really like. You won't like it, but don't ever say that I said that.'

I asked him what Brother Roberts was like.

'Fuck me, have you met him already?'

'Yes, I met him in the refectory having tea.'

'Did he say anything to you?'

'He asked me my name and touched my face with his hands.'

'Did Brother Price see him doing that to you?'

'Yes, and he seemed a bit angry too.'

'You're in a bit of trouble so.'

Over the next few weeks my minder was more forth-coming.

'If both of them like you at the same time, you're fucked, that's all I'm saying. Never, ever, ever let either of them know which one you like best.'

He whispered this to me, seemingly afraid that some of the other boys might overhear what he was talking about. What on earth did he mean by this? I had only known these two men for such a short while so how could I be so important to them already? Nothing like this had happened with the nuns, I had been nobody's favourite there. I must have looked terrified because he shrugged and held up his hands to appease me.

'Look, all I know for definite is that if anything happens to you, I'll be killed by Brother Price.'

I nodded uncertainly. He tried again.

'You know that Brother Price has put his eye on you, don't you, the way he swung you around on your first evening here? That means you're special; you'll find that out for yourself in good time. Remember now: never ever tell him a word that I've told you. Will you promise me, Michael? Please, I'm serious.'

I heard the anxiety in his voice so I fervently promised not to repeat a word, even though I didn't really understand what he was talking about.

Settling In

INITIALLY THE REGIME at St Joseph's was very difficult to get used to. The Brothers ruled with a rod of iron, or more precisely, with a leather strap. Almost from the outset there was a very liberal use of the strap for the most minor infringements of the rules. Boys were beaten severely and in some cases within inches of their lives. Fear hung in the air like smog, and laughter was seldom heard.

Boys were placed in dormitories in terms of age. Being eight years old I ended up in the lower dormitory, on the ground floor, near the Brothers' private entrance to the monastery. In bed at night, I could hear the occasional car that travelled along the main road, just outside the big wall. The lower dormitory had approximately a hundred beds in it. The beds were three deep from front to back, stretching from one end of the dormitory to the other. There was also a row of beds placed against the side walls, on either side of the exit that led to the washroom and toilets at the top of the stairs.

My bed was number fifty-two. (Much later I discovered that I had been assigned that bed on the specific instructions of Brother Price.) It was right beside the door that led directly into the Brothers' private quarters. To the right of that door was the refectory where we had our meals.

Brother Murphy was in charge of that lower dormitory. He and I took an instant dislike to one another. He was a Kerry man with absolutely no sense of humour. His demeanour was always sour and the boys easily annoyed him. I was fascinated by his withered left ear. His response to the most minor of irritations was the wielding of the strap that he wore on his left hip as if it was a gun. He strutted about the place trying to instil fear into us boys, with the occasional glance at a nearby mirror as if to check out his own toughness. While I recognised the potential danger I always considered him to be a bit of a clown. He was a lightweight posing as if he had gravitas and he was certainly no Brother Price. When giving out the weekly changes of clothes he always gave me the ugliest, tightest fitting clothes. More often than not Brother Price would bring me back to the clothes room to find more suitable items for me to wear. It humiliated Brother Murphy to have to hand over the keys of the clothes room.

Everybody knew I was Brother Price's 'special pet' and gave me a wide berth. He looked in on me in the lower dormitory most nights, deliberately passing by my bed and making some comment. I didn't read anything into it at first but after a time I wished that he wouldn't do it because it made relations with Brother Murphy very unpleasant. Another boy asked me one night why Brother Price always passed by my bed. I had no answer.

Trouble blew up for me quite unexpectedly one Sunday morning at Mass, of all places, when Brother Price caught me smiling at Brother Roberts on my way back from receiving Communion. He glared at me, full of rage. In my young ignorance I didn't really think much of it. That afternoon, however, he was on yard duty and everybody could see that he was as mad as hell with me.

'That's it Michael, he has it in for you. He's going to beat the shite out of you. Watch out now,' warned one of the senior boys.

I couldn't understand why smiling at Brother Roberts was such a big deal. It certainly didn't occur to me that Brother Price might be inflamed with jealousy. That evening I was waiting in line with the other boys; we were going into the hall to see a film. Brother Price pounced, pulled me roughly aside in full view of everyone. He barked at me to go to the dormitory and wait for him there.

I was quite annoyed with him for embarrassing me, but then, when he appeared in the dormitory, a few minutes later, my irritation was replaced by fear. His face was white with rage and I thought that he was going to beat the daylights out of me. Instead he told me to undress and get into bed. I thought it was strange as it was still bright. When I got under the covers he gave me a sharp slap across the face with the palm of his hand. I was stunned and started to cry.

'Ha! Where is Brother Roberts now? Hey? I'll teach you to smile at him like that.'

I had no idea what he was talking about. His rage was such that I decided against asking what I had done wrong, and was beside myself trying to understand what was happening. I said that I was sorry in the hope of being allowed to dress and go back to see the rest of the film, but he was having none of it. Vaguely, I sensed that whatever was going on between him and Brother Roberts – whose name he almost spat out – had something to do with me. My mind churned up the yard conversation with the older boy. I had broken the rule of never letting either of them know which one I liked best. Smiling at Brother Roberts at Mass obviously signalled to Brother Price my preference. The truth was I *did* prefer the gentler Brother Roberts to Brother Price, who scared me a little, most of the time.

'You're not to get involved with Brother Roberts in any way and that includes smiling at him. Do you understand me, Michael?'

While I surely did not, I replied that I did, hoping he would leave me alone. I kept crying while my mind raced. Instead of leaving, however, he hauled himself over and sat down on my bed, his hand hovering near my face. I was terrified that he might give me another slap or, worse still, a few licks of the leather that hung from his hip. He seemed to take pleasure in my fear. Inwardly I resolved never to show any smiles to Brother Roberts in case I missed more films in the future. I don't know how long he sat there in silence, but I must have fallen asleep. When I woke up Brother Price was gone, and in his place was Brother Murphy, standing over me with a mean grin on his face.

'Well, Clemenger, how is Brother Price now?'

That night some of the boys asked me what had happened with Brother Price. I told them I was beaten because I had smiled at Brother Roberts. It was all over the dormitories within a minute. They went very quiet and quickly got into bed.

Brother Roberts
Makes His Move

THE RELATIONSHIP BETWEEN Brothers Price and Roberts, whatever it was prior to my arrival, declined steadily into internecine war. They vied openly for my affection and attention. I bitterly resented being put in such a bewildering position, not knowing which way to turn.

What did they see in me? I was quite small for my age, fair-haired, with greyish-blue eyes. I was always quick to smile and combined an enquiring mind with, perhaps, just the right amount of shyness. Most of the time I stared at the ground until I was spoken to, but once addressed I was articulate and unafraid to ask questions.

When I was about nine years old Brother Roberts stopped me one evening, as I was leaving the chapel after the saying of the rosary.

'Michael Clemenger, I want a word with you.'

The other boys raced past me on their way to the refectory.

'Don't be worrying about missing supper. I have

arranged it with Brother Lane. Come along, I have something special to show you.'

He brought me into the closet, where the soutanes were stored, and picked out a long black gown and white vest to go with it.

'Now Michael, let's go to my room.'

Nervously I followed him into the private residence of the Christian Brothers, down a long corridor with one window that looked directly into the seniors' dormitory. The lights were on, allowing me to spot a solitary boy in one of the beds. Brother Roberts pointed out the individual rooms of the Brothers, which were dimly lit. We passed a bathroom, prompting him to ask me if I wanted to use the toilet.

'No, sir!'

In truth I was somewhere between terrified and bewildered at finding myself in such proximity to the private lives of the Brothers.

When we arrived at his room, which was almost the farthest from the chapel, he pulled out a set of keys and opened the door.

'In you go, Michael.'

I distinctly heard Brother Murphy praying aloud in the room next door.

'Oh, don't mind him; he's always at that sort of thing. You'll get used to it in time.'

Locking the door behind us, he told me to get undressed. Bewildered, I removed my clothes until I was standing naked, shivering and completely unsure of what was expected of me. He sat on the only chair, which was right beside the bed.

'Get into the bed, Michael, if you are cold.'

Glad to cover my nakedness, I jumped into the bed; it was much softer than my own. It had lovely white sheets, two pillows and a couple of heavy blankets. On the wall straight ahead was a picture of the Sacred Heart and a crucifix. Books were scattered on a nearby table, black hats hung from the hat stand and a black brolly stood beside the door. The room was very cosy. Despite this, however, I felt ill at ease. There was something not quite right about the way Brother Roberts had stared at my body.

'Would you like to be an altar boy, Michael?'

I nodded fearfully.

'Well, so you shall.'

He pulled back the bed clothes and began stroking my arms and chest. His hands were trembling, but warm. Leaning over me, he kissed me on my shoulders, neck and even my ears. Frozen, I kept my eyes on the crucifix opposite me. It struck me that Jesus was almost naked on the cross. I had never noticed that before. Heavy grunting and moaning brought me back to an appalling reality. Brother Roberts' lips crushed against mine, sucking them hard as if he was eating a ripe orange. I could hardly breathe. In panic I tried to push him away, but he was too strong for me; I was utterly terrified, and actually thought I might die, such was the suddenness and ferocity of his attack.

After maybe ten minutes it was over. He quietened down and his breathing returned to normal. I sat upright in the bed.

'Stand out on the floor, Michael, and try on the black soutane.'

Meekly, I did what I was told and put on the robe with his help. Gently he combed my hair with a brown brush and stroked the back of my neck with his hands.

'Look in the mirror, Michael. Do you see how beautiful you look? My, you will make a fine altar boy.'

Opening a drawer he took out a bag of sweets and said I could start eating right away. I was also presented with a sweet drink, yellow in colour, and told to sit down on the bed again.

'You are going to be my top altar boy. Would you like that, Michael?'

What could I do but nod my head helplessly.

'Promise me, Michael, that you'll say nothing of this to the other boys. Some of them might get jealous and try to hurt you. You're going to be my favourite boy, which means I'll always take care of you. Just you wait and see. Get dressed now, leave the soutane on the chair and I'll take you down to the kitchen for your own special supper.'

In the Brothers' kitchen a tray, bearing my name, sat proudly on a table covered with a tea-towel.

'Go on, Michael, have a look at what's underneath the towel. It's your reward for being such a good boy.'

At this point I was feeling rather overwhelmed by the whole episode and found it hard to take in what was happening. There was a knock on the kitchen door. Brother Roberts answered it, and whoever it was went away.

'Do you like the buns, Michael?'

'Yes, sir.'

I couldn't understand why I was being rewarded as I hadn't done anything.

'Remember, Michael, you mustn't tell anyone that you were in my room. It will be our little secret.'

Fretting that the other boys would guess where I had been anyway, I asked him what I was to say if anyone asked me anything.

'Don't worry your little head about that. I'll take care of everything.'

When I finished the tea, cakes and yellow drink he wiped my mouth clean with his handkerchief, kissed me and sent me on my way.

'Off you go now, back to the playground.'

To my horror, who should be on yard duty but Brother Price. Glaring suspiciously at me, he asked where I had been.

'Brother Roberts was fitting me with a soutane, for to become an altar boy, sir.'

'Oh really, and did it take you all this time?'

'No, sir.'

'Well then?'

'Sir, he brought me to the Brothers' kitchen to give me tea and cakes.'

'And by any chance did he give you sweets?'

'Yes, sir.'

'How many?'

'A bag of sweets, sir.'

'Where are they now?'

'I ate them, sir.'

'All of them?'

'Yes, sir.'

It was only then that I realised I had left at least half a bag of sweets on Brother Roberts' bed.

'Tell me, Michael, where did Brother Roberts have you try on the soutane? Was it in the chapel or some place else?'

'In the chapel, sir.'

His eyes bore right through me. *My God, he knows I'm lying*, I thought.

'In the chapel? Are you quite sure, Michael?'

'Not the chapel, sir, in his room.'

Lowering his voice, he asked me why I hadn't said so in the first place.

'Because he told me not to, sir.'

'And did anything else happen there, Michael?'

'No, sir.'

'Are you sure? Answer me truthfully now. I'll know if you are lying.'

'Nothing happened, sir.'

'Indeed, indeed.'

He came closer, looking straight into my eyes. The whole school was watching us. I betrayed not a flicker as I held his gaze. If I broke down the boys would know that Brother Roberts had done something to me. How else could I explain the tea and buns? The whole situation was a nightmare. Suddenly, to my immense relief, he moved back from me.

'Okay, Michael, you can go.'

Walking quickly away, I headed for the handball alley. Some of the boys started to follow me, but Brother Price let out a roar.

'Get away from him, the lot of you, or you will all get the strap.'

I must have looked as tired as I felt because he asked me if I wanted to go to my bed instead. I said yes immediately and ran all the way to the dormitory, grateful to be alone at last. I was asleep before my head hit the pillow and never woke up until the following morning.

Brother Lane

APART FROM MY bewildering experience with Brother Roberts there were other worries. There was the constant threat of violence. One Brother, in particular, was known for his brand of sheer viciousness.

On my first encounter with Brother Lane, even before I knew of his infamous reputation, I sensed the badness in him. He was the smallest of all the Brothers, but he more than compensated for his short stature with the level of his ferocity. As I watched him walk about the monastery with a perpetual sneer on his face, it seemed to me that he held an individual hatred for every single boy. Nobody liked him, not even his spies. When he appeared on yard duty, bodies literally scattered in all directions. Some of the more senior boys hissed through gritted teeth that he was a 'murderer'. A photograph hung outside the sick bay of a boy named Joseph Pyke, a well-built, handsome redhead, with a strong chin and confident smile, that many Monoboys believed had been kicked to his death by the bad-tempered Brother. Apparently this boy had been a firm favourite with Brother Roberts, who had taken the photo. It was also

Brother Roberts who had put it up on the wall, possibly to make a point to 'the murderer'.

Brother Lane was in charge of the refectory and, therefore, responsible for the feeding of the boys. The Brothers themselves had their own kitchen and, judging by the lovely smells that emanated from that quarter, they ate very well indeed. Each table seated up to twelve boys and was supervised by an older boy whose job it was to ensure that no good food ever went to waste. As soon as the meal was finished the table leaders had to present the leftovers plate for inspection. Generally the boys were so hungry that they would have eaten the legs of the table. Meanwhile Brother Lane sat on a high chair so that he could oversee the entire operation. His beady eyes scoured the masses below, with menacing intent. Any infraction would drive him into a show of rage. This was when he was at his most dangerous. He never acted immediately; instead he would take out a matchstick from his pocket and chew violently on it for an undetermined amount of time. I never saw him spit out any of the stick and thus believed that he swallowed it, splinter by splinter. His attack was always sudden, no matter what. He would leap down from his high stool, run headlong at his intended prey, drag him to his feet and charge with him straight ahead; all the while he would be shouting like a lunatic, out of the refectory and into a small room off the kitchen, known as the dungeon. A few minutes later he would arrive back and resume his reading of the paper as if nothing had happened.

There were a number of different versions about what exactly happened to Joseph Pyke, but here's the one that I heard most often.

On the day in question Joseph Pyke was in charge of one of the tables. For some reason he forgot to check the contents of the all important plate that held the leftovers, which were only ever potato skins. That particular day the spuds were so bad and soggy that some of them were completely inedible. Unfortunately, for poor Joseph, the Cork man was in a foul humour. Brother Lane inspected the plate with his pen and, upon seeing the bits of rotten potato on the skins, flew into a blind rage. He kicked Joseph from his elevated position on his high stool, catching him full in the chest.

According to eyewitnesses Joseph fell backwards, unconscious before he hit the floor. He died three weeks later in the local hospital, in February 1958. By the time I arrived, in August 1959, the reputation of Brother Lane was a ferocious and frightening one.

Even before I met him other boys warned me, several times over, never to make direct eye contact with Brother Lane unless he specifically told me to look at him. We finally came face to face, in the refectory, one dinner time. He seemed aware of my standing with Brothers Price and Roberts.

'So you're Clemenger, Brother Price's and Roberts'

little pet. Well, I hope you're not expecting any special treatment from me. You're a small wee butt of a boy, aren't you, Clemenger?'

I was so fearful of him that I could hardly reply.

'Cat got your tongue, boy?'

'No sir, I'm just afraid, sir.'

'And so you should be. Get on over to table number four and sit down.'

When I reached my seat I felt that I had survived a major shock to the system.

Somehow I knew that he was going to be trouble for me. I didn't want to end up dead like poor Joseph Pyke and resolved to myself, from that day onwards, that I would do whatever it took to prevent such an occurrence. I seized my opportunity the very next day in the yard when Brother Price arrived to take over from Brother Lane. I ran over to Brother Price, in full view of Brother Lane, crying hysterically. Brother Price immediately picked me up, full of concern. Brother Lane left the yard in disgust. Brother Price called over two senior boys and told them they were in charge until his return. Taking me by the hand he led me into an empty classroom, where he sat on the teacher's chair and lifted me up on to his lap.

'Well, Michael, tell me what's the matter.'

I blurted out what Brother Lane had said about him and Brother Roberts. He became very angry and muttered something I didn't understand. However, I was consoled when he added that if Brother Lane ever hit me I would be the last boy he'd ever hit in St Joseph's.

'Don't you worry now, Michael.'

He stroked my face and head in full view of some of the boys, who could see in through the classroom window. I didn't care as long as word got back to Brother Lane, via his spies, that I had nothing to worry about from him as far as Brother Price was concerned.

These spies were out-and-out sneaks that the Brothers relied on for information about the boys. They were usually in the thirteen to fourteen years of age bracket, and reported on their fellow pupils to curry favour with their Brother of choice. I never knew what their rewards were. It wasn't an easy life. For one thing everybody knew who they were so they usually found themselves isolated from the rest of their class, while rival Brothers made life difficult for one another's spies. However, I understood why they did it. It was their way of surviving the brutal regime, just like making the most of being a 'favourite' was mine.

For a while afterwards Brother Lane completely ignored me. I grew brazen, thanks to my 'protectors', and returned in full the sneers he sometimes threw my way. Other boys thought I was mad and playing a dangerous game, but fixed in my mind was the image of a dead Joseph Pyke. I was determined he wasn't going to do the same thing to me.

To be doubly sure I also told Brother Roberts about Brother Lane's attitude to me at meal times. Some of the boys told me that he had been very fond of Joseph Pyke, whom he believed to have had great potential as an Irish dancer. However, Brother Roberts explained that since Brother Lane had complete charge of the refectory he couldn't readily interfere. Seeing my disappointment, he winked at me.

'Don't worry, Michael, there's always more than one way of dealing with difficult situations.'

On a day to day basis, however, the boys at my table were more concerned that Brother Lane might take out his anger on them. The head boy told me that the best way to avoid trouble with 'the murderer' was to give him no excuse to strike.

'Do you see this potato?'

'Yes.'

'Well, all you have to do is cut it in half, and squeeze each half until there is nothing left, only the bare skin. Do this every fucking day of your life while that murderer is around. Do you understand, Michael?'

I nodded anxiously.

'All right then. Some day you will be in charge of a table so make sure you pass this on to the other boys.'

*

One morning Brother Price called me into his room. It was a few months after my arrival in St Joseph's.

'Do you know how old you are today, Michael?'

I didn't understand what he meant. He pulled me onto his lap.

'Today is the first of November and it's your birthday, the day you were born nine years ago.'

Still puzzled, I waited for further explanation.

'You see, Michael, everybody is born to a mother and father on a certain day of the year and this is their special day.'

He held me very tightly and began to sing 'Happy Birthday' quietly into my ear. Later, in the yard, he told the other boys that it was my birthday and to be extra nice to me.

Word soon reached Brother Roberts' ears and that afternoon he called me into the sweet shop beside the handball alley. I was struck by the smell of the various sweets and toffees.

'So, Michael, I hear it's your birthday today.'

'Yes, sir.'

'Well, we can't let that go by now, can we?'

My mind was full of Brother Price's words and I asked Brother Roberts what a mother and father was for and, if I had them, where were they? He was a little taken aback at my sudden line of questioning.

'Go on, Michael, put your hand into the jar of sweets and fill that little bag beside the table.'

Eagerly I filled the bag to the top, looking at him expectantly.

'Now, never you mind about your mother and father. I'll take their place and look after you.'

With that he gave me a great big hug and told me to run along and play. I shared my sweets with some of the other boys and in all the excitement of the day I forgot, for the moment, any thoughts about having a mother and father.

A few weeks later, Brother Price asked me what I wanted for Christmas.

'You'll have to write it down so that I can send your letter with all the others to Santa Claus.'

Once again I stared at him, in bewilderment.

'Come on, Michael. You must know who Santa Claus is?'

'No, sir.'

'Are you telling me that you never celebrated a birthday or heard of Santa Claus in St Philomena's?'

'Yes, sir.'

For a moment I thought he was going to cry. Instead he hugged me and assured me that I would get a very special present from Santa Claus this Christmas.

Some of the other boys told me that Brother Price was in charge of giving out the Christmas presents. They were made up on the floor of the fifth class' room. The bigger boys could see them through the window, all the parcels laid out with our names on them. Being far too small to see in I could only imagine this wondrous sight.

On Christmas Eve night we all went to midnight Mass and had a late supper afterwards. It was hard to get to sleep with the excitement of Santa's arrival. Sure enough, at 9 o'clock the next morning, after breakfast, Santa was driven into the yard on a tractor and trailer. The noise of the engine was deafening. In our turn, as our names were called out, we stepped forward to shake hands with Santa and receive our Christmas present. I was less interested in my present than I was in Santa, who seemed familiar to me. When I shook hands with him I knew immediately that it was Brother Price. For some reason I felt angry with him. Nevertheless I played along while all the presents were handed out. Santa left on the tractor and trailer and Brother Price reappeared a few minutes later, walking around the yard, chatting to the other boys. There was great excitement over the presents that included toy guns, bows and arrows, tanks and boats. Brother Price avoided talking to me, perhaps because he knew that I had recognised him. In truth I felt rather let down; to discover that there was no such thing as Santa Claus after only finding out about him so recently.

At least the food was a bit better for the holiday. We had a feast that included a good helping of meat, tapioca pudding, lemonade, fruit and extra slices of bread. Apart from that, the day itself wasn't great. We spent most of it outside, unsupervised. The senior boys were in charge until the Brothers finished their dinner at 6 o'clock. This meant lots of fighting amongst the boys, which in turn meant a good few beatings when the Brothers found out who had been causing trouble.

I didn't sleep well that night, although I was tired after all the festivities. In my head I kept hearing Brother Price telling me that I had been born to a mother and father. The Baby Jesus had His mother and father with Him in the manger, so where were mine?

The School Chaplain

HE WAS A strange man, Father O'Neill. He had been living in St Joseph's for some years and before that was supposed to have spent a period of time on the missions in Africa. A dour, sullen man, he never spoke to any of the boys if he could help it. His primary role, it seemed to me, was to say Mass every morning at 7.30, after which he disappeared for the rest of the day. Many of us disliked having him hear our confession because of the way he shouted his responses. He could clearly be heard by anyone outside waiting their turn for the confessional. Furthermore, rumour had it that if anyone broached the subject of their sexual abuse the priest would repeat it back to the relevant Brother and a big beating was sure to follow.

One morning after Mass Brother Roberts asked me to come to his room. I did so rather reluctantly and was pleasantly surprised to find he wasn't alone. There sitting in Brother Roberts' chair was Father O'Neill.

Two breakfast trays lay on the Brother's bed, showing the remains of eggs and scraps of toast. A jar of marmalade sat beside a large teapot. Brother Roberts poured me a cup of tea and gave me the scraps of food. I thanked him and ate them standing up. Throughout, Father O'Neill looked at me very sternly.

'So, you are Michael Clemenger.'

'Yes, sir.'

'Don't call me sir, call me Father.'

'Yes, Father.'

'Brother Roberts has been telling me that you would be a suitable boy to clean my room in the mornings. Would that be the case?'

'Yes sir, I mean, Father.'

I could hardly hide my surprise at being offered such an important position in the school and at my age too.

'Are you an honest boy?'

'Yes, Father.'

'Do you say your prayers well?'

'Yes, Father.'

'Have you ever stolen anything?'

'No, Father, never.'

Brother Roberts looked on approvingly, but said nothing. After a few more questions Father O'Neill turned to Brother Roberts and wondered if I wasn't a bit too young for such responsibility.

'Indeed he is, Father, but he's the best boy I can find for the job and besides I'll keep a good eye on him.'

'Very well then, if you're happy with him, that settles it.'

With that, Father O'Neill left the room saying that

he would be away for the rest of the day, but would leave his door open. After he was gone Brother Roberts told me to go off to school. I was to come back after dinner. Word soon got around the yard that I had landed the plum job of looking after Father O'Neill's room. There were some jealous looks, but nobody said anything to me.

After dinner I made my way back to Brother Roberts' room and knocked on his door. He was lying on the bed as if he had been sleeping. He got up, washed his face and dried it with a towel.

'Now, Michael, this job of cleaning Father O'Neill's room is an important one. I picked you especially for it so I hope you won't let me down. Anyway his room is just two doors away from mine so I'll be able to look in on you most mornings. Always check in with me before you head off. Right then, off we go.'

Before he opened his door he gave me a kiss on the lips. I never knew what he was going to do next. When he opened Father O'Neill's room it was full of cigarette smoke. Brother Roberts opened the window at the other side of the room to let the smoke out. When the smoke finally cleared I took a good look around. Directly inside the door, to the left, was a high double bed with lots of pillows. Standing beside it was a tall, old-fashioned radio, about four feet high, with a row of knobs at the front. Brother Roberts followed my gaze.

'Remember, Michael, never turn on the radio. It

upsets Father O'Neill because he has it fixed on his favourite stations and doesn't like them changed.'

I nodded and continued with my inspection. Against the wall, beside the window, was a high, black armchair with cushions that sat next to a black chest with a lock on it. A large wardrobe with a mirror stuck on its front stood to the right of the door. There were ashes everywhere on the floor, the bed and even on the radio. What a messy old *fecker*! I thought. Brother Roberts' room was very clean in comparison.

My tasks every morning were simple. First I was to open the window to let out the smoke, and then I had to make the bed, sweep the floor and tidy any clothes I found lying around. Finally I was to take his breakfast tray back to the kitchen and wash the cutlery. Brother Roberts told me that it should take about half an hour to do everything properly.

'Take your time, do it right and make sure that Father O'Neill has no complaints.'

With that he left me to get on with it. It was strange to be finally alone in the priest's bedroom. I felt a great sense of honour and responsibility. I soon got used to the routine though I changed the format of duties slightly. Usually I opened the windows first to let the smoke out and then I would take the tray back to the kitchen minus the scraps of toast and cold tea that he might leave on the tray. By the time I returned to his room the smoke was usually gone. I would then make the bed, fluff out the pillows and pick up any clothes that Father O'Neill dropped on the floor. Next I swept the floor with a sweeping brush that was kept in a cupboard beside Brother Murphy's room. After that I emptied the three ashtrays into a bin, cleaned them out and replaced them strategically around the room.

I took my time, stretching out the cleaning to a good forty-five minutes. Initially Brother Roberts inspected my work as soon as I was finished, but after a few weeks there was no need as Father O'Neill told him that he was more than satisfied with me. Occasionally the priest left a slice of toast and half an egg on his plate by way of reward. I was most grateful for these scraps which helped to keep the hunger at bay. I often felt guilty eating these scraps, knowing that the boys next to me in class were going hungry, but what was I supposed to do?

Generally the food in St Joseph's was pretty dreadful; both in quality and quantity. We were at the mercy of the cooking abilities of the eight boys who worked full-time in the kitchen. There were four meals a day, though they were hardly 'square' ones. Breakfast at 8 o'clock was a small bowl of porridge, so thick in consistency that it stuck fast to the spoon, followed by two thin slices of bread with a scrape of Stork margarine and a tepid cup of either tea or cocoa. Dinner was five hours later, at 1 pm: boiled potatoes in some kind of soup where, the odd time, a carrot said hello. Sometimes there was cabbage or cauliflower. I don't remember any meat. The meal depended on the strength of the potatoes; they were good in the summer months and fairly rotten throughout the long winter. After this we had a dessert of either semolina or rhubarb with custard. The dessert bowl was tiny and the portion was less than half-full. If one of the servers went above the invisible line of 'less than half-full' he would be beaten by Brother Lane. At 4 o'clock we were given one slice of bread and Stork margarine, with another barely warm cup of tea or cocoa. This exact meal was repeated at 6.45pm, as our supper. Sometimes there was a blob of jam. On Sunday evenings we were given a treat for our supper at seven, one slice of bread fried in meat dripping. Overall it wasn't enough food for growing boys, especially when the weather was cold and miserable. Most boys went to bed hungry at night. The bread was strictly rationed, so there was no such thing as an extra slice except on Christmas Day.

I never developed a fondness for Father O'Neill, though I cleaned his room for six years. He wasn't a nice man, possibly because of his many physical complaints. His stomach always gave him trouble and he had diffi-culty with his feet. Often he wasn't able to say Mass because they were so swollen. Over time his collection of various medications spread out across the room. The different coloured boxes always caught my attention. One of the best things about the job was that Brother Roberts mostly stayed away because he hated the smell of smoke. Father O'Neill never sat down ever and asked me about myself or paid me even one little compliment about my housework. However, he did tell me once that I was a good altar boy because I was so good in answering the responses of the Latin Mass. That was high praise indeed, especially coming from someone who normally went through altar boys like a knife through butter. He got rid of a lot of them chiefly because they didn't respond well to the Latin Mass.

In time the Brothers got used to seeing me in the private quarters though some of them didn't like it, in particular Brothers Murphy and Lane. I used to enjoy their obvious discomfort when I passed them on the corridor. Brother Lane's room was on the landing just next to Father O'Neill's. His door was never locked and I was determined to have a look inside it. One morning, after he left for the refectory, and all was quiet, I tiptoed inside. What a shock was in store for me. Expecting it to be as comfortable as Brother Roberts' or Father O'Neill's I found it to be the exact opposite. For a start the walls were completely bare, no pictures or crucifixes. The single bed had just one blanket and no pillows whatsoever. A razor and brush sat on a single chair. The wardrobe was home to a solitary blue shirt on a hanger and a pile of dirty socks. At the bottom of the wardrobe, however, were two brown leather straps. I picked one of them up and was surprised by how heavy it was. It turned out that both straps had small coins stitched into the top of them. Typical of Lane, I thought, that he would actually take the time to sew small coins into his straps. I couldn't remember ever seeing him wear either of these on his hip. And how come he had extra leathers anyway? Even if he wore the same one for years on end it would be very hard to wear it out. I closed the wardrobe and took a last look. Biros and note papers were the only features of normality. I thought the room was creepy, and also that it perfectly summed up Brother Lane's lack of personality.

Brother Murphy's room, on the other hand, was completely different. He had enough pictures of saints, Jesus and Our Blessed Mother to decorate his own church. Amongst all the portraits were three large crucifixes with a set of rosary beads hanging from each of them. Books lay everywhere in complete disorder. I wondered how he managed to get into his bed at night. He must have had to step on some of the books.

Often when Father O'Neill and I were walking in the corridor Brother Murphy would pass by, pretending not to see us, chanting some prayer to himself. Then when he decided he 'saw' us he would deliberately drop his large, black Bible at the priest's feet. In the beginning I used to help him gather up the pictures and odd bits of papers that fell out of the pages. After a while Father O'Neill told me not to bother stopping as the Brother was only doing it to get his attention. Sure enough, I began to notice that he only ever dropped the black book in the presence of Father O'Neill, who would roll his eyes to the heavens and walk away muttering something along the lines of 'That idiot'.

I often heard Brother Murphy chanting while I was next door with Brother Roberts, being kissed and mauled. He always seemed to be around to see me both enter and then leave Brother Roberts' room. Sometimes he sat on the stairs as if timing the length of a typical visit. As I opened Brother Roberts' door to leave he always made sufficient noise to, I presume, let Brother Roberts know he was around. Once he asked me what went on in there.

'I'm learning the Latin Mass, sir.'

'Hmmph! A likely story indeed.'

On another occasion he confronted me on the stairs and asked me if I had been in his room.

'No, sir. I only go into Father O'Neill's and Brother Roberts' rooms.'

'Don't ever let me catch you in mine or it will be the worst for you, you little brat.'

I repeated his words back to Brother Roberts and together we knocked on Brother Murphy's door. Words were exchanged and Brother Murphy was put in his place. I heard no more from him on the matter.

Brother Price's Favourite Boy

BROTHER PRICE'S ROOM was next door to Brother Lane's. I wanted to have a peek inside but had to be careful because you never knew where Brother Price might be at any given time. Then, one morning, I got my wish when he told me that he wanted to see me before that evening's rosary. When I knocked at his door he called for me to come in. I was taken aback to find him wearing an open necked white shirt, trousers and standing in his bare feet.

'Come in, Michael, come in.'

I was very nervous of him and was sure he could sense it.

'I see that Brother Roberts has put you in charge of Father O'Neill's room. How are you getting on there?'

'Fine, sir.'

'Brother Roberts is good to you, isn't he, Michael?'

'I don't know what you mean, sir.'

'Oh come on, Michael. Why do you think he put you in charge of Father O'Neill's room?'

'I have no idea, sir.'

'Well, you are only ten years old. Usually that's a job given to an older boy.'

I had no idea where this conversation was leading but knew that I had to be careful.

'I want you to come and see me on Saturday morning, at 11 o'clock. Some of the older boys will tell you the time. And you're to wear your Sunday best because we're going for a walk down the town together.'

I spent the next couple of days wondering what Brother Price was going to do to better Brother Roberts. That Saturday morning he took me by the hand and led me out by the Brothers' private entrance and headed towards the town.

'Get to know this route, Michael, because from now on you'll be going down the town every morning to fetch the *Irish Press*.'

He left it at that for the moment.

'Would I have to wear my Sunday suit for that, sir?'

'No, but you'll have to dress smartly for going down the town.'

It was a blustery morning, the trees bowed in the wind as if to greet me. Walking along the wide road I fancied that I could smell freedom. Cars beeped us as they drove by, Brother Price waved gaily at their owners. I felt like I was ten feet tall. The townspeople we met on the road greeted the Brother as if he was someone of importance. Occasionally he stopped to talk to a gentleman, the conversation usually centred on the weather. Once or twice he even introduced me to these strangers. About a quarter of a mile from St Joseph's he pointed out a street sign, Rock Street.

'Do you see that butchers' shop on the corner? A couple of times a week you might be given an order for the butchers. All you have to do is hand in the note. They'll deliver the meat themselves.'

He brought me into the shop and briefly introduced me to the two men working there. Next we called into the little newsagent's shop where I was introduced to two sisters and a rather tall man. Brother Price informed me that every morning I was to go to the shop at nine in the morning to collect the *Irish Press* and then I had to return at four for the *Evening Press*. There was a standing order so I had no need to bring money with me. I liked the women immediately though the man was somewhat reserved.

'I'm giving Michael a trial run for the next few weeks to see how he gets on. If you find him suitable then he'll become the regular boy who will collect the daily papers for me.'

As Brother Price exchanged a few words with the ladies he reached into his pocket and pulled out a three-penny piece. Handing it to me, he told me to buy myself sweets.

I had never seen such a coin before and was fascinated by its shape and colour. Of course I had seen small change before, on Father O'Neill's dresser, but had never touched it. One of the women filled a bag with sweets and gave me back a penny, which Brother Price told me to keep.

On the walk back to St Joseph's my head was spinning. I didn't know what to make of it all. In such a short space of time I had two of the best jobs in the monastery: being in charge of Father O'Neill's room and leaving the monastery twice a day to collect the newspapers for Brother Price. What would the other boys think of me? To be honest, though, I didn't really care. Brothers Price and Roberts were the main players in St Joseph's. I was beginning to understand the rules of the game and also understand that there would be a price to pay later. But for now I forgot my worries.

Those walks to town were something of a turning point for me. I didn't notice it at first, but gradually it dawned on me that people seemed a little afraid of me. As I approached, mothers would shield their children as if I was a barking dog that could bite them. Curious children peeped out from behind their mothers, sneaking a good look at me in safety. Grown men slipped into doorways, looking suddenly busy. When I had passed by they stepped back out onto the road again to continue about their daily business. Few people greeted or even smiled at me. They talked about me as if I was deaf.

'Oh him, he's the Monoboy. Sure he's a nice looking lad, but he must have something wrong with him to be put into that awful place.'

Of course I had no idea what they were talking about. Were they right? Was there something wrong with me? Over the years I developed my own negative attitude towards them. Not wanting to lose my daily walks out of St Joseph's, I was obliged to hide my intense dislike of them all. When I met anyone on the road I stared them straight in the eye without blinking. Sure enough they always blinked first and turned away. Little victories like that became an important part of my day. I strutted in and out of the shops as if I hadn't a care in the world. I wouldn't give them the satisfaction of showing me any pity. With the *Irish Press* in my hands I trotted smartly along the road, flicking through the front pages intently, pretending to be unaware of the many pairs of eyes upon me. Occasionally the ladies in the newspaper shop slipped me a few sweets for which I thanked them. I never enjoyed eating them because I thought their kind gesture was made purely out of pity. The other boys, however, never made the distinction as they gobbled them down ravenously.

As I got older I became more troubled by the sight of the children in the town clinging to their mothers. A raging jealousy began to emerge from somewhere deep inside of me. Reluctantly I acknowledged the idea that I must be different from those children since I had never experienced such love and affection. Where were my mother and father? Why didn't they come to visit me? More importantly, why did they give me away? Had I done something so bad that they did not want me? The tears would flow as I made my way back to the monastery. In this mood I often went to see Brother Roberts. He never had any satisfactory answers and I always regretted asking him because it became an excuse for him to stick his tongue down my throat.

Brother Roberts' Wednesday Ritual

SINCE BROTHER ROBERTS first kissed me that day I tried on the soutane, he would take every chance he got to stick his tongue down my throat. I think it frustrated him, however, that he felt he didn't have enough time with me to do more. So, he devised a way of being alone with me, on Wednesday evenings, in order to 'explore' me inside out.

How I hated Wednesdays. It was the day of the week that I dreaded the most, when Brother Roberts made a grand entrance into the playground with me on his mind. What frightened me most was that he was making a public show of his affection, summoning me to him. Dutifully I accompanied him to the sick bay. As we left the yard there was always a momentary silence before the boys resumed their play again. When Brother Price was on yard duty there was little he could do to save me from the clutches of his older colleague.

On reaching sick bay Brother Roberts would be in a state of mounting sexual excitement. He ran the bath and got me to undress. I was sure the boys in the yard were only too aware of what was happening to me, which added to my intense shame and embarrassment. Generally baths were not the norm. Boys usually showered on a Saturday afternoon, supervised by either Brother Roberts or Price. After stripping himself naked, he squeezed into the bath beside me, whispering sweet nothings to calm me. In such close proximity there was little room to escape his passion. The only way to survive intact on these occasions was to pretend that they were happening to a third party and that I was merely an observer. Although this was very difficult to do with Brother Roberts' tongue halfway down my throat. It was only during these episodes that he was in any way rough with me. In my terror my body would go rigid. Not that he was capable, at these times, of acknowledging my fear. My naked body seemed to arouse him all the more. Roughly manipulating me as if I was a loofah, he would kiss me on my back and legs, all the time breathing heavily. I did not like him to get on top of me in case I drowned. Somehow I managed to avoid such a fate by suggesting that I wash his back for him. He always liked to lead in all sexual activities and didn't like me suggesting anything to him. I felt that he enjoyed the fear in my eyes.

Generally his baths lasted about an hour. After satisfying himself, which was usually signalled via a loud grunt, he lay back in the bath and reheated the water by turning on the hot tap. He would seek to reassure me, by repeatedly whispering in my ear. I just wanted to be out of there and playing in the playground, but that rarely happened. Usually it was my bedtime by the time he was finished. After lifting me out of the bath he would place a big white towel around me and sit me on a chair, while he attended to himself. Once dressed he was transformed back to his normal self, the roughness encountered in his sexually excited state gone for another week. His touch became gentle and caring once more. My body was dried as if it were a piece of delicate china, followed by a heavy sprinkling of fine talc powder, which was tenderly applied.

He usually brought a change of clothes for me. After fixing my hair and planting a few more kisses on me he cleaned the bathroom and took me back to his room for what he called a reward. I was not interested in such rewards, but always asked him not to let me back into the playground when he was finished with me. At first he seemed surprised, but then he agreed. It became a game for him thereafter. Together we would sneak out the back entrance, after the bath, through the dormitories and back to his room. He enjoyed the intrigue of it all, which no doubt added somewhat to his sexual excitement. He always made sure that I was in bed before the other boys came to the dormitories. I always pretended to be asleep, but I never fooled Brother Price.

When the others were in bed Brother Price would sit on the side of my bed.

'I know you're not really asleep, Michael.'

Slowly and reluctantly I would stick my head just above the bedclothes to be greeted by inquisitive eyes that were bursting to ask me a thousand questions. But he never did, in the beginning, much to my relief. I rarely slept much on Wednesday nights with the confusion of it all.

Telling Brother Price

BROTHER ROBERTS WAS the first to treat me 'like that', but it wasn't long before I found out what it meant to be a favourite of Brother Price. In truth it meant the same thing, only different.

Brother Price's sexual intimacy with me was very different from that of Brother Roberts. He was less in your face, more circumspect, with less hands-on kind of activity. While he was younger than Brother Roberts he seemed less sure of himself when dealing sexually with me.

Usually he operated at night. The tell-tale sign, after lights out, was the dreaded sound of the sliding door at the chapel end of the dormitory. I am sure most of us boys' hearts missed a beat as he walked quietly along the rows of beds. Many of us pretended we were fast asleep so that he would pass by. However, if he put the 'glad eye' on you, it didn't matter if you were genuinely asleep or not. It was quite difficult to relax, never mind sleep when he was in that state of mind. I always knew when it was my turn even before the door slid open. I would catch him looking at me very intently, with drops of saliva lodged on the sides of his mouth. His time of arrival was usually around 10.30 at night. I knew this because I always noted the time on the green clock that stood on the table beside his bed. As I walked through the dormitory I would feel the eyes of the other boys upon me, filled with relief, I'm sure, that it was me making this awful journey tonight.

His room was usually dimly lit. He liked it that way as it made him feel more in control knowing that I was afraid of the dark. He was always sweating profusely and always dressed the same, in a loose nightgown and black slip-ons. Half whispered instructions to undress and face the wall with outstretched hands would be issued. This format never changed in all our encounters. Brother Price was most insistent that under no circumstances should I look behind me no matter what noises I heard. If I did, he promised I would receive a good thrashing. Because of this I never actually saw him naked. As with Brother Roberts I did my utmost to pretend that the events were happening to a third party and not to me. Strange noises and grunts emanated from behind me, accompanied by the creaking of the bed. A low gasp or moan told me when it was over. The whole act usually lasted about ten minutes.

Thereafter his voice returned to normal and his previous agitation disappeared. Stretching my naked body across his knees he would rub copious amounts of Vaseline on my bottom and thighs, moaning quietly to himself. I never understood what he was saying at these times. After he was completely satisfied he would instruct me to get back into my nightshirt and sit awhile on the bed. Then, with an intense look about him, he would question me about what I got up to with Brother Roberts. I always tried to deny that anything untoward went on but one Wednesday night, after Brother Roberts had been particularly rough with me and had laughed cruelly at the sprouting hair around my privates, I decided to tell Brother Price everything about the weekly baths. Maybe I just wanted to tell another adult; secretly I hoped that Brother Price would do something to help me.

'Sir, Brother Roberts always takes his clothes off first and fills the bath with water. He is very big and hairy down there and he likes me to touch him to make him even bigger. When I've taken off all my clothes he grabs hold of me, pressing himself against my body while holding onto me very tightly. He grabs my bottom and tries to stick his finger inside me, which really hurts. He only takes it out when I get afraid and start to shout at him,

'"Please stop! Stop! That hurts, sir."

'"Okay, Michael, okay. Be quiet now. Get into the bath."

'Usually I get in first and he throws water up around my bottom. Then Brother Roberts stands beside the bath and gets me to kiss and lick his privates. It tastes funny.

'"That's a good boy, Michael, my favourite boy."

'After a few minutes he gets into the bath and asks me to wash him very carefully around his privates and bottom. He has a big scar across his belly; it's horrible to look at.'

While I was describing all this Brother Price, who had lit his pipe, pulled on it furiously. His eyes were wide open and I was scared that he liked what I was telling him and would want to do the same thing.

'After I finish rubbing his privates and bottom Brother Roberts grabs hold of me and tries to kiss me on the mouth.'

Brother Price asked me if I liked that. I told him no.

'Why not?'

'Because Brother Roberts sticks his tongue so far down my throat that I can hardly breathe.'

'And does he kiss you anywhere else, Michael?'

'Yes, sir, on my privates, bottom and feet.'

'He kisses your feet?'

'Yes, sir. Brother Roberts likes feet.'

'Hmmm, indeed. Go on, Michael, then what?'

'Well, sir, then he tries to get on top of me, which scares me. He's so heavy and I'm afraid I won't be able to keep my head out of the water. It's like he goes a bit mad. He rubs his privates with his hands and when the stuff comes out of it he rubs it all over my body. Then he's back to normal and he's kind and gentle again.'

'What would happen then, Michael?'

'He would say I was his favourite boy, sir. His most lovely boy.'

'Indeed. Indeed.'

'Then he pulls the plug, gets out of the bath and dries himself with a big towel. By the time he's finished I'm freezing because all the water is gone. When it's my turn he rubs me all over with the towel and whispers in my ear,

'"Remember Michael; don't tell anybody about this, it's our special secret."

'Then he rubs talcum powder all over me.

'"We mustn't forget the little toes now, must we, Michael?"

'And as he does this he keeps pulling me towards him, to kiss me again on the mouth.'

'Do you like him kissing you, Michael?'

'No, sir. I told you I hate it. When he puts his tongue inside my mouth he starts to touch my private parts again.'

'Tell me, Michael, do you have these baths in the Brothers' quarters?'

'Only once or twice, sir. He prefers to do it in sick bay, usually on Wednesday nights.'

'Were you ever disturbed those times in the Brothers' quarters?'

'Yes, sir. Brother Murphy knocked on the door and asked who was in there. Brother Roberts just told him to go away, that he would be a while.'

'How long did the baths last in the Brothers' quarters?'

'I don't know, sir, but they weren't as long as the ones in sick bay.'

'Do any of the Brothers know that you were in the bathroom with Brother Roberts?'

'I don't know, sir, I don't think so.'

'Tell me, Michael, is that why Brother Roberts put you in charge of Father O'Neill's room and made you head altar boy?'

'Maybe, sir, I don't know. He told me that he liked to see me as much as possible, and that he liked having me around the Brothers' quarters so that we could have time alone in his room.'

'Does he do those sorts of things to you in his room too?'

'Yes, sir, except there is no bath.'

'Sit back on the bed, Michael. I've no more questions for you. Just have a little rest.'

As I lay back on the bed I began to worry about what Brother Price might do with what I'd just told him.

'Sir, you won't say anything to Brother Roberts, will you?'

'Absolutely not, Michael, you can be sure of that. He doesn't need to know I know. Why do you ask, anyway?'

'Because he would probably take all my jobs away from me.'

'Don't worry your head about that. I've heard myself

that Father O'Neill is more than pleased with you cleaning his room while Brother Burke says you're a lovely altar boy.'

I was mightily relieved by Brother Price's words.

'Okay, Michael, get up. We'll go and have a cup of tea in the Brothers' refectory.'

Brother Price was giddy in a way that I had never seen him before. He seemed delighted with himself; perhaps he felt that he had one up on Brother Roberts now.

Before I could leave he would always ask if any of the senior boys had made any improper sexual advances towards me.

'They better not if they know what's good for them. You would tell me, Michael, if anything happened, wouldn't you?'

'Yes, sir.'

Over the subsequent years I don't believe that Brother Price ever betrayed Brother Roberts' secret. In fact, from then on, when Brother Roberts made his grand entrance on Wednesday evenings, Brother Price seemed much less concerned and agitated, as if he didn't mind so much, now that he knew exactly what was going on in the bathroom on Wednesday nights.

*

I knew about some of the senior boys who tried to interfere with the smaller boys in the showers and toilets but they never gave me any trouble. Many of them knew about Brothers Price's and Roberts' interest in me, and, for their own sakes, gave me a wide berth. It was some comfort to be gained from an appalling situation but it wasn't absolute. For instance I always knew that I was most vulnerable to a sexual assault from older boys when the two Brothers were away on holidays.

A few days into the summer holidays, one of these senior boys made a move on me, on the way back from the chapel after evening rosary. I will call him 'Jim', but that's not his real name. He was a big brute of a fella with very large hands, maybe fifteen or sixteen years of age. I knew nothing of him; he wasn't one of the usual suspects.

'Clemenger, I'm going to have you. I'll see you later.'

Filled with fear I told him that if he touched me I would tell Brother Price when he returned from holidays.

'Fuck you and fuck Brother Price, you little runt.'

When eventually he did strike it was in the middle dormitory. He grabbed me from behind and threw me onto a bed.

'No point shouting, Clemenger. There's no one here to save you now.'

Violently he grabbed hold of my trousers, pulled them down around my ankles and fell on top of me. He was very strong and powerful.

'Keep still, I want to kiss you.'

Holding my head steady he thrust his tongue down

my throat while trying to grab my privates with his left hand. It hurt like hell. I was afraid that he might kill me so I kept still. He didn't care how I was feeling.

'Turn around, you fucker, I want to get at your arse.'

Repeatedly he tried to stick his thing into me, but it wouldn't fit.

'You're too tight, but I'll have you, keep still.'

Despite repeated efforts he failed to have his way. In his frustration he started to beat me hard on the bottom with his clenched fists. All in all he landed me about eight blows, all the time cursing me until finally he stopped. Grabbing me by the throat he threatened that he would kill me with his bare hands if I ever mentioned him to Brothers Price or Roberts. For the next few weeks I walked about with very sore buttocks that were black and blue. My assailant assumed that he had frightened me so much that I wouldn't dare to tell on him. He was wrong.

Brother Price arrived back about two weeks later. As was his custom he called me to his room to resume his normal sexual escapades. On seeing the traces of bruising on my buttocks and legs he became upset. I eagerly explained what had happened, but was not prepared for his reaction.

'The boy's name, Michael. IMMEDIATELY!'

A chill went through me. I had never seen him so angry before.

'I can't, sir, he told me he would kill me.'

'The name, Michael.'

After giving him my attacker's name, he sat on his bed and wiped his brow.

'That sneak! It's not the first time I've heard about him. Don't worry, by the time I'm finished with him he'll be so sore he won't want to touch another boy ever again. Come with me to the kitchen for something to eat.'

After a good feed he told me to say nothing about the matter for a few days. Then he pounced. My assailant was called from the yard, having no idea that I had reported him. He left the yard with a half sneer directed towards me, but I was to have the last laugh. Within the hour I was called to Brother Price's room. There on the bed was 'Jim', completely naked with strap marks on his bottom and thighs.

'Sit on the chair, Michael. I'm not finished with this boy yet. See what I do to any boy who would dare interfere with you.'

I felt distinctly uncomfortable. Brother Price gave my assailant a few more slaps of the leather as hard as he could. Screams and cries rang out together with pleas for mercy from the helpless boy. It seemed clear to me that the Brother had no intention of stopping and I grew fearful that the boy might be killed. Jumping off the chair I stood between him and 'Jim'.

'Stop, please, sir. Don't hit him anymore, he's had enough. Please, sir.'

Brother Price, his hand raised to strike again, stopped in amazement at my intervention.

'Why, Michael? Did he stop when you asked him? I don't think so.'

'Even so, sir, please stop. He's had enough. Please.'

My voice was trembling.

'All right, Michael.'

He threw his leather on to the bed.

'Get dressed and get out of here. And if you even so much as look in Michael's direction again you'll get more of the same. In fact I'll finish you off.'

Over the next few days 'Jim' was confined to bed due to the severity of the beating. In spite of myself I felt some pity for him and, unknown to Brother Price, visited him every day bringing him comics, books and sweets. His only concern was that Brother Price might see me with him and he would get another beating. I reassured him that nothing would happen. However, I did ask him to promise that he wouldn't interfere with any other boys in the future. He said he was sorry for what had happened.

'By the way, Michael, why did you stop Brother Price? I don't think I'd have done the same in your place. You're a good boy, Michael. I know from some of the boys that you want to become a priest. I hope you do some day.'

'Jim' left the monastery a few months later. I never forgot his assault on me but also, more importantly, I never forgot the reaction of Brother Price. He became extremely protective towards me in the succeeding years, putting the word out that under no circumstances was I to be touched by any of the senior boys.

Brother Breen and
Brother Murphy

FORTUNATELY I COULD read and write by the time I arrived at St Joseph's. There were about three hundred boys in the monastery in August 1959, and not many of them went to school or had much learning. Some worked in the various trades such as bakery, farming, carpentry, tailoring and shoemaking. Boys considered to be less than clever usually got these jobs, according to their particular level of intelligence: thick, slow, backward, idiots and 'amadawns' were common labels used by the Brothers. These labels must have had a devastating effect on their concept of self, long after they had left the orphanage.

I was placed in the third class, which was under the care of Brother Breen, one of our oldest teachers. He was very tactile. During religious instruction he often sat me on his knee, rubbing my legs with his enormous hands. I wasn't afraid of him because he constantly told me that I was a very bright boy. He was the first person to introduce me to the Irish language. I had little understanding of the grammar, however, which frustrated both of us, and found myself unable to learn it by rote as I had done with the Catechism. When Brother Breen was pleased with my scholastic efforts he slipped me a few sweets in class.

My copybooks in Irish, English and Maths had seen better days. Their pages were well worn, with the names of previous owners crossed out in turn as each new pupil ascribed their own. I often wondered what became of these previous students or, more importantly, what would become of me when I had to pass the books on and have my name crossed off by a new owner. The only time I ever saw Brother Breen – who didn't carry a strap on his hip – lose his temper and slap a boy on the back of the legs, with his hand, was when he was trying to teach us Irish. He called us a class of 'amadawns' when no hand went up to answer the '*cúpla focail*'.

Anyway, after two years, I was transferred to Brother Murphy's class. A native Irish speaker, his classroom was more like a newspaper shop. About thirty boys sat amongst the clutter of tea chests full of tattered newspapers written in Irish. From the ceiling hung out-of-date calendars that swayed in the wind when the old creaky door opened. There was a long blackboard that stretched from one side of the classroom to the other. On my first morning I realised, much to my horror, that most of the writing on the blackboard was in Irish. *My God*, I said to myself, *I'm in for it now with this clown*. To be fair to Brother Murphy he was never boring. From one end of the day to the other he wandered around the classroom as if on a sacred mission to educate these unfortunates that God had placed in his delicate care. Except that he was anything but delicate. He laboured like a madman, determined that, if it was God's will, and given the strength of the strap he swung liberally from arse to arse, we would, one day, walk out of his classroom as 'native Irish speakers'. Alas, alas, it was all in vain.

'Amadawns is all that God has sent me. I cannot get Irish into these fools, no matter how hard I try. And only God Himself knows how hard I try.'

With that he continued to lament *as Gaeilge*, pacing the floor and even growling to himself. I thought him the height of entertainment and never wanted to miss a day in his class. Not everyone agreed with me, particularly the poor unfortunates he often beat within inches of their lives. While he taught other subjects, like English and maths, his great love was Irish and he frequently slipped in the '*cúpla focail*' even when teaching maths. The dumb faces looking back at him, including my own, would always invoke a response of 'amadawns, amadawns', and with a roll of the eyes he would move reluctantly on.

Possibly his second favourite subject was religious instruction. I think he fancied himself as a priest. He never went anywhere without his black Bible, which he would fondle incessantly, flicking through the pages for divine inspiration. As far as I was concerned he was at his most entertaining when he embarked on one of his religious chants. From his throat there would emanate such pieties that it was hard to reconcile his vicious streak with such a religious countenance. In fact he used the Bible to play mind games with us. Closing his eyes he would begin to chant, almost appearing to lose consciousness. Then, suddenly, an eye would pop open in the hope of catching some poor boy laughing at him. With flight of foot he would strike and dispatch his prey to sick bay for repairs.

Depending on the ferocity of the attack the victim might appear back in class within a few minutes, or days, to make his apology. Brother Murphy, with a disdainful wave, would tell the lad to sit down again. More often than not boys were only able to sit on one cheek of their bottoms as a testimony to the savagery of the beating.

On the hour, every hour, the brown clock would ring out, whereupon Brother Murphy made us stand and say a prayer to Our Lady. Even at such a tender age I was enthralled with the concept of time. Brother Murphy was always saying that everything has its own time. I wondered where time went to. Did it go back to Heaven because it belonged to God? I hadn't yet learnt how to read the brown clock myself. The other boys told me that I had to wait until I reached fifth class, and even then it was only ever taught by Brother Price. Therefore, when Brother Roberts taught me how to tell the time I had to let on to Brother Price that I was learning something new. I think he knew that I could read his watch already, but he said nothing.

All the Brothers wore watches on their wrists. On one occasion Brother Breen, noticing my fascination with his watch, let me hold it. His was the only one that had a black face. It also made a noise when I held it up to my ear. I asked him where the noise was coming from, but didn't understand his 'tick-tock' answer. Furthermore I couldn't fathom how watches kept going in the dark when you couldn't see them.

Brother Burke

BROTHER BURKE WAS a very old Christian Brother who had been living in St Joseph's for years. He took no part in any activities in the school and was only seen at the morning Mass. He was fairly small, bent down with age and walked with difficulty, requiring the support of a big brown walking stick.

One Friday evening when I was about twelve years old Brother Roberts called me to his room. Reluctantly, with a heavy heart, I made my way to his room, expecting his usual putting his tongue down my throat. He seemed to have been waiting for me because as soon as I arrived he combed my hair, telling me that we were going to visit one of the other Brothers who was poorly. As we walked along the quiet dark corridor I wondered who it could be. Halfway down the corridor Brother Roberts told me to use the Brothers' toilet as we could be with the sick brother for a while. He tapped on a door that I wasn't familiar with. A voice cried loudly 'come in, come in'. When the door opened a gush of smoke swept past me into the corridor. Holding me tightly by the hand Brother Roberts walked me into the room.

'Hello, Brother Burke, how are you feeling this evening?'

The room was nice and cosy with a little fire in the grate. For a second or two I couldn't see Brother Burke. Then out of the corner of my eye I spotted a tiny figure lying in the bed, propped up with pillows. He looked like a ghost: pale, sweaty and coughing frequently.

'This is Michael Clemenger. He's going to clean your room for you every Saturday morning at 11.30.'

'Come forward, boy, let me see you.'

I stepped very close to the bed so that he could get a good look at me.

'Ah, yes, so you are Michael. Sit by me, I think I know you. Brother Roberts, doesn't Michael serve Mass for Father O'Neill most mornings?'

'He certainly does. He's the best boy I ever had, Brother, the best indeed.'

Somehow I don't think that Brother Burke understood the true meaning of what was being said.

'If Michael cleans Father O'Neill's room, then he's good enough for me. He can start tomorrow morning. Now Michael, I won't be here so just come into the room and give it a good tidy. Good boy.'

I duly arrived at Brother Burke's room at 11.30, the following morning. On the stairs I ran into Brother Murphy who was surprised to see me in the Brothers' quarters on a Saturday morning.

'What are you doing here at this hour of the day?'

Needless to say I took great delight in telling him that I had just been assigned to clean out Brother Burke's room every Saturday morning. He actually snarled as he brushed past me down the stairs.

The elderly Brother's room was quite dark with lots of holy pictures hanging on the walls. A big statue of Our Lady stood on the mantelpiece. Above the fireplace he had stuck up several photos of himself as a younger man, some of which included him posing with whom I assumed to be his family, while others showed him standing under a blue sky, surrounded by exotic looking people, probably from the years he spent away on the foreign missions.

The duties were similar to those of Father O'Neill's room. Brother Burke was a heavy smoker and on the table beside the bed I often counted five or six pipes that were in use at any one time. I cleared out the ashes, actually filling a bucket to the top, and then I carefully carried it to the coal shed without any accidental spills along the way. He also loved candles and had a lot of them stacked in a corner of his room. There were also lots of prayer books and rosary beads scattered in various places around the room. I imagined he must say his rosary in bed because, while straightening out the covers, I often found a couple of sets of the beads at the top of the bed or on the floor beneath it. I usually finished his room in twenty minutes and would spend the rest of the time going through his books.

Sitting in his arm chair amongst his books, pictures and beads it was easy to forget, just for a little while, that I was an orphan in St Joseph's. The whole atmosphere in this little room lent itself to my fantasy that one day I could be like Brother Burke or Father O'Neill. I found it comforting to be surrounded by props of holy books, beads, prayers, statues and crucifixes. If I offered up my circumstances to Jesus in time I might become worthy of the honour of priesthood. In all my prayers to God I was very definite with him that I didn't want to become a Christian Brother. After leaving Brother Burke's room I usually slipped into the chapel to pray earnestly to become a priest. Ironically my desire to become a priest was reinforced by my visits to Brother Burke's room rather than Father O'Neill's.

I never had any complaints from Brother Burke about my work. Occasionally he left sixpence or a shilling on the side table with my name on it. I was careful always to take the money back to Brother Roberts' room.

'I was right about you, Michael. I have known boys to take money like that and put it in their own pockets.'

Brother Burke's generosity greatly enhanced the number of sweets I received over the succeeding years.

Father O'Neill's Sermons

EVERY SUNDAY, AT midday, we assembled in the chapel for Father O'Neill's sermons. He never performed these with much enthusiasm, but saw them, I think, as a necessary chore. He plodded up the aisle when we had been quietened down by the reliable Brother Murphy. Most of his sermons were forgettable, but I paid particular attention since I imagined that one day I might be giving similar sermons in far away Africa. The idea of joining the priesthood was really beginning to take root in my mind, although I told nobody about it. A few themes could always be relied on to pass the half hour. Father O'Neill's pet hates included telling lies, stealing, impure thoughts and masturbation. Regarding lying and stealing, he usually referenced them in the context of our future employment.

'It is important to uphold the good name of the school at all times. The world out there is a hard place and you always have to be on your guard.'

The example often cited was the case of a hotel manager interviewing applicants for a job in his hotel.

After each interview the man deliberately dropped a pen on the floor. Most of the boys went through the door without hearing the pen fall. It was during the last interview, however, that the boy heard the pen falling. He immediately retrieved the pen from the floor and handed it to the owner, who promptly told him he had the job. The moral of the story was that good manners go a long way.

Father O'Neill's whole demeanour stiffened when the topics of impurity and masturbation came up. In his eyes these were grave sins against the Almighty. Brother Murphy could always be relied on to cough appropriately as if to remind us to sit up and listen. Sombre in his gestures, the priest would slowly remove his glasses, replacing them with another pair and begin to read with great solemnity from the Holy Bible. He frightened the bejasus out of us with his pious ferocity. Hell was waiting for any of us who dared to indulge in such practices. It was most important that we prayed to Our Lady: Three Hail Marys for purity, both day and night. I heard it said in the playground that some of the older boys had gone to confession and told him of the sexual abuse they were being subjected to at the hands of the Brothers. Outraged at such accusations, he reported them to the Brother Superior who promptly dismissed them out of hand as lies and fiction. The complainants usually got a good hiding for their troubles.

What caused Father O'Neill to expand his chest to its full extent was that dreadful and most filthy habit of all, masturbation. His voice literally quivered with disgust at the very idea. Apparently it was particularly abhorrent because it was a sin that could be committed without anybody knowing. Even the word itself was enough to upset poor Brother Murphy as he feared just hearing it was enough to put bad thoughts into our simple minds. I was always fascinated with the way that masturbation terrified both priest and Brother equally.

'No! No! No to masturbation!'

Father O'Neill frequently bellowed out this mantra, clenching his fist for emphasis and clinging to his Bible for support. It brought a laugh to my mind when he solemnly announced that he would always know who the masturbators were. Hair would grow on the palms of their hands and eventually they would go blind. It was God's way of punishing such vile and disgusting acts committed in the dead of night. For such sinners hell was surely waiting, where there would be much wailing and gnashing of teeth. Prayer was the only thing that could save us from a fate worse than death. After frightening the shite out of us he would slowly descend from the altar carrying his two pairs of spectacles. I couldn't help wondering why Father O'Neill would need two pairs of glasses. His eyesight must have been very bad indeed.

One of these Sunday sermons, however, struck a particular chord with me, about Jesus preaching to a large crowd. The adults were pushing the children back, slapping them out of the way, so they could get closer to Jesus. Seeing this, Jesus cried out for them to stop what they were doing and let the children approach. Father O'Neill continued.

'Suffer little children to come unto me. It were better that a millstone be tied around their necks and they be cast to the bottom of the sea rather than harm one of these my little ones.'

I was completely taken aback, as I am sure were many of the boys around me. Considering what he knew about the sexual abuse carried out by some of the Brothers, and his inaction on our behalf, I thought he had a brass neck. What a hypocrite he was. Over the years I had heard him repeat this 'suffer little children' nonsense several times over. He seemed able to dissociate the words of the Gospel from the grim reality of what he surely knew was happening all around him. Moreover, the Brothers themselves failed to make the connection between these words and their own deeds. I lost any remaining respect for Father O'Neill thereafter and came to appreciate that talk was cheap. Action was what counted.

In bed at night I often wondered where Jesus was in all this. Father O'Neill was fond of saying that God will not be mocked and that His eyes were all seeing. That kind of threat was always associated with the hidden sins of impurity and masturbation. Well then, didn't God or Jesus see what the Brothers were doing to us? And if so, what was He doing to protect us? I was starting to have doubts about this Jesus.

The Typical Day at St Joseph's

AT 7 O'CLOCK every morning the Brothers assigned to each dormitory burst through the doors, shouting and clapping their hands loudly. A bad morning was when they pulled the bedclothes off us, hurling insults at our sleepy frames. I hated having to wash in cold water, especially during the winter months. Then I had to endure the 7.30 Mass with the usually cranky Father O'Neill. After Mass I joined the other boys in the refectory for breakfast. When the meal was finished I cleaned the rooms and fetched the newspaper, making sure to be back on time for assembly at 9.30. This involved being lined for inspection by the superior along with the cobbler and the tailor. We were examined to determine if we needed new boots or a change of clothes. Despite the bad food we constantly grew out of our clothes. Then the boys assigned to the farm, carpentry, tailor's shop or cobblers would fall out and disappear. The rest of us went off to our various class rooms with little enthusiasm. We all met again, in the early afternoon, for a dinner fit only for pigs. If we didn't eat it we starved. The beautiful smells of cooking coming from the Brothers' quarters only increased our hunger pains.

Surviving Brother Lane's half hour at meal times was always foremost in our minds. Many of us would have gladly missed dinner rather than have to cope with his terrifying glares. After dinner we played in the yard until the nurse appeared. How we dreaded the sight of this harmless old woman, with her large spoon of cod liver oil that she eagerly stuffed into us. 'It's good for you boys,' was all she would say when boys tried to resist or spit it out. At 2 o'clock we went back to school or work until 4 o'clock whereupon tea and a slice of bread would be served in the refectory. Most of the younger boys then played in the yard until six in the evening.

A senior boy assigned the task would ring the Angelus bell, which was beside the toilets, and we would all march off to the chapel for the rosary. We all had our own rosary beads, which we were expected to have with us at all times. The various mysteries in the early years were said by Brother Roberts, but as his deafness became more obvious he was replaced by Brother Murphy. Supper was at 6.45pm and usually consisted of a couple of slices of bread, weak tea and Stork margarine. After wash-up it was out to play in the fields on a summer's evening or, in the years St Joseph's had a television set, watch TV until 9pm. Bed followed soon afterwards and so the years went on and on.

*

One Saturday morning, sometime in September 1961, Brother Price assembled all the boys in the playground and announced that we were going to get a television set. I had no idea what he was talking about. On the following Monday afternoon a van arrived at the school with a big box. One of the men went up to the roof and placed an aerial on the chimney. With due ceremony Brother Price turned on the TV, but there was neither picture nor sound. In the excitement he had forgotten to plug the set into the socket on the wall. Some boys started to jeer and shout but Brother Price didn't see the funny side of it and gave them a slap of the leather he carried on his hip.

My earliest television memory was an ad for Lyons – 'the quality tea'. I found the advertisements more interesting than the regular programmes. In a short time all the boys were TV addicts, which helped to keep the monastery running smoothly. The TV usually went on at 7.30pm, after the prayers and supper, and was switched off at 9pm when we were all marched off to bed. Television personalities, such as Bunny Carr and Seamus Ennis, soon became favourites. After about a year the novelty wore off and most of the boys preferred the films that came to the school every weekend. Usually the film arrived by car at about a quarter to five on a Friday evening and was placed strategically in a window in the Brothers' private quarters. There was always a cheer from us when we caught a glimpse of it. Most of us loved westerns, as well as gangster and war movies.

Some of the Brothers were not keen on having us gathered together in the dark, watching films. For Brother Murphy, in particular, it was an opportunity for the worst type of sin, with the possibility that the boys would touch each other's private parts. I found it very amusing, watching him walking up and down the rows of boys with his little flash lamp.

'Where are your hands, boy? Keep them out in front of you where I can see them.'

Most of the boys took advantage of the darkness to hurl insults at him.

'I'll get you, don't you worry. I know who said that! You'll be sorry, you lot of curs.'

Then there would be a chorus of voices shouting at him.

'Please sit down, sir; we want to watch the film. Please, sir!'

With that he would slither back to his seat at the back of the long hall. I don't think he liked films very much and he was always whinging that TV was bad for our eyes. During the changeover of the reel he flashed his lamp to let us know that he was still around. Many of the boys hated him, but I always enjoyed his 'tomfoolery' no end.

After the showing of the film one week Brother Price asked me to wait behind as he wanted to speak with me.

'Well, Michael, did you enjoy the film?'

'Yes, sir.'

'Do you know where the films come from, Michael?'

I must confess I never gave it much thought.

'Dublin, Michael, where you come from. They have to go back there every Monday morning on the train. I need somebody trustworthy to take them to the train station on Monday mornings. Do you think you could manage that for me?'

'I think so, sir, but I don't know where the train station is, sir.'

'That's all right, Michael. We'll take the film there on Monday morning together and I'll show you where to go.'

This meant that now I had gotten all the top jobs in the school – and at such a young age. Being favoured by Brothers Price and Roberts certainly made life a little more bearable, but few of the other boys were aware that there was a price to be paid for such generosity. There certainly were lots of rumours, especially about Brother Roberts, giving one or two boys a 'special wash' on Saturday nights, which was bath night for all of us. These boys were always upset in themselves for a few days afterwards. I never said anything about either Brother despite regular promptings. In fact nobody said anything at all. I saw boys being taken from their beds at night but, like everyone else, I pretended not to see it. It was a big secret that everyone knew about but no one, neither Brothers nor boys, ever spoke about.

1962 All Ireland

KERRY WAS A great county for the football and every September they were expected to win the Sam Maguire cup. If they didn't win the Kerry people would say that they were only lending out the cup for that year. For us boys in St Joseph's it was hugely important that Kerry won because not only did it mean we had a day off school, but also that some of the Kerry players would visit us with the Sam Maguire cup.

Kerry won the all Ireland final in 1959, the year I arrived at St Joseph's, but I didn't have any interest in the sport back then. When we got the television, however, I got to know such Kerry legends as Mick O'Connell, Mick O'Dwyer, Johnny Culloty and the Sheehy brothers. Naturally we were terribly disappointed when Kerry lost in 1960 and 1961 but then we watched them win in 1962. Brother Ryan, the superior, duly informed us that some members of the Kerry team would visit the school on the following Wednesday, at half past two. In the meantime we would be scrubbed from head to toe, have our hair cut and be wearing our Sunday best for the visit.

Even the Brothers were excited at the possibility of meeting Mick O'Connell, so I think it's fair to say that we were all disappointed when only a few players arrived with Sam on the Wednesday, including Johnny Culloty, who played in goal, and Niall Sheehy. There was no sign of Mick. Niall Sheehy was huge. When I was introduced to him he lifted me up in the air. He had a winning smile and was a real gentle giant. He gave me the Sam Maguire cup to hold and shouted at the rest of the boys,

'Now lads! Up Kerry!'

With that we all started shouting 'Up Kerry! Up Kerry! Up Kerry!'

The Brothers put on a big scoff and we all got sweets, lemonade and oranges. The Kerry players seemed mighty impressed with the jolly atmosphere between the Brothers and us, not realising, of course, that it was all a sham. We were under strict orders to behave ourselves. If we didn't we'd probably end up in sick bay. The visit lasted about forty minutes. Brother Ryan thanked the players for their visit and rewarded us with a day off school. He ended his short speech by asking for three cheers for our visitors. Just before he got back into the car Niall Sheehy came over to shake my hand and say goodbye. I was thrilled with myself.

When they were gone we changed out of our Sunday clothes and headed for the playing fields to re-enact the great final all over again.

Confirmation, June 1963

ONE SATURDAY MORNING, in 1963, just after St Patrick's Day, Brother Roberts informed me that I would be making my Confirmation. The relevant instruction would be provided by Father O'Neill and Brother Price. The idea of becoming a soldier of Christ, thanks to the sacrament of Confirmation, meant nothing to me while talk about renewing my 'baptism vows', whatever they were, made no impression on my mind. Nevertheless my excitement grew as the big day approached, not least because it would be my first time to see a bishop.

A few weeks later Brother Price called me to his room. Apparently there was a serious problem that could prevent me going forward for confirmation: there was no written evidence to prove I had ever been baptised. It was shocking news. How could I become a priest, I thought to myself, if I wasn't even a member of the Catholic Church? I must have looked upset.

'Don't worry, Michael, I am sure that everything will work out just fine.'

I took comfort from that, as he always made things all right.

For the next few weeks I waited anxiously. The time was spent praying for Pope John XXIII, who had died that May, and hoping that God would send a new pope who would continue the good work of the Second Vatican Council. My eyes glazed over during the Sunday sermons when Father O'Neill extolled the many, many virtues of this council. Meanwhile confirmation suits were picked out for us, usually hand-me-down suits worn by boys in previous years, which explained their distinctive smell of mothballs. These suits only made an appearance one day a year. No word came from Brother Price about what was happening until the Friday before the event, when he called me to his room late in the evening.

'Listen carefully to what I'm going to tell you.'

My mind was racing ahead. Please God, let the news be good. I so want to be a priest when I grow up.

'Michael, my boy, you'll be making your Confirmation after all. We found the evidence we needed. Do you want to know the details?'

'Yes please, sir.'

'Well, it's a strange one all right. It seems that you were born in Dublin, but you weren't baptised in your local parish.'

He coughed slightly.

'The problem arose because you were baptised in a neighbouring parish. A church called St Nicholas of Myra in Francis Street, in the centre of Dublin.'

'What does that mean, sir?'

We were sitting side by side on his bed and he placed his arm around my shoulder.

'Oh, don't bother your pretty head about such things for the moment, Michael.'

I persisted.

'Have I any parents, sir?'

'Why, of course you have. We all have. How do you think you came into this world otherwise? It's just that things don't always work out so that children can stay with their parents.'

'Is that what happened to me, sir?'

'I'm afraid I don't know the answer to that question, Michael. Perhaps you'll find out the answer yourself one day. But you're a nice boy; everything will work out fine for you.'

He seemed very uncomfortable talking about my parents.

'Let's change the subject, shall we? You know that you have to have a confirmation name. Why not take the name of our new Pope, Paul VI. Michael Paul Clemenger, that has a nice ring to it, doesn't it?'

After a little more fondling he told me to go to the yard to tell the other boys my good news. Just before I fell asleep that night, I wondered about my baptism in a strange church.

The great day finally arrived on the fourth Sunday in June. The sun was shining as we clambered onto the minibus that was taking us to St John's Church for the ceremony. The boys were giddy with delight. I was less so because Brother Lane was in charge of us. I glared at him out of the corner of my eye. It was just my luck that he'd be here to spoil the fun. When we arrived at the church he issued a frightful warning: basically if we misbehaved he would skin us alive.

To my surprise the church was already packed. The town children, who were making their confirmation alongside us, were already in their pews. They delighted in the fuss being made of them by their families. I didn't know about my classmates, but the sight of those doted-upon children produced a profound sense of bitterness and resentment in me. In fact I came very close to tears. Yet, despite the pain, I couldn't tear my eyes away from them; the giddy excitement of the parents, the affectionate grandparents, the aunties, uncles, sisters and brothers. The atmosphere in the church was tremendous. Music was playing, the hundreds of people were making a racket and anxious-looking altar boys were rushing about the place. Why wasn't I being carried away on the contagious wave of excitement? Instead, I had never felt so lonely in all my life. *Yes, Michael, you're an outsider because you have no parents.* My inner demons danced a jig inside my head. *Where were my kisses, my hugs, my happy family? Far away in Dublin*, I thought bitterly. *I was so much an outsider my own parents hadn't even wanted me.* Love was being paraded before my eyes, but it had nothing to do with me. I could see it but never experience it. A silent rage was born in me that day, one that still generates bitterness and overwhelming feelings of isolation all these years later.

The music grew louder and with great fanfare the bishop made his grand entrance. My eyes never left the families in front of me. From the back seat I had a good view of the proceedings. The bishop spoke eloquently about the love and pride the families must be feeling on this most joyous day. His remarks were obviously only addressed to them, and certainly not to us poor boys from St Joseph's. *Feck him. Feck the lot of them. I'm on my own? So be it. I can look after myself.*

The children were brought forward to the bishop, who smiled at each of them in turn and patted them on the cheek. Photographs were taken for the albums. Finally it was the turn of the boys from St Joseph's. Being almost last in our line I had time to take a closer look at the happy families in the pews. Their looks of pity infuriated me. Well, I for one didn't need their pity. I was as good as any of them. On being beckoned forward by Brother Lane I rose to my full height of 4 foot 10 inches and marched as if to meet my enemy in battle. I believed a thousand pairs of eyes were upon me and I was determined not to buckle.

Fixing my eyes firmly on the bishop, I took great pride in the fact that he blinked first. Turning aside he uttered some prayers and patted my cheek. It was over in seconds. I heard him say 'Amen' and made my grand exit convinced that I had won a great fight. Walking back to my pew I paused briefly to take a last good look around the whole congregation, taking in the grand design of the church, from ceiling to floor. Some of the other boys were delighted at my antics. They knew what I was doing, as did Brother Lane. He glared at me menacingly, but I didn't give a damn about him. All I knew was that I had grown up that day. The steel spine was fully formed now. I would go forward henceforth, not as a soldier of Christ, but as my own man, afraid of none of the feckers. I was an army of one. My feelings of being different now had definition. I was an outsider driven by hate and isolation. My dream of becoming a priest reinforced my sense of my own worth; I would not be defined by others. I refused to draw on their opinion of me, good, bad or indifferent. I would survive the experience of being unwanted and unloved though the pain might never go away.

In the days following my Confirmation my perception of my circumstances began to crystallise more clearly. Up to this, I had just accepted things as they were without much thought. But now my feelings took on a new urgency. A strange anger seized me. Images of happy families enraged me. An abiding resentment against the world replaced my tears. It was poor consolation to be continually told that God had a plan for each of us and that he loved us enough to die on the cross for our sins. What sins had I committed to end up in this place of misery?

As I carried out my chores in the town my mind was continually asking questions about the people I saw. Did their children have to put up with being pawed and slobbered on by old men? Were they being beaten within inches of their lives? Were their futures bright? It seemed to me that it had already been ordained; they were destined to success while we orphans were doomed to failure. I began to loathe the town children, especially if I saw them with their parents. How I longed to change places with them. I envied them as I made my way back to the monastery, careful not to wet the newspaper with my tears. Instinctively I knew that I would have to find some coping mechanism, otherwise I would not be able to continue going down town.

From that point on, I would pretend not to see them. I would project beyond them as if they didn't exist. Many rosaries and prayers were said by me along my hill of Calvary. Adopting an air of quiet superiority, I groomed myself carefully, and wore the best clothes I could find. My shoes were spick and span and I kept my hair in place with a comb that was a present from Brother Roberts. I cultivated good manners and presented myself with a confidence that I never felt internally. I became a very good actor, always smiling for the town folk and performing above myself, in their view, despite my poor circumstances. How I hated their condescending manner, their embarrassed half smiles and gestures of fear that I might attack their children.

It was during this period that I began to wet the bed and suck my thumb at night. An astonished Brother Price transferred me from the middle to the senior dormitory so he could keep an eye on me. I also became fearful of the dark and couldn't sleep if I couldn't see the nightlight. Brothers Price and Roberts grew very concerned about me. The former had me moved to the bed that was directly under the nightlight. Underneath the light hung a huge portrait of a boy who was similar in age to me. His name was Saint Dominic Savio. Brother Roberts gave me a little booklet about his life that I read from cover to cover. Sometimes when I was in the yard Brother Price allowed me to go to the chapel to visit Our Lady, for whom, he knew, I had special devotion. Before her statue I would fervently recite the rosary and offer up my tears. Between these visits to the chapel and the constant prayers to St Dominic I slowly began to dissociate myself from the reality of the hell that was St Joseph's.

I could only survive if I cloaked myself with a religious piety and viewed my suffering as a preparation for the afterlife in Heaven. In that frame of mind I learned to cope with my circumstances. Walking down the town became less problematic and my bed wetting stopped suddenly, though I continued to suck my thumb for years to come. I got to love the bed and would often pretend to be unwell knowing that Brother Roberts would give me a few days off sick. This usually occurred at the weekends. In my own bed all my dreams usually came true and nothing bad ever happened.

The Lay Staff

MR CANTANELL WAS our music teacher. I have only fond memories of this man. In a place of gloom, misery, tears and floggings he did his best to brighten up our lives with music. A quiet, shy man with delicate hands, he could barely move his head because of a growth behind his neck. Some of the boys nicknamed him 'Banana Neck', but never had the guts to say it to his face. His movements were slow and deliberate, and he moved about the band room as if he was in a perpetual state of conduction. Brother Roberts introduced him to me somewhat reluctantly as he would have preferred to keep me in his dancing class where he could mould me. However, even he agreed that I didn't have dancing feet.

Mr Cantanell seemed to sense from my first meeting with him that Brother Roberts had a particular interest in me and that he should keep an eye on me. Even though Brother Roberts was getting old he still exercised power in the school when it suited his purposes, especially in relation to me.

'You're a lucky boy, Michael, that Brother Roberts cares so much about you that he would personally introduce you to me. That has never happened with anyone else.'

I just looked straight at him and said nothing. I worried that perhaps he knew something already.

'So, which instrument would you like to try?'

He brought me over to the press and opened it.

'Go on then, pick one.'

I took out a trumpet. It was shiny but felt quite heavy in my hands. Mr Cantanell took the instrument from me.

'You are quite small and delicate for your age, aren't you, Michael? Perhaps something smaller would be more suitable.'

He picked out what looked like a tin whistle; I had seen one being played on the television. Telling me that it was actually a piccolo, he placed it at the side of his mouth and started to play a tune on it. Then he handed it to me.

'Go on, try it for me.'

I blew into it, but no sound came out of it. There was little improvement over the next few months, despite the music teacher's best efforts. He advised me to forget music and that I would never be any good at it. I was both relieved and surprised because he never got angry with me in all that time.

One evening Brother Roberts called to see Mr Cantanell about me.

'Well, how is Michael getting on?'

I could see that Mr Cantanell was nervously searching around for a diplomatic answer. He hated any unpleasantness. To his surprise I answered for him.

'It's no use, sir. I can't seem to get the hang of this instrument and besides I don't have the ear for music like some of the other boys.'

Brother Roberts, in some surprise, looked at Mr Cantanell.

'Not to worry about Michael then. He wasn't very good with his feet so it's no wonder that he's no better with his hands. He only does well with the schooling.'

This last remark he seemed to express more to himself.

However, he did ask Mr Cantanell to keep me on in the band room until something else turned up. I don't know which of the three of us was the more relieved, although Mr Cantanell was certainly pleased that Brother Roberts had asked him a favour. Over the next few months I did little in the band, save risking damage to my ears during the heroic attempts of Mr Cantanell to make other boys play their instruments in tune. To be fair to him, if he spotted any boy with the potential to be a musician he encouraged him in every way.

He often called me to his room after dinner. I never worried about him. Sexually abusing boys wasn't his style and he had no reputation for that sort of thing among the others. When I knocked on his door he gleefully shouted out to me to come in. Locking the door behind me, he took out from the cupboard a case containing his pride and joy, a violin that had seen better days, and caressed it lovingly. In all the time I knew him, he never once let me handle that sacred instrument. Sheets of music were placed on a stand and then he would seat himself royally on an old chair and start to play. On and on he would go, performing one melodious tune after another, bringing himself into a state of anxiety as he went. Beads of sweat would fall copiously from his forehead, often onto the violin itself, which he never noticed until the end. Often he would ask me to face away from him and shout out in his excitement:

'Michael, Michael, is my bow hopping?'

'I don't know, sir.'

'Well, you must listen because if the music is played right, the bow should glide along the strings not hop. Music, Michael, is played with the heart and appreciated with the ear.'

I believe that Mr Cantanell lived for that period every afternoon, when he could indulge his real passion, playing the violin. It seemed to give him the resolve to go on for the rest of the day and I was happy to have been a part of it. On one occasion, while putting his violin back in its case, he surprised me by asking what I would like to be when I grew up. I told him I wanted to be a priest and go to the foreign missions in Africa. He was surprised at my answer.

'So you would like to be a priest, Michael. How are you at school?'

'I'm very good at school, I think, sir.'

'Well then, perhaps one day.'

He always treated me most kindly after that. Though he was never tactile with us boys, on my last day he gave me a gentle hug and wished me luck. I don't think I ever spoke with him again though he did smile at me whenever we met in the yard.

*

Archibald was the caretaker, an old shadow that rambled from dormitory to dormitory at all hours of the night. He was a strange fella indeed. I don't ever recall him speaking in all the years that I was in St Joseph's. You always knew he was around from the smell of the foul tobacco that he smoked incessantly and the tapping sound of his cane. Part of his job was to wake the habitual bed-wetters and get them to go to the toilet. I once asked Brother Roberts about him. He told me that old Archibald was a retired garda. Nothing else was said.

None of the boys ever had a good word to say about him. Every two hours, throughout the night, he appeared in the doorway of the dormitory and turned a key in a hole in the wall. The key was then returned to a brown box that he carried across his chest. One night he saw me coming out of Brother Price's room at about 11.30 at night. He seemed surprised but said nothing as I hurried back to my bed. He didn't live in St Joseph's and cycled to and from the monastery on his big, squeaky bicycle.

*

Mr Quinlan was in charge of the tailor shop. He was a very quiet and reserved gentleman despite the high demands made on him by the growing number of boys. He inspected us every morning, at assembly, but never got involved with us in any way, save in regard to clothing. Brother Roberts assigned me to the tailor shop when I was about twelve years old, personally introducing me to Mr Quinlan. They had some understanding between them. Brother Roberts told the tailor that there would be times when I wouldn't be in the workshop but that he shouldn't worry because I would most likely be with him.

Mr Quinlan was generally indifferent to any of the boys in the tailor shop who weren't good with their hands. There were some boys who showed promise and with proper guidance could become good tailors in their own right. I certainly wasn't one of these. It took me forever just to thread a needle. After trying to use the sewing machine a few times, Mr Quinlan advised me to keep away from it. He laughed out loud one evening when in my attempt to sew a patch on an old pair of trousers I accidentally sewed it onto the trousers I was wearing. Repeatedly he complained to Brother Roberts that I was the most useless boy to have ever come into his work room. Nevertheless Brother Roberts insisted that I stay, which I did for the next four years. I certainly didn't see tailoring in my future; I wanted to be a priest not a tailor.

Imagine my surprise when one day Mr Quinlan introduced his two sons to me, telling me that they were both studying for the priesthood. I was green with envy. The youngest boy struck up a friendship with me. He used to bring me booklets about the Missions, which fired my imagination and stiffened my resolve to follow him into the priesthood. One evening, when things were quiet, I disclosed to him my wish to be a priest. He seemed very surprised indeed.

'Why, how can this happen for you, Michael?'

'I don't know.'

'You have to have a good education to become a priest. Can you even read or write?'

Indignantly I said I could.

'Don't I serve on the altar for the Latin Masses in the school and the convent?'

'But why do you want to become a priest?'

Tensely I replied that I didn't know why, I just wanted to, that's why.

'You know, Michael, you don't just decide that you want to become a priest. You must have the vocation. It's a special calling by God.'

I felt he was trying to discourage me in my desire by putting road blocks in my way. During all the time I knew him, and even after his ordination, he never encouraged me to pursue my dream. I was really disappointed in him and became more reserved in his company. During my secret visits to the chapel I prayed very hard to Our Lady and Jesus for this special calling or vocation, as young Quinlan liked to call it. I became obsessed with the idea of vocation over the next few years, often talking in broad outline with the various missionaries I met about how I could acquire a vocation. Frankly none of them ever talked to me seriously about it.

In the tailor shop I was assigned to cleaning up after work in the evening and doing the ironing. I knew I was useless and would never make a tailor. Mr Quinlan had no interest in me, but tolerated me at the insistence of Brother Roberts. Occasionally Brother Price put in an appearance in the tailor's shop, much to the annoyance of Mr Quinlan, who was obliged to listen to long conversations about God knows what. Brother Price would rabbit on while Mr Quinlan nodded very occasionally. The former would sit against the radiator and stare at me in a very disconcerting way. One evening I asked him when I would get long trousers like other boys.

'Don't worry about that, Michael; you'll never be in long trousers as long as I'm in this school. You have a beautiful pair of legs and I want to be able to see them.'

In fact I never did get to wear long trousers until after he left the school. Mr Quinlan, I am sure, never understood the real reason that Brother Price came so often to the tailor's shop when he had no business there.

Mr Quinlan also performed jobs for the town folk. People would want trousers shortened, sleeves turned up or patches put on sleeves. When they were done he sent me down to the draper's shop with the parcels, where I received payment in a sealed envelope that I brought straight back to him. Every Friday, about 5 o'clock, Brother Roberts went around the various trades to collect the monies made from any outside jobs. He carried a small, flat, red box in his pocket, along with a notebook. Often he called me out of the tailor's to accompany him on his rounds. He didn't really need me at all. Perhaps he was just making a point to both Brother Price and the senior boys. He could be quite possessive really. When he collected the monies he brought them back to his room, counted them and wrote up the accounts in a little notebook. He was a lovely writer and his work was always very neat. After his usual sucking on my lips he'd give me a few sweets and send me on my way. Mr Quinlan never asked me where I had been, on my return. If I was ever delayed, which was often, the other boys cleaned up for me. Many of them knew but never said anything, and neither did I.

The Sunday Walks

THE FIRST THING I did, when I woke up on Sunday mornings, was to look out the window hoping and praying it was raining. I was always delighted if it was lashing down cats and dogs. The greyer and blacker the sky, the more confident I was that the dreaded Sunday walk around the short ring of Kerry would be cancelled. My joy was heightened by the disappointment of Brother Lane who normally took us on these treks. However, I was often disappointed by the weather. If the rain held off I would have to put on my best clothes and line up with other boys, in foul humour. It wasn't so much the treks themselves that I hated, but the initial walk through the town, past the pitying eyes of the townsfolk. I always tried to hide behind the bigger boys so that I wouldn't be recognised. Furthermore, a walk with Brother Lane was not necessarily a pleasant stroll but rather a brisk silent trot, with no talking allowed. Brother Lane performed his usual Sergeant Major routine, full of bluster and fury. He liked to pick on me to make a point.

'Get on, Clemenger, you cur, get a move on there or you'll feel the full force of my boot up your backside.'

I always stared at him defiantly knowing that he wouldn't touch me with Brothers Price and Roberts around. Therefore he was always highly irritable with me, partly because he couldn't instil fear in me but, more importantly, because the other boys knew this and he lost face with them.

I liked it when we were out of the town, free from the prying eyes. We could relax then. While the beauty of the hills was undoubtedly breathtaking I never had much of an appreciation for them. I didn't live in beauty. My colours were grey and sombre. No birds sang in my garden, no beautiful flowers gave off a scent. There weren't any images of tranquillity to caress in my mind's eye as I walked along. Some boys used these walks to try to make an escape. With such high numbers it was difficult for Brother Lane to make sure nobody ran off. No matter how hard he tried, a boy or two would usually be missing before the return to the monastery. Naturally this made him mad but he always had the last laugh when the missing boys were duly returned by the police. Then Brother Lane would exact his sweet revenge by beating the living daylights out of them before despatching them to sick bay for repairs.

I never understood why boys ran away from the monastery in the first place. They were always caught and, when they were brought back, given a good hiding for their troubles. Running away was considered very brave by many of the boys and the more times a boy ran away the better they were thought of by the rest of us. I never had any desire to run away. After all where would I go? Could I really survive in some farmer's outhouse eating nothing but raw carrots? Surely I was better off where I was?

St Joseph of Cupertino

ONE FRIDAY EVENING Brother Roberts told me that a film was to be shown that weekend about the life of St Joseph of Cupertino. My first thought was that the boys were going to be very disappointed. We were used to enjoying our John Wayne westerns and Humphrey Bogart gangster movies, so much so that we often acted out what we had seen on the big screen. I assumed Brother Roberts was referring to the saint that the school was named after.

'No, Michael. Our patron was the father of Jesus and the husband of Mary. This St Joseph was born much later in Italy and died a very holy man. Sit on the bed there and I'll tell you his story.'

He spoke about St Joseph's poor background and his lack of education that didn't hinder his desire to be a priest. Brother Roberts explained that only God gives people a vocation to join the priesthood. I asked him about this word 'vocation' that I had heard before but didn't fully understand.

'Well, a vocation is a special calling by God himself where he selects very good people to serve him on the altar and say Mass. Even I cannot say Mass because I am a Brother and not a priest. Not everybody is called to this vocation, Michael.'

At this point Brother Roberts didn't know that I wanted to be a priest, though he often said that I was very holy. Usually holy people who love saying their prayers, and love Jesus and his parents, Mary and Joseph, can be called by God to be his priests. I did ask him what was the difference between Jesus and God.

'They're one and the same. We'll talk more about this when you have seen the film.'

That Saturday night, needless to say, I paid special attention to every detail in case Brother Roberts asked me any questions. I think it's fair to say that not many of the other boys were too impressed with the film. Indeed they were mightily relieved when it was over. However, it made a powerful impression on me, one that has stayed with me for forty-five years. The fact that he was what Brother Murphy might have called an 'amadawn' really appealed to me. In many ways he was a bumbling fool who was neither particularly clever nor gifted with his hands. He was always getting into trouble and upsetting those around him. Despite all these flaws and imperfections his feet sometimes left the ground when he was praying. I thought that he must be stretching towards the sky to be nearer to God. The film actually moved me to tears several times, and this seemed to amuse some of the other boys. I looked forward to being questioned by

Brother Roberts about what I had seen, and he was certainly delighted by my searching questions.

'Ah yes, I knew you would ask about St Joseph's feet leaving the ground. No, Michael, it wasn't a trick; it was God's way of showing St Joseph's fellow friars that he was specially favoured despite his lack of education. Being lifted off the ground like that is called levitation, and it's a gift that is only given to the great saints. When St Joseph died he went straight to Heaven without having to spend any time in purgatory.'

This word 'death' interested me and I asked Brother Roberts what it meant.

'Death comes to us all, Michael; all of us must die and be judged by God himself. If we are good we go to Heaven and if bad we go to hell for all eternity. But if we are bold and commit venial sins we must go to purgatory to make up with God for offending him.'

My only experience with death was seeing a cow lying dead in a field.

'Do animals go to Heaven when they die, sir?'

'Oh yes, Michael, they certainly can.'

That's good, I thought to myself. Brother Roberts asked me if I was tired.

'A bit, sir.'

'Well, then, lie on the bed and have a little sleep.'

After about an hour he woke me up, gave me a few kisses and hugs and told me to go down to supper. I didn't sleep much that night for thinking about these extraordinary words like 'vocation' and 'death'. It was strange to think that I must one day die, like Joseph Pyke, and be buried in a graveyard. It gave me a great fear of the dark. I consoled myself that if I became a priest I would have been chosen by God himself, which meant that when I died I'd be carried straight off to Heaven by him. And, of course, I would be very, very old by the time this event took place.

I prayed all the way to the railway station the following Monday morning, carrying the film reels extra close to my chest. On reaching the station I succumbed to my desire to hold on to the film until the very last second.

'Come on, Michael,' I heard a voice behind me say, 'the train is about to leave.'

Reluctantly I handed it over and stood to watch its final departure from me. As the train pulled out my eyes welled up with hot, blinding tears. Full of confusion and frustration I slowly made my way back to St Joseph's, by way of the newsagents for the newspaper. I comforted myself with dreaming about becoming a priest. After all St Joseph of Cupertino, despite his lack of education, succeeded, so why wouldn't I? All I had to do was pray harder and longer. Perhaps St Joseph of Cupertino would put in a good word for me.

Summer Holiday

THE ANNUAL ONE day trip to Ballyheigue was the only holiday we ever got in St Joseph's. It usually occurred in the first week of July. On that special day it was as if the lights were switched on in a very dark room. We got away with 'murder' and duly behaved badly, loudly and happily. The day always began with a quick inspection of the weather. It's funny but I don't remember the day ever being spoilt by rain. At 9.30 in the morning the buses arrived to take us out the road to Ballyheigue.

I always sat with Brother Price on the bus. He was at his most relaxed on these trips. Brother Lane remained his usual miserable old mongrel self – the boys knew that he couldn't touch us on the holiday – while Brother Murphy sat tense and straight, holding tightly onto his black Bible as if to protect himself from us poor 'amadawns'.

Finally there was the school principal, Brother Ryan, otherwise known as 'mallet head', on account of his massive head and extremely short neck. We had very little to do with him. Even as a young child I could plainly see that the man suffered in our company. He didn't know how to deal with boys in any way, was awkward in the simplest conversation and when he did smile it appeared rather strained. Resolutely he fixed his eyes on the road in case any boy said anything to him. *There must be a special type of Brother sent to St Joseph's*, I mused to myself, because most of them shared the same traits of being miserable and malicious, and unable to have the briefest 'normal' conversation with the boys in their charge. *Feck them, they're not going to spoil this day for me*, I thought. I am sure other boys felt the same. If they couldn't pretend to relax, for just one day, that was their problem, not ours.

The journey took one hour. At our destination we were lined up and given our instructions. For example we couldn't get into the water without permission, and when we heard a whistle we were to immediately return to the buses to be fed. Most of the boys didn't give a damn about lunch. All they wanted to do was run wild along the beach, playing cowboys and Indians among the sand dunes. I preferred to walk alone and barefoot along the shore, watching the birds flying gracefully overhead. Every now and then they landed on the sea to stick their faces into the water. Lying on my back on the warm sand I loved to gaze into the clear, blue sky, fanta-sising that if it parted, like the Red Sea for Moses, I might have a glimpse of Heaven itself. Perhaps the huge roar of waves was what God's voice sounded like when He is angry.

In no time at all one of the Brothers would blow a whistle, interrupting our various activities. The treats we received on holiday were called 'scoffs'. Naturally their rarity only added to our delight. Lunch for every one of us was an apple, an orange, a small bag of sweets and sandwiches with some kind of meat in them, followed by lemonade, orange or tea. It was such a pity, I thought to myself, that we couldn't eat like this every day. I knew the Brothers certainly did because I often saw the leftovers on the plates in their dining room, thanks to Brothers Price and Roberts; bits of sausages, tomatoes and blobs of eggs. Once the meal was over, and permission obtained, the boys scattered again in all directions.

It was my habit to hang back after dinner and stay close to Brother Price. Secretly I didn't trust some of the older boys who might start to pick on me, and I wasn't the only one. A group of us, younger and smaller, preferred to walk with him along the beach. He loved to show off his particular talent at skimming stones across the water, something I could never do. My stones would land once on the water with a disheartening plonk before sinking immediately.

'It's all in the wrist, Michael.'

Occasionally we saw a boat pass by and would wave to the people on board.

'Can we go on a boat, sir?'

'No, Michael, I don't think so. Those things are very

expensive to hire. If you like, though, you can climb on my back and pretend that I'm a boat.'

I'm sure he regretted making such a wonderful offer because he was obliged to spend the next hour giving us all jaunts in and out of the sea. When he was finished he lay down exhausted, sweating profusely under the hot sun.

'Be a good lad, Michael, run back to the buses and get me a bottle of lemonade and a towel. One of the Brothers should be around.'

As luck would have it, the only Brother lying beside the buses was Brother Lane, who was reading his book.

'What do you want?'

I blurted out Brother Price's request.

'A likely story indeed, Clemenger. Pull the other one. Do you think I'm going to fall for that cock and bull? Be off with you now, you cur, or you'll feel my boot up your backside.'

He must have forgotten he was only wearing his sandals.

I turned back hesitantly towards Brother Price, but had only taken a few steps when the bad-tempered Lane told me to wait. To punish him I pretended not to hear his call.

'Clemenger, get back here immediately. Are you deaf?'

Reluctantly he gave me a large bottle of orange and told me to get lost. I stood my ground.

'But sir, Brother Price asked for a bottle of *lemonade*, not orange.'

Looking as if he wanted to rip my head from my body he roughly exchanged the orange for the lemonade.

'Now clear off, you little cur.'

Grabbing a towel I complied, chuffed at having got the better of him. When I thought I was far enough away from his glare I opened the bottle and took a few slugs to celebrate my victory over Joseph Pyke's murderer. When I eventually got back to Brother Price he wanted to know what had taken me so long.

'I don't think Brother Lane believed me, sir, when I told him what you wanted.'

'That bloody fool!'

Exasperated he took the lemonade and towel from me. Looking at the bottle he asked me had I taken a drink.

'Yes, sir. I had a drop. Sorry.'

Uncertain of what his reaction might be, I was relieved when he merely shrugged.

'That's all right, Michael. You probably needed it after dealing with Brother Lane.'

After taking a few gulps he wiped himself down with the towel and gave the bottle back to me, telling me to share it with the other boys who were with us. Then he fell asleep while the rest of us occupied ourselves running up and down the shoreline, always careful to stay within shouting distance of him.

In another while the whistle rang out again. We made our way back, with Brother Price, for more scoffs.

Brother Lane approached Brother Price, asking him had he sent me to fetch a bottle of lemonade and a towel.

'Yes, Brother, I did. You should have believed him in the first place as he is an honest boy, which you know full well.'

I was standing about three feet from both of them and overheard the whole conversation. Brother Lane solemnly walked away with his tail between his legs. *Serves him right*, I thought, *trying to catch me out in a lie so that I would get a beating from both of them for being dishonest.*

At 5 o'clock the final whistle blew; it was time to go home. I would gladly have swapped all my days at St Joseph's to stay forever on the beach in Ballyheigue. The boys were counted and, much to the relief of Brother Ryan, there was no one missing. Only then would he address us.

'Well boys, did you enjoy the day?'

After a quick tidy up, we reluctantly boarded the buses again for the return journey back to the greyness of St Joseph's, leaving behind the fresh air, salty waves, shrieking gulls and a beach covered in our footprints, for another year.

Possessed by the Devil

ONE EVENING, IN the playing field, Brother Price called me aside.

'Michael, are you left handed?'

'I don't know what you mean, sir.'

'Which hand do you hold the hurley with?'

'This one, sir.'

Taking the hurley from me, he showed me how it should be held.

'In the right hand, Michael, always the right hand. Okay, try that now. Hit the sliotair.'

I couldn't hit it out of my way.

'It feels very awkward, sir.'

He called to one of the boys to fetch a football.

'Kick it normally as you would.'

The ball went a fair distance.

'Now try it with the right foot.'

I didn't kick it half the distance.

'Which hand do you write with?'

'My left, sir.'

'Indeed. Why?'

'I don't know, sir.'

His face grew stern.

'Michael, how many boys or Brothers do you see writing with the left hand?'

'I haven't ever noticed, sir.'

'Well I do. None, none and none. Get out of that dirty habit of writing with your left hand. Do you understand me, Michael?'

'Yes sir. I'll try.'

He snorted in anger.

'You will do better than try. Do you understand?'

'Oh yes, sir.'

Over the next few years I grew out of the habit of writing with my left hand for fear that Brother Price would give me a good hiding. Over time he reinforced his command with a few sharp slaps on the offending hand. I was always puzzled that none of the other Brothers seemed to have any trouble with me being left handed.

Once, when he was in a particular good mood I asked him why I shouldn't write with the left hand.

'Well, Michael, it's simple really, people who write with the left hand are possessed by the devil.'

He said this with such ferocity that it frightened the shite out of me. However, I reckoned that maybe there was no room for the devil since I was already being possessed by both him and Brother Roberts. Nevertheless I don't recall ever seeing a Christian Brother writing with his left hand. Changing from writing with my left hand to my right hand did nothing to improve its legibility. Today my family and friends say that my hand writing is harder to read than a doctor's, particularly if I'm tired.

Bing Crosby

IN THE AFTERNOONS, while cleaning up after dinner, one of my delights was to listen to the radio. One day I heard a voice singing that made the hairs stand up on the back of my neck. I was spellbound by the melodious tone and asked one of the older boys who the singer was.

'That's old Bing Crosby. He's never off the radio, there's always somebody requesting some song of his. I think he's bloody awful. I much prefer Cliff Richard or Elvis Presley meself. Don't tell me you like that kind of singing.'

Over the next few weeks I listened out for Bing Crosby on the radio. In the playground I told Brother Price that I had heard Bing Crosby and liked him very much. To my surprise he told me that Bing Crosby was his favourite singer.

'Come to my room later. I think I have some articles about his life that I can lend you.'

Sure enough when I knocked at his door, he surprised me with some pictures of Mr Crosby, a book on his life and a few records. I was delighted with myself.

'You can keep the pictures, Michael, but I need the

book back when you're finished with it. Come down to the TV room now and I'll play some of the records.'

The other boys teased me for liking what they called 'that auld fool', but Brother Price soon put manners on them with a few slaps from his leather. One boy in particular was most persistent in pestering me to the point of telling me one Saturday that Crosby was dead. I was so upset that I burst into tears and ran to Brother Price.

'Don't be silly, Michael. Of course he's not dead. Who told you such nonsense?'

After giving the boy a good hiding Brother Price made it very clear to the rest of the boys that if there were any more remarks made about Bing Crosby being dead he would thrash them all.

I raced through the book about Bing Crosby's life. It transpired that his mother's people were Irish, from Co. Galway, and that she had emigrated to America in the 1890s where she married and had six children. Bing was born in 1904 and was a famous singer in America by the time he was thirty. He married a woman by the name of Dixie Lee and had three sons with her. Unfortunately she died of cancer in 1954. He married again, in 1957, and had three more children. Not only was he a famous singer, he also became a movie star, winning an Oscar for the 1944 film *Going My Way*.

Brother Price called me to his room one evening, to tell me that *Going My Way* was coming to the school and that he had ordered it especially for me. I was ecstatic.

'Don't tell any of the others and if there's any trouble, I'll bloody well sort them out.'

When finally I got to see the film and discovered that Bing Crosby was actually playing a priest I was filled with pure joy. When he sang that song for the old priest who hadn't seen his mother for years, the tears ran down my cheeks and I didn't care who saw them. I would have endured a thousand years of jeering for those precious moments.

Most of the other boys thought the film was bloody rubbish. However, with Brother Price and his leather on the prowl looking for potential victims to slay for their impertinence, none ventured to complain. I went to bed that night absolutely delighted with myself. When Brother Price came by my bed I thanked him repeatedly for the film. This show of genuine appreciation from me pleased him very much.

'I'm not finished yet, Michael. There's more to come. Go to sleep now.'

He was as good as his word. One summer day he called me in the yard and announced to the other boys that I would be watching TV on Saturday nights. It turned out that there was a Bing Crosby season on, and over the next few weeks I got to see most of Bing's 'Road' films with Bob Hope. Brother Price would leave me a few sweets and an apple or orange. He showed me how to turn on and off the television set.

'Remember, always take the plug out of the wall

when you are leaving and lock the door behind you. Leave the key on the window outside my room before going to bed.'

It was a wonderful perk to my position as his 'favourite'.

I don't know what the other boys ever made of the situation, but I always had great fun, getting into my bed after 9 o'clock on a Saturday night with all those jealous eyes peeping out at me from under the bedclothes.

The Graveyard

I HAD BEEN living in St Joseph's for almost four years before I discovered that it had its own graveyard. One evening Brother Roberts called me from the playing field. After his customary hour of sucking on me like an orange (which I was well used to by now) in his room, he walked me down towards the handball alley, stopping before a small gate. It was a beautiful summer's evening. Pointing at the small roadway he asked me had I ever been down there. When I said no he pulled out a bunch of keys and opened the gate. Taking my hand in his he led me to the end of the roadway.

'Look to your right, Michael.'

In front of me lay a series of markings with square shaped stones at the back wall.

'Do you know what they are, Michael? They're the graves of Christian Brothers who lived in the school many years ago and are now dead. Do you know what dying means or what it's like to be dead?'

'Being dead means not being able to move about or get up when you want to.'

'That's not a bad answer, Michael. We all have to die one day, even you.'

'Like Joseph Pyke?'

'Yes, like poor Joseph Pyke.'

His voice quivered slightly as he ran his fingers through my hair.

'And, sir, will you die and be buried here?'

'Yes, I too will die, but I don't think I'll be buried here. There's no more room left so I'll probably be buried in the local cemetery, which is outside the town.'

I began reading each headstone in turn. There were seven in total. The youngest Brother was only twenty-nine years old when he died, while the oldest was sixty-two. Brother Roberts seemed to be in a very reflective mood so I decided to ask him a few more questions.

'Sir, why was I born?'

'I don't know why, Michael, but I'm certainly glad that you were.'

'What will I be when I grow up?'

'I don't know, Michael. You tell me.'

Looking him straight in the eye I told him that I wanted to be a priest. I was relieved that he knew at last. To my intense relief he didn't dismiss the notion out of hand, but suggested that I pray a lot about the idea.

'Have you ever mentioned this to Father O'Neill?'

'No sir.'

'Perhaps for the time being it might be wise to keep your secret to ourselves.'

I sensed from the tone of his voice that he suspected Father O'Neill wouldn't approve.

'Would you like to be anything else, Michael? Say, for example, a Christian Brother?'

'I don't think so, sir.'

He smiled to himself at this.

'Tell me, Michael, where do dead people go?'

'Most of them go to Heaven after spending some time in purgatory.'

'And the others?'

'They go to hell, sir, for all eternity.'

'Why?'

'Because they commit sins of impurity in thought, word, deed and action, sir.'

'Who told you that, Michael?'

'Father O'Neill, sir. He always says that masturbation and impurity with other boys are grave sins that merit only hell, where there will be wailing and gnashing of teeth.'

'Does he indeed, and do you believe that?'

'I'm not sure, sir.'

'Do you commit masturbation and impurity with other boys?'

'Oh no, sir.'

I felt a little uncomfortable at the direction our conversation was taking and my heart was beating very fast.

'Tell me, Michael, how often in a week would Brother Price call you to his room? Be careful with your answer now because I have my spies.'

'At least once a week, sir.'

'Don't worry, Michael, I don't want to know the details.'

I was mightily relieved at this.

'While you are in his room does he ever talk about me?'

I pretended not to understand.

'Come, come, Michael, surely you know what I mean.'

I tried to reassure him that I never told Brother Price anything about what we did together, despite the Brother's constant questions. Next he asked me the dreaded question that I had always felt was inevitable. Holding me around the waist he drew me close to him.

'And which of us do you prefer, Michael? You can tell me, it won't get back to Brother Price.'

The question was not that hard to answer really. Of the two of them I owed my position – that is all my jobs of responsibility – to Brother Roberts. Brother Price was merely following his lead, in his attempts to better him. Therefore, I threw my arms around Brother Roberts.

'You, sir.'

A broad smile fell across his face.

'That's my boy, my favourite boy. I knew the answer, but I just had to ask to make sure.'

He hugged me for what seemed like ages.

'Come on, Michael, graveyards are quite dreary places. Let's go to the kitchen for tea and scones.'

He danced attention on me in the kitchen. Suddenly the door opened and Brother Lane walked in. I froze under his hateful glare. He mumbled something that caused Brother Roberts to walk towards him; with that the former turned on his heels and stormed out of the room.

'Be careful of him, Michael. He has a terrible temper and is liable to do anything when he loses his head.'

I took the opportunity of asking him about the rumours circulating that Brother Lane caused the death of Joseph Pyke.

'Ah, it's best not to worry your pretty head about such stories. We just have to be careful when *that* fella is around.'

The emphasised *that* was enough. It was impregnated with hidden meaning whose significance was not lost on me.

The Black Missionary

ONE MORNING AFTER Mass, in around 1962, Brother Roberts called me aside and told me to dress nicely as we would be going across the road to the convent run by nuns. It was common for priests called 'missionaries' to come home from places like Africa and China to Ireland for their holidays. They usually lived in the convent for some of their stay. Most of the missionaries were men in their fifties or sixties. They were polite and often left a threepenny piece for me after their stay. I thought that because they lived so far away they were heroic figures and I seriously hoped to be like them when I grew up.

It was the missionary ideal of 'saving black souls' in Africa that began to plant firmly in my young mind the desire to become a priest. This was reinforced by one of the nuns in the convent when she said to me in an aside that I would make a lovely priest because of my love of the Mass. The convent became a place that I liked to visit. The Reverend Mother seemed to like me, often praising me for my good conduct in church. When I was about fourteen years old the Reverend Mother called me into her office.

'Michael, there is a priest coming to say Mass here next week. I've spoken to Brother Roberts about it and he's happy for you to serve his Masses.'

Normally Masses were said in the convent anytime between 9.30am and 3.00pm. The visitor had requested to say his Mass at noon.

'Don't worry; he'll be finished by 12.45pm, so you'll be back in time for your dinner. Now there's another thing, I just wanted to warn you that this priest is different from any of the other priests you have met.'

I stared at her and waited politely for more information, my mind racing through all the priests I had ever met.

'Well, Michael, I don't want you to be frightened but it's just that he's black. That's all.'

She seemed more uncomfortable about it than I was. When I didn't react to her news she turned business-like.

'Just make sure you're here for 11.45am. Run along now.'

The following Monday morning, I got my first glimpse of the visitor. He was a big, powerful looking man; his hands were enormous, much bigger than even Brother Price's. On seeing me approach he completely disarmed me with the warmest of smiles. Against his dark face his white teeth seemed to sparkle and light up the whole room.

'Hello Michael, I'm Father — .'

I gulped nervously. There sure were a lot of letters in his name. He laughed at my face.

'Just call me "Father", Michael. All right?'

Between us we sailed through the Mass without any mishaps, much to the relief of the Reverend Mother. Back in the sacristy she hustled me back to St Joseph's. She did the same thing the following day, only this time Father ran out of the sacristy and called me back.

'Don't mind the Reverend Mother, she doesn't mean any harm. I am busy for the rest of the week but on Saturday I'm free and you and I can have a long chat. Would you like that? I expect you have a lot of questions you want to ask me?'

'Yes, Father, thank you.'

I really liked him and wasn't bothered in the least that he wanted to spend some time with me. After all it was only Brothers who touched me, never priests. In comparing him to Father O'Neill I began to realise what a dour character our chaplain really was. That Saturday morning, after Mass, Father instructed the Reverend Mother to bring some tea and biscuits as he wanted to have a chat with me. She seemed a little surprised but didn't say anything.

'Pull over a chair, Michael, and sit next to me. Tell me, are you afraid of me at all?'

'No, Father, why should I be, after all you are a priest.'

'I'm a priest all right but still some people seem afraid of me. Why do you suppose that is?'

'I don't know, Father, perhaps it's because you're black, but I'm not afraid. I've seen lots of black men before, you know.'

'Have you now?'

'Yes, Father, in the movies, Tarzan movies especially. Usually the black men are chasing Tarzan up the trees, blowing arrows at him with long tubes.'

He roared with laughter. With that, the door opened and in walked the Reverend Mother carrying a tray covered with a white linen cloth. She made an effort to sit down, but Father was most insistent that he would like to be alone with me for a little while.

He gently lifted the cloth off the tray to reveal the nuns' best china and a plate full of biscuits. What a treat! He poured me a cup of tea. Petrified that I'd drop the cup I sat as close to the tray as I could. When he passed me the plate of biscuits I was careful not to be greedy and take too many. After all I had to go back across the road and eat a dinner fit for pigs.

'Tell me, Michael, how old are you?'

'I am thirteen or fourteen years old, Father, I think.'

'Do you mean you don't know?'

'I suppose so, Father.'

'Have you any parents?'

'Yes, Father.'

'How do you know?'

'Because Brother Price told me so, Father.'

'Why then are you not with them?'

'Brother Price told me it was because I was born before they were married, Father.'

'Have you ever seen them?'

'No, Father. I mean I don't think so, Father.'

'Are you sure, Michael?'

'No, Father, I'm not sure. I only know what the Brothers in St Joseph's tell me.'

'How long have you been in St Joseph's?'

Boy, I thought to myself, *when am I going to get a chance to ask* him *some questions.*

'I've been here for four or five years, Father.'

'Do you know where you were before that?'

'St Philomena's Home, in Stillorgan, Co. Dublin, Father.'

'Where will you go after you leave St Joseph's?'

'I don't know, Father. Anyway I have to stay in the monastery until I'm sixteen years old.'

'Who told you that?'

'The older boys, Father. They all go when they reach sixteen. I'll have to leave too, Father.'

'Would you like that?'

'I'm not sure, Father.'

Why on earth was he asking me all these questions?

'What do you want to be when you grow up?'

Well, this was one question I had been waiting to answer.

'I'd very much like to be a priest, Father.'

My answer seemed to surprise him somewhat.

'You would like to be a priest? Can you read and write?'

I told him I could do both rather well.

'Good indeed, Michael. Do the school authorities know of your desire?'

'Yes, Father, some of the Brothers know.'

'Does your chaplain know?'

'I don't think so, Father. I clean his room almost every day, but he has never said anything to me about it.'

'How are you at your prayers?'

'I am very religious, Father. I pray all the time, even at night, although sometimes I fall asleep while I'm saying them.'

'Do you know what a vocation is, Michael?'

'Yes, Father.'

'You do? Well then, tell me what it is.'

I was reminded of being asked my catechism for my Holy Communion.

'A vocation is a special calling by God/Jesus to say Mass every day in memory of his passion and resurrection every day for the rest of your life.'

'Anything else?'

'Yes, Father, to hear confessions, forgive sins and give absolution.'

'This is all very true, Michael, but God also says that while many are called, few are chosen. God may or may not be calling you to priesthood. He may have other plans for your life.'

I was completely stunned. It had never entered my head that I would be anything other than a priest. Reading my dismayed expression, Father sought to reassure me.

'Pray a lot, Michael, and leave it all in the hands of God. He always knows what's best; also you should have a special devotion to Our Lady. Will you do that for me?'

'Yes, Father.'

'Okay, Michael, you can go back to St Joseph's now for your dinner. Go with my blessing, and pray for me as I will for you.'

With that he made the sign of the cross over me, *pater et filius et Spiritui Sanctus*.

Brother Murphy's Hurley Stick

DESPITE THE FACT that Brother Murphy was from Kerry, a great county for the football, his great sporting passion was hurling. Both Brothers Price, a Kilkenny man, and Lane, a Cork man, found this strange. He spent a lot of time practising his skill in the school's playing fields, and had a great selection of hurley sticks, usually bringing three or four onto the field with him. Trouble erupted when one of them went missing. He had us search high up and low down but it remained at large. This, Brother Murphy just couldn't accept. For months after he could be seen searching through the old sheds for the stick. It became an obsession with him, and he soon convinced himself that some of the boys had stolen it.

When he was in charge of the yard he ordered the older boys to go to the playing fields and search every square inch, in the hope that it might be found lying in some ditch. One evening, when he was in charge of the rosary, he actually asked for a special prayer to be said for the return of his precious hurley. We looked around at one another in disbelief.

'Prayer, boys, is very powerful. Prayer can achieve miracles.'

When, after a week, this didn't produce a result he complained that we weren't praying hard enough. Then he came up with the theory that the reason our prayers didn't work was because one of us – who was doing the praying – was the bold thief of his hurley.

'Confounded robber, whoever you are. Don't worry, you will be caught and God help you when I find out who you are.'

A few weeks later he burst through the chapel door, to make one final throw of the dice. Walking slowly towards the altar with his head bowed, looking neither left nor right, his trusty black Bible clutched against him in a passionate embrace, he halted at the front of the chapel and prostrated himself before the altar, lost in silent prayer. What an actor, I thought to myself. Other boys were already beginning to laugh despite their best efforts to retain their composure. There was no response from the Brother. Picking himself up, he turned and faced us.

'We are all gathered here to pray. Prayer is most powerful with God. He never fails to grant the request of the sinner, no matter how grievous his crime. It's not too late to repent, God is waiting for you. He will not refuse a contrite heart. But, of course, you must want to be forgiven. And there is no need to be scared. I will be like Jesus; I too will forgive the boy or boys who have stolen my hurley. Now I'm going to close my eyes for five minutes to give the thief time to go and get it. There will be no more said about it after that. I am ready to forgive.'

With that he closed his eyes and, with outstretched hands, began to chant his prayers. It was one of the funniest things that I have ever seen in my whole life. In spite of the risk we collectively succumbed to uncontrollable laughter. After all he couldn't beat us all up. He managed to ignore us for five minutes more, continuing against our laughter with his chanting. Thereafter his face changed from one of serenity to one of withering rage. An eye suddenly popped open.

'Clemenger, I'll make an example of you.'

Suddenly you could hear a pin drop while fear gripped at my heart.

He closed his eyes again and went back to his prayers. This time the chapel was in complete silence. Another few minutes went by and he came around to the front of the altar rails, to see if his blasted hurley had mysteriously reappeared amid all the excitement. It hadn't. Seeing that he was about to speak again, I got up from the pew and made to leave.

'Clemenger, come back here, you little cur.'

'I'm going to see Brother Price.'

'Don't worry, Clemenger, he won't help you.'

I ran out of the room, slamming the door behind me. He told the boys that I would pay the price for whoever had dared to steal his hurley.

Brother Murphy did not act immediately. He never did. When he wanted to beat up a boy he would give him three or four weeks to fret about it, reminding the intended victim on a daily basis that he would soon be very sorry. The long, torturous wait was nearly worse than the actual beating because it meant the victim couldn't let his guard down for a minute, for weeks on end. Once he had told the others that he was going to make an example out of me that was it. A beating was inevitable but no way was I going to play scared for the next month.

The following morning, during communion, I stared right at him, placing the paten very close to his Adam's apple. After cleaning Father O'Neill's room I met him on the stairs. I don't know what came over me but I found myself blocking his path.

'Do you think I'm afraid of you? Well, I'm not. Do you want to hit me now? Get on with it then, you madman.'

I felt nothing but contempt for the cruelty of this Brother and was determined to show him that I was not intimidated by him, like so many of the other boys.

He made a lunge at me, but missed. I stood my ground, telling him that I was ready for him.

'Just wait, Clemenger. I'll get you, don't worry, you cur.'

'Well, madman, I won't make it easy for you.'

Shocked by my behaviour and not wanting to act in the

Brothers' quarters he went back to his room muttering to himself.

Over the next few days I never gave him an inch, knowing that a beating was coming. All the boys thought that I was mad, but were delighted at my behaviour. When finally he attacked me it was in the TV room while he was in charge. I didn't hang around and met him head on. He lunged at me and I lunged at him. It was an unequal fight. I was very small for my age and all it took was one or two swift blows to put me flat on my back. Once I was down he landed a few kicks on my knees and shoulders as I tried to protect myself. Then I received a vicious kick that caught me full on the testicles; the pain was so severe that I could offer no resistance. In a rage he continued to kick me, again and again, alternating with throwing a few more punches.

'Now you see, boy, what happens to anyone who crosses me.'

Lifting me off the ground as if I was a piece of paper, he flung me towards the stairs. The other boys pleaded with him to leave me alone but he kept attacking me. At one stage I found myself tumbling down the steps with continuous blows being landed on my body. I was out cold by the time I hit the last step. It was only then that he stopped. Meanwhile some of the boys ran to get Brothers Roberts and Ryan.

I finally regained consciousness the following day, much to the relief of the superior, amid rumours that I might actually die. When I came to, Brother Ryan was the first person I saw. He was standing at the bottom of the bed. It took a few moments to realise that both Brothers Price and Roberts were sitting on either side of the bed, each holding my hand. The pain surged through me to such an extent that I started to move violently in the bed.

'Where does it hurt, Michael?'

'All over, Brother Roberts, especially on the right side, in my private parts, sir.'

I felt silly saying 'private parts' to him, seeing how he knew them as intimately as I did. Brother Price seemed to be trembling. He turned to his superior.

'See what he's done. This won't be the last of it, you know.'

'Yes, you're right, Brother, but is the boy clean down there? For God's sake get on and wash him, the doctor is on his way up.'

It was almost comical, watching the two of them, Brothers Price and Roberts, pussyfooting around which one of them would wash me down there. Eventually they decided that one of them would wash while the other dried. Surely Brother Ryan understood that there was more to this scene than strained politeness. He was witnessing peculiar behaviour between the two most powerful Brothers in the school. They supervised the day to day running of the place while Brother Ryan was more of a figurehead, with little or no contact with us boys. It was obvious that he had no idea who I was and was, therefore, relying on the two Brothers for information about me.

The sliding door opened and in walked an elderly gentleman escorted by one of the senior boys who showed visible surprise at seeing me alive. Brother Ryan went to meet the man he then introduced to Brothers Price and Roberts. For a few moments they spoke aside from my bed. The discussion appeared heated with Brother Ryan particularly agitated. Then the doctor approached the bed.

'Well, young man, what have we here?'

He placed his hand on my forehead and I instinctively recoiled.

'Don't worry, Michael. I'm not going to hurt you.'

Brother Roberts told me to relax and listen to the doctor.

'Tell me, Michael, where does it hurt the most?'

'In my private parts, sir.'

'There's no need to call me sir, Michael. Will you pull the blanket down and show me exactly where it hurts?'

Being completely naked, I was a little hesitant. When I tentatively rolled down the blanket he let out a gasp.

'My God, what happened here? The boy is black and blue. This isn't right. How did this happen?'

He looked at Brother Ryan for answers but none were forthcoming and, naturally, the doctor turned back to me.

'Michael, do you know how this happened?'

I looked at the three Brothers standing around my bed. It was obvious that they didn't want me to say anything incriminating.

'I think I fell down the stairs.'

'Did someone push you?'

'Maybe doctor, I'm not sure, I didn't see them.'

'It's all right, Michael, never mind about that for now.'

He proceeded to examine me and I saw for myself that there was a big lump on the right side above my privates. The pain was horrific when he touched it.

'Ah now, that doesn't belong there, whatever it is. Sit up, Michael, and bend forward. How is the pain now?'

'Much better, doctor.'

'Okay then, lie back down, child.'

He fixed the blanket over me and turned to Brother Ryan.

'I want to admit the boy to hospital to have it repaired.'

'That's not possible.'

'Why not?'

Brother Ryan shrugged his shoulders.

'Well then, there's no more to be said on that score. I'll give him something for the pain in the meantime and I'll be back to see him on Wednesday. We'll talk then.

'Goodbye for now, Michael. I want you to stay in bed for at least a week. You're not to get out of bed for anything, even to go to the toilet. Do you understand?'

'Yes doctor, sir, thank you.'

Brother Ryan told the doctor that they would make sure I had all my meals brought to me.

'That'll do for now, I suppose.'

Touching me lightly on the cheek, the doctor and Brother Ryan left my bedside. I could see the former wasn't very happy. I suppose Brother Ryan didn't want anyone to know that such vicious beatings were commonplace. Maybe in a hospital the doctor's questions would have to be answered, and those answers would reflect very badly on his school.

After they were gone Brothers Price and Roberts sat on the bed eyeing each other nervously. Brother Roberts was the first to speak.

'Maybe we should take it in turns to look after Michael. What time would suit you, Brother?'

'Evenings are better for me because I teach most days until four.'

'That's settled then. I'll go and get something nice for Michael's tea.'

When he left, Brother Price gave vent to his feelings.

'This won't stand, Michael, it won't be forgotten. Indeed, you look pitiful! God help us that you weren't more seriously injured or killed.'

'Like Joseph Pyke, sir?'

'Yes, I suppose so.'

He tried to avoid my gaze, in order to hide his tears from me. Suddenly he caught hold of me and drew me towards him.

'I'll make everything all right, Michael. Do you hear me? Now, lay back and rest. Remember you're to stay in bed for a few days. I'll have one of the boys bring up a potty for you. Get some sleep and I'll call back later.'

I was asleep for maybe twenty minutes when one of the senior boys came in with a potty and an old newspaper to wipe my bottom, should I need it. He tried to be funny and make me feel better.

'Hey Michael, have you ever tried to wipe your arse with the *Irish Press*? The bloody paper keeps slipping and if you're not careful you'll end up spreading the shite halfway up your back and all over your feckin' hands.'

As much as I wanted to, I couldn't laugh with the pain.

'Guess what, Brother Murphy isn't in the school. Some say he's gone on holidays for two weeks. Or maybe he's never coming back, all thanks to you.'

I thought I was going to be terribly bored in bed, but I quickly got used to the lifestyle. My breakfast was brought to me on a tray by a senior boy; unfortunately the food itself was even worse than usual. The porridge was like putty and clung grimly to the spoon no matter how hard I shook at it. Lumps of it were stone cold and there was a marked absence of milk. The next delight was a mug of greyish water that vaguely passed for tea. Sitting beside the tepid liquid was the scrawniest piece of bread, which was far from fresh.

Johnny, my 'waiter', beamed mischievously at my obvious dismay.

'Compliments of Brother Lane. He sends you his best regards, Michael.'

Once again I was unable to laugh thanks to the shooting pains in my groin. Brother Price came by before school to see how I was.

'Did you enjoy your breakfast, Michael?'

'No sir, it was really awful with cold tea and a tiny bit of stale bread.'

'That Lane!'

With that he left the dormitory in silence.

I was still hungry but settled down to try and sleep again. Just then the door slid open. I couldn't believe my eyes when in walked 'the murderer' bearing another tray of food, followed closely by Brother Price.

'Leave it on the bed beside Michael; I'll do the rest.'

I hardly dared to look up while 'the murderer' never so much as glanced towards my bed. Nevertheless I never had any problems with my meals after that. Brother Price smiled wryly as he watched his colleague leave.

'Brother Lane is really all right. You just have to keep an eye on him.'

Brother Roberts visited me every day after dinner. He wasn't much of a talker, and didn't really engage in small chat. Generally he preferred to bring me presents, sweets, religious objects or pamphlets. We would read the pamphlets together as he held me close to him. One day he brought me a book about the life of the recently deceased Pope John XXIII. I thoroughly enjoyed it, and read it from cover to cover at least three times. Seeing my appreciation he presented me with another book, this time about Pope Pius X. It was a great read but I was a little disturbed by the photograph of the Pope lying dead with a cross in his hands.

'Don't be upset, Michael. Pius is in Heaven. He's not really dead, but alive with Christ and his blessed Mother in Heaven. Tell me now, if you had one wish that I could grant, what would it be?'

'To be responsible for cleaning the altar on my own.'

'Really, you would like that? Okay, then! I'll show you what to do when you're better. I'll leave you now to sleep.'

And with that he planted a load of kisses on my cheeks and lips.

At about 7pm Brother Price appeared. He had a look at my privates and remarked that the swelling was gone down. So perhaps I would be up and about in a few days.

'Do you know why you have a lump there?'

'No, sir.'

'The one on the left is in the normal position while the one on the right isn't where it's supposed to be. Either as a result of the kick you got or from the fall down the steps.'

'Do I need to go to hospital, sir?'

'No, Michael, I don't think so. However, you'll have to be careful. That means no more contact sports like football or hurling.'

Sensing my disappointment, he added some good news.

'And, of course, there'll be no walks around the short ring of Kerry for the foreseeable future. It would be too much for you in your present condition. Would you not agree?'

My face immediately brightened up.

'Oh yes, sir.'

'Now let's talk about other things. What about films? Can you tell me what your favourite films are?'

'That's easy sir. *St Joseph of Cupertino*, *Going My Way* with Bing Crosby, *Devil at 4 O'Clock* with Spencer Tracey, *Casablanca* with Humphrey Bogart and *High Noon* with Gary Cooper.'

'Gosh, you have a good memory for films. Now tell me who you like on TV.'

'Well, sir, I only like one programme on TV, *The Fugitive*. Dr Richard Kimble goes to a different place every week and always does something good for someone. He has to keep going from place to place because there's a detective chasing him for killing Mrs Kimble. But he didn't do it, sir.'

'Hmm, I don't think that's such a good programme, Michael.'

'Really, sir. Why not?'

'Because it gives some boys the idea that it's a good thing to run away from the school. Then, once they're caught, they have to be punished with a beating, which is a bad thing.'

I had to agree with Brother Price. I often heard these runaways telling their mates not to believe everything they see in the movies.

Brother Price was very anxious that I get up and about as soon as possible.

'Staying too long in bed might make you forget how to walk again. You wouldn't want that to happen now, would you?'

'No, sir.'

During the second week of my convalescence he took to helping me out of bed in order to walk me around the large room. Initially I could only accomplish this by leaning heavily on him. Gradually, though, I could manage on my own and was feeling well enough to stay up most of the day. Within two weeks I was completely mobile and able to resume my chores, much to the relief of Brother Ryan who remained anxious about me for a considerable time after my recovery.

Fire!

BROTHER MURPHY HAD played his cards and now it was my turn. Emboldened by the knowledge that he couldn't beat me up a second time, I set out to annoy him as much as I could. When he was receiving Holy Communion I always placed the paten close to his neck.

'Steady, Clemenger, steady.'

Father O'Neill would whisper as I snapped the paten away before the bread had even reached Brother Murphy's lips. When I met him on the stairs I deliberately blocked his way.

'Move Clemenger, you cur, or you'll get more of the same.'

I would stare at him silently, thinking, *Just try it, you madman.* During one of these impasses a very stern Brother Price came out of his room.

'Michael, is there a problem?'

'No, sir, Brother Murphy is just talking to me and calling me a cur.'

'Is he indeed? Come with me, Michael.'

I followed him downstairs to Brother Ryan's office.

'Wait here; I want a word with the superior.'

About five minutes later both Brothers Ryan and Price came out.

'Get on with your duties, Michael. We'll talk to Brother Murphy.'

I don't know what happened but, thereafter, Brother Murphy studiously avoided me, day and night. Feeling robbed in some way, my hatred for him raged away inside me. I was determined to have my revenge. After giving it a lot of thought I decided to burn down his classroom. The place was full of old papers; it would probably be an easy enough job. I told one boy my plan. He thought I was mad and tried his best to talk me out of it but my mind was not for changing. The following Saturday morning I took a box of matches from Brother Burke's room. I would have to act fast because I couldn't be going around the yard carrying a box of matches.

Three days later, in Brother Murphy's class, I put my plan into action. After catching his trousers on a nail that was sticking out of one of the desks, the Brother went behind the blackboard to take off his trousers and mend them. Immediately I crept down to the back of the room and coughed to cover the sound of my striking the match that I then flung onto a pile of old newspapers. To my horror the papers wouldn't light, probably because they were so damp. However, there was some smoke. And that was enough. The class suddenly erupted.

'Fire! Fire!'

My classmates and I ran from the room, shouting at

the tops of our voices, leaving Brother Murphy behind, spluttering in the smoke as he tried to save his rubbish. An ambulance arrived into the yard and parked on the square where we played marbles. Two men sprang out of the vehicle and rushed inside. By now there was total pandemonium in the playground. Brothers Price, Lane, Roberts and Ryan were at the door of the school doing their best to restore order. Out came the two ambulance men with Brother Murphy, minus his trousers. With a struggle they had to get him into the ambulance and that was the last we ever saw of Brother Murphy.

Brother X

HE CAME TO the school sometime in the sixties and from the first moment I laid eyes on him I knew that he was a 'wrong one'. His exaggerated smile, which was devoid of warmth, didn't in any way camouflage the eyes of a sneak. A rather unimpressed Brother Price introduced the new Brother to the school.

Brother X made the classic mistake of trying to run before he could walk, attempting to impose himself on us from the get-go. He loved to walk about the yard flashing his leather that swung liberally from his hip. Every now and then he would touch it fondly, as if it represented his life's worth. Both Brothers and boys considered him a bit of a gobshite and he had little standing within the community.

Brother Price was now head teacher. A lay teacher was put in charge of 5th class and Brother X in charge of the 3rd and 4th classes. At this stage the number of boys in St Joseph's was falling. The lower dormitory was now completely closed leaving only the middle and upper ones which were under the charge of both Brothers Price and X.

The new Brother fancied himself as a bit of an authority on music. It wasn't long before he began to conflict with the duties of Mr Cantanell. There could only be one winner in that contest, between the bully and the gentleman. Inevitably Mr Cantanell withdrew gracefully. Brother X became my teacher twelve months later when a lay teacher left, and he was a pretty poor one. His communication skills were pitiful and he had a tendency to repeat himself over and over again. He may have been a Christian Brother, but he was certainly no teacher.

He used to bring some kind of contraption into the class that played music. I had never seen one before and thought that it must be some kind of newfangled radio; in fact it turned out to be a tape recorder. He taped songs off the radio so that he could teach us to sing them.

'Come on, boys, we have to learn these songs about fighting for our independence in 1916.'

None of us had a clue what he was talking about and he never bothered to explain. What had songs got to do with something from years ago? He could never join the dots for us; things were just thrown out there in the wind without explanation or context. Luckily for me, I was soon transferred to Brother Price's class. In spite of the ongoing and wholly unpleasant nightly sessions in his room, I was able to recognise him as being a far better teacher.

After a while, rumours began to circulate that X liked little boys 'in that way'. To me that was the code to be very careful when he was around. At first I paid little heed to him and had little to do with him. However, when he bumped into me in the Brothers' private quarters he was extremely curious to know why I was there. Brothers Price and Roberts weren't long in letting him know that it was none of his business. Brother Price in particular was much offended that Brother X was asking questions at all. Brother X had taken a room near to his, which was a huge source of annoyance to Brother Price, as this meant that Brother X would be aware of my comings and goings. One evening Brother Price told me that if I had any problems with Brother X I was to come and tell him straight away and he would sort it out. I assured him I would.

One day when Brother X was outside on yard duty I snuck into his room to see what it might tell me about him. He definitely enjoyed washing himself and smelling nice; there were a large number of fancy aftershave bottles along with five or six bars of soap on his wash stand. What luxury. There were several combs and brushes and some kind of hair cream too. There were no dirty socks on the floor in his room, no overflowing ashtrays and no religious paraphernalia strewn about the place. His room was absolutely spotless. The bed was perfectly made while three or four shirts hung majestically on brown hangers in the wardrobe. Two new leathers sat neatly on a small table just inside his door. The top of his locker held a selection of photographs of him and his family. He was far too neat for my liking so it didn't surprise me when I heard the rumours. What was surprising, however, was that he had the arrogance to try and interfere with Brothers Price's and Roberts' favourite – me.

It happened when Brother Price was away from St Joseph's and Brother X had to take his class. Quite unexpectedly he placed his hands on my neck and shoulders and lingered there a while. I couldn't believe it. When he finally moved away one of the boys whispered to me.

'Wow, Michael, he's sure put the glad eye on you.'

I don't know if Brother X heard him. It was obvious I was in trouble when, at the end of class, he asked me to stay behind. I tried to leave the room but he stood in my way.

'Did you not hear me, Michael Clemenger?'

'Yes, sir, but I need to go to the toilet.'

'Indeed. Stand aside there and let the other boys out.'

My classmates rushed past me, mightily relieved they weren't in my shoes, and I was left alone with him. They knew as well as I did what was going to happen next.

'Tell me, Michael, what is it that you do in Brother Price's and Brother Roberts' rooms in the evenings and at night?'

'I don't know what you mean, sir.'

'Come on, boy, of course you know what I mean.'

'Sir, if you want to know you better ask them yourself.'

Then he asked me straight out about what was really on his mind.

'They interfere with you, boy, don't they?'

'No, sir! Of course not, sir.'

I felt my face getting hot.

'You can ask them yourself, sir. They'll tell you themselves. They don't do anything to me.'

I could see that he was getting excited in that way, the more I denied that anything was happening and the more my voice quivered with my nervousness. I felt trapped.

'Did you like it when I put my hands on your neck and shoulders?'

'No, sir, it scared me, sir.'

'Oh, really? And does it scare you when Brother Price or Brother Roberts put their hands on you?'

'You better ask them yourself, sir.'

'No, boy, I'm asking you.'

'I've nothing to say, sir.'

'Did the Brothers tell you not to say anything, Michael? Is that it?'

I kept my head down, staring down at the floor. He came towards me and tried to grab hold of my arms, but I was too quick. I ran away from him, keeping my distance as he tried to catch me.

'Stand still, boy. Do you hear?'

I kept on running around the classroom shouting at the top of my voice.

'I'm going to tell Brother Price about you, sir.'

Eventually he got hold of me just as I reached the door. He pulled me to him and I think he was trying to kiss me, but I was uncooperative and fought him off.

'Keep still, you little brat.'

When finally he realised that he wasn't going to have his way with me he gave me a few slaps of the leather, on my backside and legs.

'You're a bit of a pup, Clemenger, aren't you? Mention this to Brother Price and you'll be sorry.'

He opened the door and I ran out. I didn't stop running until I reached Brother Roberts' room. Brother Roberts seemed genuinely shocked and angry that Brother X would have the audacity to interfere with his favourite boy. He reassured me that he would deal with Brother X in his own good time.

However, it was a completely different story when Brother Price returned and heard what happened. He brought me with him as he barged unannounced into Brother X's room. A startled Brother X attempted to show fury at the intrusion. Ignoring him Brother Price told me to sit on the bed and for the next ten minutes or so I watched him give Brother X a fierce bollocking. By the time he was finished I thought Brother X was on the verge of tears. He just sat there on the radiator with his head bowed. Brother Price told Brother X that he would be moving to the other end of the corridor because he couldn't bear to sleep near him. He also warned that if there was a repeat of this nonsense the superior, Brother Ryan, would be informed. Finally he told him that he and I would be having tea and cake in the Brothers' refectory and he hoped we wouldn't be disturbed.

'I understand fully, Brother Price.'

I thoroughly enjoyed my tea and cake that evening. Over the next few days I made sure that the whole story got around with the result that some of the boys weren't quite as afraid of Brother X from then on, while I had absolutely no more problems with him.

The Death of Brother Breen

BROTHER BREEN HAD retired from teaching in around 1963. I used to see him walking briskly around the town in the course of my travels. He always greeted me with his polite smile and looked hale and hearty. Then, in April 1965, while out on one of his walks he collapsed in the street and was rushed to the nearby Bon Secours Hospital. We were called to the chapel by Brother Price to say a special rosary for his recovery. It didn't seem to be too serious. Based on daily reports about his progress, everybody expected him home soon.

So it came as a great and profound shock when a few days later Father O'Neill informed the entire community at Mass that Brother Breen had died suddenly at around six that morning. Nobody could believe it. I went through the motions of the Mass in a state of bewilderment. At breakfast a lot of the boys looked genuinely upset. School was out and we all mingled in the yard, searching our memories for events that tied us individually to Brother Breen. He had always been nice to me and, although tactile, never interfered with me in that way and was the first person ever to tell me that I was clever.

Brother Price took charge of the arrangements, organising both Brothers and boys.

'Okay, gather around, boys. I need six volunteers to act as pall bearers for Brother Breen's funeral.'

He was speaking in a language that I didn't understand: pall bearers, funeral? These were new terms for me and many of the other boys. The older boys knew what they meant from Joseph Pyke's death in 1958. Since there were no volunteers Brother Price shouted out that he would pick out six boys himself. Not being very tall I hid behind some of the taller boys.

'It's no use hiding, Michael; I need you for the Mass. Fall out.'

With that he quickly named five other boys.

'Now, you lot, get washed and change into your best clothes. We're going to visit the hospital to pay our last respects.'

I wondered why, since the man was dead, and wouldn't notice us standing in front of him.

At about 11 o'clock we walked down the town and into the Bon Secours Hospital, where we were met by Brother Ryan, Father O'Neill and the Reverend Mother, who also managed the hospital. As we all made our way into the room I had an attack of nerves.

'I don't want to, sir. Please sir, I'm too scared.'

Squeezing my hand Brother Price told me it was okay, that he would be standing right beside me. There was a chill in the room. Brother Breen lay on the bed all swollen up. His face was the colour of Father O'Neill's stole and his hands were as white as snow. The other boys were visibly upset and unable to control their tears. There were a lot of prayers being said with such repetition that I felt it would be impossible for Brother Breen's soul not to go immediately to Heaven.

'You can touch his hands, Michael, if you want to.'

I did so tentatively. The skin was very soft though icy cold. A pretty pair of rosary beads intertwined his fingers. A strong, pungent smell was coming from the body, which remained in my nostrils for weeks after the poor man was buried. We recited the rosary with Father O'Neill and were told to say our goodbyes. When we came back that evening Brother Breen would be in the coffin and we wouldn't see him again. I made the sign of the cross on his hands and was completely taken aback when I saw his black watch on his wrist. I couldn't believe it, why was Brother Breen still wearing a watch if he was dead? On the way back to the school I asked Brother Price about it but he gave me no reply.

At about 5.30 that evening, following an early supper, the six of us boys, together with Brothers Price and X, returned to the hospital. We waited outside the main entrance. It was a beautiful evening and I could hear birds singing away. Father O'Neill arrived in a black car with Brothers Ryan and Roberts and walked past us. Then a bell rang out, the doors opened and a procession led by Father O'Neill moved off down the hall.

'Get ready, boys, line up there on each side. Michael, you walk in the front.'

It was my first time to see a coffin. On the sides were lovely brass handles while on top was a small white cross and a plate with Brother Breen's name and date of birth on it. I did a quick calculation. Brother Breen was sixty-eight years old. The coffin was placed in the shiny, black hearse and the back door closed down on it. Flowers were placed on top of the hearse. Taking our places each side of the car, we marched off slowly down the road.

The next morning the coffin was in the chapel.

'Michael, you will help Father O'Neill at the Mass and at the graveside after Mass.'

I don't recall who told me that. Just before the Mass Brother Breen's brother and sister arrived. His brother was the spit of him, although he was thinner and younger. I can't recall anything about the sister except that she looked older than both of them.

A much larger group of boys were allowed to attend the funeral in Rath cemetery. On the way through the town people lined the street as we passed, furiously blessing themselves and muttering some prayers. Otherwise the journey was uneventful until I happened to find a threepenny piece on the road. Sweets on the way home, I thought. At the graveside I approached the coffin with Father O'Neill. Only then did the enormity of death finally strike home. A cold shudder ran through my bones. Father O'Neill cried out the prayers as the coffin was lowered into the cold earth. The brother and sister dried their eyes and the small crowd made the responses while I thought I could hear the ticking of the black watch on Brother Breen's wrist. Then Father O'Neill leaned down and picked up a small piece of clay. He threw it onto the coffin, made the sign of the cross, sprinkled holy water over the grave and that was that.

Father O'Neill, Brother Ryan and the other Brothers came in turn to shake hands with Brother Breen's relatives. Brother Price told the boys to go back to the school.

'Michael knows the way home.'

We went via the nearest shop and spent my three-penny piece on sweets. A gloom descended on St Joseph's that weekend. The boys didn't say much to each other about Brother Breen's death but I'm sure I wasn't the only one with questions. Brothers Price and Roberts would answer mine. I wondered who would answer theirs.

*

Brother Breen's death affected me for months afterwards. In fact, it became something of an obsession. I felt my faith being shaken to its core. The consolation of Jesus sounded hollow in the coldness of the clay.

'You think too much, Michael.'

This was the common refrain from Brothers Price and Roberts whenever I raised the subject. By now I was fourteen years old and beginning to lose the security and innocence that childhood brings. I had many questions for God/Jesus. I was less willing to simply believe, full-stop. The more I learned about God the less sure I became. The Brothers had no answers and I could hardly approach that old fart Father O'Neill. I would have to find my own answers inside my head. What was the point of my existence? Where would I end up when I died? Why had I to be good, avoid temptation and desist from committing sins against purity? What was Our Lady's role in my life? She was known as the mother of the church but she was no mother to me. The more I thought about these things the more angry I became.

The Brothers behaved with profound cruelty, both physically and sexually, against us. Why were they getting away with it when God was looking down? Why did the police not believe the runaways who told them about the abuse? Why did God not rescue us? Where was the God that cried out 'suffer the little ones to come unto me'? These words filled me with rage. Father O'Neill often spoke about the hypocrites, the Pharisees in the Gospel, who incurred God's righteous anger when citing the case of the woman caught in adultery. I began to believe that Father O'Neill was also a hypocrite, in that he was fully aware of the sexual and physical abuse and did nothing about it.

As far as I was concerned both Father O'Neill and God were conveniently blind to our suffering. Shame on both of them. Maybe Brother Breen and Joseph Pyke were the lucky ones, free from fear and pain.

How could I be a priest with all these questions? Would God want me while I entertained such thoughts of anger? I didn't try to hide them from God. I often spent long periods before the Blessed Sacrament pouring out my heart to Jesus but I never received the slightest consolation despite storming Heaven with my prayers. Often I got up from these visitations more confused than ever. In my desperation I would go to the statue of our Lady, plug in the flex and light up the crown on her head. In the dark of the evening, through my tears, I imagined that I saw her smiling down upon me. Nevertheless I didn't feel any more assured.

Perhaps the whole thing was a hoax and there was no God after all. In truth I didn't like to pursue this thought, it made the world too lonely a place. Sometimes I snuck into the Brothers' garden in search of answers. There I felt my faith readjust itself again; being physically close to nature made me feel sure, once more, that there must be a God. Yes, nature provided me with reassurance about the possibility of an Almighty Father. It seemed to me that God was simply better with flowers and trees than he was with human beings.

If Brother Breen was sixty-eight years old when he died then I could live for another fifty-three years. But what would be the point of that if my life was so miserable now? Perhaps it would be better to die at thirty-three years, the same age that Jesus died on the cross. At least I wouldn't be able to commit as many mortal sins as I would if I lived to be sixty-eight.

Life, death, religion and the meaning of it all was giving me a headache. Perhaps Brothers Price and Roberts were right.

'Michael, you think too much, it only makes you miserable.'

Brother Lane Again

FOLLOWING THE BEATING by Brother Murphy I was exempt from going on the usual Sunday walks with Brother Lane, which infuriated him. However, one Sunday after dinner, he cornered me.

'Right, Clemenger, you little cur, fall in with the rest of them.'

'But sir…?'

'Never mind what somebody else told you, fall in or you'll feel the true force of my boot up your backside.'

About three miles out I sneezed suddenly and pop went the testicle up into my groin. I fell to the ground roaring with the pain.

'Get yourself up or I'll kick the shite out of you, Clemenger.'

'I can't, sir, the pain is very bad.'

He hesitated for a moment, unsure what to do with me.

'Please, sir, leave me with another boy. I'll be fine in a little while.'

'Don't you dare tell me what to do.'

'Yes, sir, sorry, sir.'

He couldn't afford to leave me lying on the side of the road so he called one of the boys over and ordered him to carry me on his back.

'But sir, he's too heavy.'

Oh, come on, I thought to myself, *with what they're feeding me you could put me in your pocket.* Another boy, Pat, stepped forward. He slept beside me in the dormitory and was always friendly to me.

'I'll carry him, sir. I don't mind.'

'All right then, pick him up. We can't spend the whole day moping about over this cur.'

With that Pat bent down and gingerly placed me on his back.

'I'm sorry, Pat, if I'm too heavy.'

'Don't worry, Michael, sure you're not heavy at all. A load of hay for the cattle is much heavier than you.'

I must have fallen asleep on Pat's back because when I woke up I was in the playground with all of the other boys. Pat asked Brother Lane what he should do with me.

'Put him in bed I suppose. But don't think, Clemenger, that you can try that trick with me again.'

In the dormitory I thanked Pat for his kindness.

'Sure it was nothing. Should I bring some supper for you?'

'Don't risk it, Pat. It's not worth you getting a hiding from that fecker. Can you try and get a message to Brother Price instead? Be careful though, "the murderer" has his spies around.'

'Don't I bloody know, Michael? All the feckers have their own spies.'

Within a half an hour the door of the dormitory opened and in rushed Brother Price.

'Michael, Michael, are you awake?'

'Yes, sir.'

Pulling down the bedclothes he checked the size of the lump in my groin.

'Lie on your right side, Michael, with your legs up tight against your tummy. That will ease the pain. Rest now, I'll be back in an hour with a tray.'

I heard afterwards that Brother Price had a standing row with Brother Lane in the alcove beside the refectory, and that Brother Price got the better of the exchange.

About 8.15 that night, just before the boys' bedtime, Brother Price appeared with a tray containing a pot of tea, scones, jam and an apple.

'Sit up, Michael, and have this before the others arrive. How is the pain now?'

'It's easing somewhat, sir, thank you, sir.'

'Brother Lane doesn't like you very much, why is that?'

'He thinks I'm your pet, sir, your favourite boy.'

'And so you are. What business is that of his?'

'I don't know, sir.'

'Don't worry, Michael, leave Brother Lane to me. If he ever hits you it will be the last time he does it, mark my words.'

When the lights went out I threw the apple to Pat.

'Here, Pat, have this. Thanks for helping me today.'

I turned over and went to sleep knowing that Brother Lane intended to strike and soon.

Bye Bye, Brother Lane

IT WAS A Saturday morning in the summer of 1965 and Cliff Richard was singing 'We're all going on a Summer Holiday' on the radio. Brother Lane liked to have the radio on at mealtimes so that he could listen to the news. The tune was, I thought, quite catchy and I pretended I was dancing to it while sitting at a table in the refectory. Moving my head around I made the dreadful mistake of catching Brother Lane's eye full on. He exploded with rage.

'That's it, Clemenger; I've had it with you.'

I was sitting about twenty feet away from him. Lunging from his high chair he grabbed hold of me and ran me down the whole refectory shouting his obscene threats. I was shocked at the speed of his actions.

'Please, sir, I'm sorry, sir. What did I do wrong, sir?'

Passing through the kitchen, Brother Lane roared at boys to get out of his way. Startled boys ran in all directions. He stopped in the 'dungeon', a very small room with bare walls, the only furniture an upturned tea chest and a bamboo stick.

'Take all your clothes off and bend over the tea chest,

Clemenger. You're about to get the worst hiding of your life. You've been asking for it for a long time and now you're going to get it.'

'No, sir, I'm not taking off my clothes. You'll be sorry when Brother Price gets back.'

Brother Price was away for the weekend.

'Wilful disobedience is it, Clemenger? Are you going to tell Brother Price anything else?'

He didn't wait for an answer, just grabbed hold of my clothes and ripped them off me. Flinging me across the tea chest he proceeded to beat the living daylights out of me.

'Hold open the cheeks of your bottom, you bloody cur.'

Using the bamboo stick he proceeded to paint my bottom all shades of the colour red. Occasionally he landed sharp blows on my anus, sending sheets of pain through my whole body. He even tried to stick the rod into my anus a couple of times. The beating went on for about five minutes. When pain reaches a certain threshold it no longer has the same intensity. The last thing I remember, before finally losing consciousness, was that I was still wearing my socks.

I don't know how long I was out for but I was told afterwards that when he was finished with me, Brother Lane went back to the refectory and resumed his seat as if nothing had happened. About half an hour later he told some of the boys to clean up the mess. When I woke up I found myself in bed. My body was wracked with pain. After dinner a senior boy called out to me.

'Michael, can you hear me?'

I opened my eyes and looked at him. He pulled down my blankets.

'Fuck me! There's blood everywhere, Michael, all over your arse and legs, and there are big blisters too. What will I do? Will I call some of the Brothers? I think I better, there's blood everywhere.'

'Try and get Brother Roberts.'

About ten minutes later Brother Roberts arrived in the dormitory with Brother Ryan who told the messenger to go back to the yard and keep his mouth shut. Brother Roberts pulled back the bedclothes. Both of them recoiled when they saw the extent of the bleeding and the amount of bruising. Brother Roberts was visibly shaken while Brother Ryan was absolutely livid.

'He can't go on like this; he'll end up killing some boy before he's finished.'

Leaning over me, Brother Ryan took my hand.

'You have been very unlucky with beatings this last while, Michael. Why do you think that is so?'

'I don't know, sir. I did nothing to Brother Lane for him to beat me like this, sir. Honestly, sir.'

'All right, Michael. Clean him up, Brother Roberts. You'll be fine in a few days, Michael. I'm sure you'll be glad to know you won't need the doctor. Keep him in bed for a week, Brother, and I'll call in on him again.'

Needless to say he never laid eyes on me until I was up and about again.

After fetching a basin of hot water, cloth and towel, Brother Roberts proceeded to clean the blood off my bottom and legs. He lingered for longer than he should have but I expected nothing less from him. When he finished he rubbed white talc powder all over my back, bottom and legs. I think it's fair to say he took pleasure in it, but I was too sore to care.

'Sleep now, Michael. I'll arrange for your meals to be sent up to you.'

Leaning over me on the bed he began to kiss me and suck on my lips for a few minutes.

'Please, sir, I am very sore.'

'Okay, Michael, you go asleep now and I'll see you later.'

Brother Price arrived back on Sunday afternoon about 5 o'clock. When he heard what had happened he came straight to the dormitory and grimly inspected the damage. Noticing the white talc he enquired who put it there, nodding as if he didn't know.

'This isn't finished, Michael. I'll do nothing until you're up and about again.'

A week later I was back on my feet, although I was still a bit sore. Brother Price approached me in the yard.

'Michael, when you get this evening's paper I want you to bring it to me in the Brothers' television room.'

Having secured the paper I knocked tentatively on the door.

'Come in!'

There were four people inside. Father O'Neill was on my left as I entered the door. He pretended to be asleep when he saw me. On my right was Brother Roberts, who seemed a little agitated. And who was sitting right beside the television but the bold Brother Lane. He said something I didn't hear, causing Brother Price to jump off his chair and walk menacingly towards him.

'So, Brother, you like to beat up little boys. Would you like to try someone your own size for a change?'

I found this funny since Brother Lane was about a foot smaller than Brother Price.

'Bring the paper down here, Michael.'

I passed Father O'Neill who was wide awake now and fully aware of what was going on. Brother Lane wasn't able to get out of his chair because Brother Price was blocking his way. From behind, Father O'Neill tried to calm the situation.

'Brothers, please! This is all so unnecessary, especially in front of the boy.'

But the die was cast; there was no going back for Brother Price.

'Father, please stay out of this. This is between me and him.'

Brother Roberts stayed quiet throughout.

'What have you to say for yourself now, Brother Lane? I warned you before that if you hit Michael Clemenger he would be the last boy you would ever hit in this place.'

Part of me wanted Brother Price to deck 'the murderer', but not in front of tell-tale Father O'Neill. The priest appealed to Brother Roberts to step in, but the latter pretended not to hear him. With that he got up, saying that he was going to get Brother Ryan.

A few minutes later Brother Ryan burst through the door, shouting at Brothers Lane and Price.

'Have you both lost your minds? Michael Clemenger, get out of here and don't mention this incident to anyone or there'll be trouble. Off with you now.'

I knew who was really in charge, so I looked at Brother Price who nodded for me to leave. That evening Brother Roberts took over supervision of supper.

I didn't see Brother Lane again for a few days when he announced to the lot of us boys that he was leaving St Joseph's. There was such a roar of delight that I thought the roof would lift off the refectory. No boy ever knew the real reason why Brother Lane left the monastery though some of them suspected that it was somehow connected to my beating.

The big fallout for me was the subsequent reaction of Father O'Neill who had been friendly with Brother Lane. He was openly hostile towards me and began to complain to Brother Roberts about my work. Brother Roberts, however, was having none of it.

'He never complained about your work before. He's only starting now because of Brother Lane's departure.'

I was surprised by their friendship. Brother Lane

wasn't a particularly religious man and I wondered what they could possibly have had in common. The biggest consequence was that there were no more leftovers for me on Father O'Neill's breakfast tray. But it was worth it to have gotten rid of 'the murderer'.

Brother Z

WE OFTEN HAD new Brothers arriving, and when Brother Z arrived I soon realised that he was quite similar, in terms of temperament, to Brother Lane except that he could control his temper for longer, thereby easily leading his prey into a false sense of security. He was a tall, slippery sort of fellow, with an extremely spotty face. He differed from Brother Lane in that he actually wanted to be liked by the boys.

He arrived at St Joseph's at a time when the number of boys was falling drastically. Despite this fall in numbers the food didn't improve, either in quality or quantity. One day, during a particularly bad dinner that dogs would have turned up their noses at, I stood up in the hall and complained. I had a certain standing amongst the other boys at this stage – they looked up to me – so this probably enabled me to make my complaint, especially to a new Brother.

While he was initially stunned at such cheek coming from someone of my small frame he quickly regained his composure.

'Stand with your face towards the wall, Clemenger. The rest of you, get on with your supper.'

I must confess that I was stunned by my own bravery, or foolishness, and I knew that Brother Z would not let it pass. Nothing happened over the next three days. During all meals I was made to face the wall without anything to eat. Slices of bread and milk in bottles were given to me by other boys. In the TV room on the fourth night he called me to sit by him and pretended to be nice to me. Then, when I least expected it, he threw a punch that caught me right on the side of the neck. I ended up on the floor where I received a few more blows across the bottom and neck.

'That will teach you to complain, you little brat.'

Of course, Brother Price found out about the beating, had words with Brother Z and I never had any more trouble with him.

I wondered how long more Brother Price could protect me from these bullies. Something was going on, a change was coming, I was almost sure of it. Brother Price seemed to cling to me in his room at night, as if he was preparing to say goodbye. My instincts were to prove correct within months.

Brother Price Leaves St Joseph's

WHILE I KNEW that one day Brother Price would leave St Joseph's I had hoped it would be near the time when I myself would be leaving. There were always Brothers coming and going. Most of the younger ones usually stayed between three and five years. I can never say that I particularly liked Brother Price, but he had been an enormous help regarding my surviving a place that unhinged many other boys. He wasn't an easy man to get to know. This was probably because there were so many facets to his personality. At times he was capable of the grand gesture. On one such occasion he called me into the yard and told me to go to Brother Ryan's office and ask him for a pound. Brother Ryan gave me the pound without question. When I brought it back to Brother Price he told me to go to the shop and buy ice pops for all the boys. I brought back a box of 240 ice pops, they were a penny each. When he handed them all out he was short forty-two ice pops so I was sent back to Brother Ryan for another five shillings. When I bought the missing forty-two pops Brother Price told me to keep the change. He could be very kind at times.

However, when he was in a bad humour, he could be quite vindictive. One evening he saw me lying on the grass, in the playing fields, sucking my thumb.

'Clemenger, get over here immediately. You're a bit too old now to be sucking your thumb.'

With that he marched me over to the nearest cow dung heap and stuck my thumb in it.

'Now put your thumb in your mouth and lick it.'

Not surprisingly, I stopped sucking my thumb whenever he was around.

He was near to tears when he told me that he would be leaving St Joseph's shortly. Since I was almost sixteen, I wasn't too worried of what his departure might mean for me. At least Brothers Murphy and Lane were long gone.

'You'll be all right now, Michael; you can take care of yourself.'

Maybe I should have felt defeated, or sad and frightened but I didn't. Because I didn't need his protection anymore I had outgrown him. One might think, after six years of his 'minding' me, that I could have formed an attachment, or even affection for him but I hadn't. It is very difficult to be fond of someone you fear. My relationship with him and Brother Roberts had all been a serious game. They took what they wanted from me while I made use of their fondness for me. I did what I had to do to survive. Their 'feelings' for me gave me an easier life than most, in the school, but at the end of the day they had molested me.

He opened a drawer, pulled out his favourite pipe and handed it to me.

'Keep this as a souvenir.'

I wondered what the hell I was going to do with it. Luckily enough a boy bought it off me after Brother Price left, for the grand sum of six marbles. During his last week the Brother made a point of coming to the tailor shop and staring at me for up to an hour at a time. I am sure Mr Quinlan did not like him being there, nor did the other boys.

He called me to his room on his last night. After the usual sexual ritual he told me to dress and brought me down to the Brothers' dining room for tea and cakes. I didn't know what to say to him and just wished that he would leave. Finally he gave me one last bear hug and I went to bed. When I got up the next morning for Mass he was gone. I was glad. His going went on too long for my liking. Brother Roberts thought that I might react badly to his colleague's departure and was much relieved when I seemed to take Brother Price's leaving in my stride.

'Don't worry, Michael, I'm not going anywhere.'

I think I was reassured by that. Nobody replaced Brother Price. With the numbers dwindling to less than a hundred, by the time I left, in January 1967, Brother X at last achieved his desire to be top dog.

Yes, I thought to myself, *Brother X could probably manage this amount of boys, but he would never have managed three hundred plus, which was what Brother Price was doing when I arrived eight years ago.*

Brother Price had subjected me to experiences that no child should ever have to endure, but I couldn't help having admiration for him as a teacher.

Sweet Sixteen

I WAS SIXTEEN years old on 1 November 1966. Brother Ryan called me into his office to inform me that I would be leaving St Joseph's after Christmas.

'Go up to Father O'Neill's room at 4.30 this afternoon. He wants to have a talk with you.'

I thought this curious because the priest had had little time for me since the incident with Brother Lane.

I knocked on his door at 4.30pm sharp and let myself in at his bidding. Since he didn't invite me to sit down I stood inside the door. He never looked up once as he spoke.

'Tell me, young man, who are your parents?'

I was completely thrown by this question and told him that I knew very little about them.

'Come, come, you must have heard something about them, boy.'

'I only know what I heard from Brother Price.'

'Brother Price, indeed. And what did the esteemed Brother Price have to say about them?'

'He told me that my parents didn't wait until they were married before they had me, Father. He also said I was baptised in a neighbouring parish, St Nicholas of Myra, in Francis Street in Dublin.'

'Indeed, indeed. Do you know what that means?'

'No, Father.'

'Tell me, boy, why do the boys in the yard call you "Father"?'

'Because they know that I want to be a priest.'

'Do you indeed?'

'Yes, Father.'

Leaning forward in his chair and summoning up as much spiteful venom as he could muster, he took obvious delight in giving me the following piece of news.

'You, Clemenger, will never be a priest. Shall I tell you why? It's because you are a bastard, and a product of sin. That's why.'

The term 'bastard' was delivered with such a degree of disdain that I knew that it had to be something bad.

'What does "bastard" mean, Father? It sounds like a bad word. Is it?'

'No, it's not a bad word in itself, but its meaning is a problem for you. It's the reason that you'll never be a priest. That's the holy all of the matter. So get those fanciful notions out of your head. It cannot happen. You can never be a priest.'

His mission accomplished, he sat back in his chair. For months afterwards I thought that this conversation was the most hurtful thing I had ever experienced. It was much worse than the beatings of both Brothers Lane and

Murphy. My God, what a cruel man this priest was. I was only beginning to see his true colours. Without doubt, though he wore the collar, said the Masses and heard the confessions, he had long ceased to live up to the aspiration of his vocation. It wasn't his words so much that stung me – though to be sure I was heartbroken – but it was the shockingly curt way he told me. I saw him as a man with broken ideals who indulged his passions in food, wine and spite, while awaiting the falling of the curtain on the life lived as a lie. His goal with me was to gloat over the misfortune of my birth and to try and break down the dreams that he once shared. I felt that his anger was directed at me because I reminded him of the simple humility and trust in the goodness of God that he may once have had.

'Now, boy, get out of my sight and don't let me hear any more of this foolishness. Close the door quietly on your way out.'

I made my way to the chapel and cried before the Blessed Sacrament for nearly an hour. The other boys came to the chapel at 6pm for the rosary. The night passed in restless sleep and continuing questions.

I continued to clean Father O'Neill's room and serve his Masses. The matter was never brought up again. In fact I never had any more conversations with the priest until the day I left the school, a couple of months later.

10 January 1967

'MY BEST BOY, my beautiful boy, what am I going to do without you, Michael?'

I had no answers for Brother Roberts and by this stage, in spite of his interfering with me, I felt more sorry for him than anything else. After all he had made things relatively easy for me and had never once discouraged me in my dreams of becoming a priest. By the end he was a sickly man, much less vigorous and vibrant than when I had first met him. Still, he tenaciously stood up for me when Father O'Neill complained about my work.

It was he who came to the yard to tell me to collect my things but not before one last visit to the sweet shop. There he bought me a mixture of sweets, shoved his tongue down my throat for one last time, while trying to maintain his composure. I had never seen him cry before.

'Go now to the dormitory and collect your things.'

I passed by the remaining boys playing in the yard. We just looked at each other but no goodbyes were said. I walked through the junior dormitory recalling my fearful first night there. The beds were all empty now. I wondered where the former occupants were. Had they survived the big bad world outside? In the middle dormitory old shoes lay abandoned under beds no longer in use. Dust could be seen rising from the floor in the hazy sunlight. There was no hint of the back-breaking work that had been performed for years, to keep the place clean and tidy. The only residents these days were the spiders who slept in their cobwebs. In the senior dormitory, the only one still in use, I thought about all the crying and beatings that had taken place here. Finally, I came to my own bed. It had been my dream factory for over five years. How often had I lain here, wracked with pain from the various beatings? How often had I been taken from here to fulfil the sexual fantasies for ones who should have known better?

Hung opposite my bed, in splendid isolation, was the huge framed portrait of St Dominic Savio. I had spent hours gazing at this picture, trying to make a connection with the saint. As far as I was concerned he had unsympathetic eyes that burned right through me, especially if I had bad thoughts or dared to engage in sinful acts under the blankets when the hormones ran wild. Gathering my few belongings I threw them into a small case and with one last look at the room I left by the sliding door.

I went into the chapel. There was nobody there so I made my way to the altar, invigorated by my anger that emanated from within. Bitterly I thought this is where the seeds of my vocation were first sown. Would Jesus, who was supposedly living in the tabernacle, be able to measure the depth of my anger and react by striking me dead? By now I had had enough of this supposedly loving Son of God and His fairytale of 'suffer the little children to come unto me'. Luckily He kept Himself hidden; otherwise He would have got a mouthful of abuse from me. I never gave Our Blessed Lady a second look. Boy, I thought, what a fool I had been to think that either of them could ever love me, whatever that meant.

I couldn't leave without venting my full anger at someone, and who better than that self-righteous, condescending grossness that lay in his bed nursing his various ailments. I decided to pay him a final visit. Along the corridor I passed the empty rooms of Brothers Breen, Price, Burke, Lane and Murphy. So many memories hurled themselves at me with such violence that they only fuelled my rage. I dispensed with knocking politely on the priest's door; instead, I burst in unannounced.

'What is the meaning of this outrage, the impertinence of this behaviour?'

'Shut your mouth. This "bastard" is here to tell you that he's leaving the school in a few minutes. I just wanted to tell you first that I think you're a lousy priest.'

He seemed unable to rise or respond, probably due to his shock, so I was free to continue my rant.

'Call yourself a priest? What did you do to stop the beatings and sexual abuse you knew was happening in this place?'

He pretended not to know what I was talking about, which only increased my anger.

'Will you please leave my room at once, Clemenger?'

Kicking the end of the bed and slamming the wardrobe door beside me I told him that I would leave when I was ready. He took off his glasses, looking perplexed. Trapped by his ailing body, he could do nothing but repeat, 'Please leave, please leave.' I felt no pity.

'Shut up! This "bastard" would make a better priest a thousand times over than you could ever be. Why do you think boys gave up telling you about the sexual abuse they suffered at the hands of the Brothers? You don't know? Well, I'll tell you. Because you reported their words back to the Brothers and then the boys got extra vicious hidings for their trouble. Tell me, Father O'Neill, what kind of priest would do that?'

He looked like he was going to have a heart attack.

'Don't worry! I'm going now, but I won't forget you or those Brothers and what they did to innocent boys in this place.'

While he appeared to be relieved that I was going, I could see that I had hit home, that he had been confronted, at last, with what he knew to be true. I hoped that the echo of my words would sound in his ears for the rest of his days, reminding him of his part in the sexual abuse of little children. To paraphrase Jesus: the little children had suffered, had come to him, but had then been accused of lying. This priest's inaction had given the green light to these Brothers who were free to indulge their sexual desires with us. I kicked the end of the bed again and slammed the wardrobe door one more time before I marched out of that room forever.

I made my way to Brother Ryan's office, but he must have heard my shouting and came to meet me on the stairs.

'Clemenger, what in heaven's name is going on up there?'

'Don't you start that old shite talk with me! I was just up with Father O'Neill, giving him some home truths, particularly about all the beatings and sexual abuse that he could have prevented.'

Brother Ryan stopped dead in his tracks. I thought he was going to hit me. Glaring at him, I challenged him to try something. He pleaded with me to keep my voice down.

'Your new employer is here.'

Moving towards the parlour door he opened it, and spoke to the stern-looking woman inside.

'Sorry about all the commotion. Here is the boy who will be working for you. His name is Michael Clemenger.'

There were no further introductions. It appeared from their familiarity that other boys had been placed in her employment before. Furthermore, Brother Ryan was much too anxious to get me out of the place. Moving us steadily towards the front door he nervously bade goodbye to the woman. She appeared to hesitate for a second but the door closed firmly behind us. I imagined Brother Ryan running to Father O'Neill's room to see if he was still alive. Treading the cobbled stones alongside my silent employer, I remembered taking this same route, eight years earlier, on Brother Price's shoulders.

PART TWO

Alone in the World

Alone in the World

NOTHING IN THE monastery had prepared me for this new step. I never had to worry about making a living before, handling money or dealing socially with strangers. From the outset, however, I was determined that nobody would ever treat me the way I had been treated up to now. Therefore, I didn't take kindly to my first employer. In the car she treated me as if I was some kind of purchase and assumed that she could do with me as she wanted. I was quick to remind her that I was no pushover and she seemed to resent the fact that I had the cheek to speak to her, never mind look her directly in the eye. It was obvious from her manner that she didn't have very high expectations of me, and I was going to make sure she wasn't disappointed. If she had already decided I was going to be bad, on account of where she had picked me from, then that's what I was going to be. She pulled up outside a small hotel and gestured at the front door.

'Do you see that door, boy?'

'Please, don't call me "boy".'

'Anyway, I don't ever want to catch you going through that door.'

'Why? It's only a door like any other.'

'You don't seem to understand; when I talk, you listen.'

With that she drove us around to the back of the hotel.

'This is the only door that you are to use.'

She got out of the car, slamming the door, and went into the kitchen. Seeing that I wasn't behind her she stormed back.

'Well, are you coming?'

I made no move to get out of the car. She opened the passenger door.

'I hope you're not going to give me trouble.'

'Is this the way you treat all your staff?'

Indignant with rage, she marched into the kitchen. I remained in the car determined that I wasn't going to make things easy for her. A few minutes later she emerged again to inform me that she had been speaking to Brother Ryan. Seeing that I was less than impressed with this, she decided to change her tune.

'Come in, Michael; let's have a cup of tea before you start work.'

Having made my point I quickly got out and followed her into the kitchen. God, it was hot in there. After having tea and bread with jam on it she handed me a knife and brought me over to a bath beside the kitchen door. The bath was very similar in size to the one that I had to share every Wednesday night with

Brother Roberts. What a strange thing to think of on my first day at work. I was surprised to see that this bath was full of potatoes.

'I want all of these potatoes peeled by a quarter to six this evening.'

It was now 3.25pm, according to the clock on the wall in front of me. I laughed incredulously, telling her no, I didn't think that would be possible. She stalked off. I picked up a nearby chair and put it down beside the bath.

'You can't sit down; she'll go bloody mad.'

I looked around to see a small woman staring back at me in disbelief.

'Are you a Monoboy?'

'Yes, why?'

'Well, just none of them seem to last very long. They're not used to hard work.'

She walked away quickly before I could answer. Knowing about the other abused Monoboys only made me more determined to fail. At about 4.30 the boss arrived back in the kitchen. After briefly talking to other staff she made a beeline for me.

'You're not making much headway, are you?'

Without saying anything I glared at her and handed her my peeler. She was utterly amazed but said nothing.

'Mary, come and give us a hand with these potatoes.'

Eventually they were all peeled and ready for the party that was being held in the hotel that night. She avoided me for the rest of the evening. Mary warned me against annoying her further.

'Be careful with that one. She got rid of the other boys and she'll get rid of you too.'

'Don't worry, Mary, I'll leave myself before she gets the chance to do anything.'

Some of the other girls were quite nice to me; one of them gave me a lovely dinner at about 8 o'clock. The hotel was very busy with the guests. Occasionally I snuck a glance through the door of the ballroom as the waitresses rushed to and fro. I spent the whole night washing dishes. The sounds of the people enjoying themselves together reinforced the feeling that I was from a different planet and would forever be an outsider.

At about 1.30am things began to quieten down. Guests went home and after clearing up the ballroom the staff also went home. Mary (who was on wash-up with me) stayed behind for a cup of tea and a Woodbine. How she loved her fags!

'How long were you in the monastery, Michael?'

'Have you ever been up there, Mary?'

'No, are you mad? I wouldn't set foot inside that place for love nor money. It would frighten the shite out of me. The stories I've heard, you wouldn't know what to believe.'

'Don't worry, Mary, if you only knew the half of it.'

She moved about restlessly, perhaps nervous that I might tell her a few stories myself.

'I'm off now, Michael; have to go to my bed. Expect I'll see you tomorrow.'

The time was 2.50am. With Mary gone I was now alone in the kitchen. I didn't know what to do with myself. Not used to being up at this very late hour I just sat on a chair, utterly exhausted.

From behind me I heard the door opening. My employer was going around locking doors and putting out the lights. She saw me and cried out.

'Oh, you! I'll have to find some place for you to sleep. Come with me.'

I followed her up a flight of stairs and past a few doors. She stopped outside a door and opened it.

'There, you can sleep there.'

It was a tiny bathroom and she seemed to be directing me to sleeping on a bare wooden board that covered the bath.

'You must be joking if you think that I'm going to sleep on that.'

'That's okay, then. Do what you like.'

She walked away. What could I do but close the door and stretch myself out on the board.

I woke about 10.30 the following morning, sore all over and fighting mad. In the kitchen I met the porter. He introduced himself and made me a lovely breakfast.

'I heard that you and the boss had words yesterday. Is that true?'

'You bet it's true, but it won't be half of what I have to say to the fucker today.'

'Please mind your language; I hate to hear young people using that type of language.'

'Do you know where I slept last night?'

'Yes, that's where all the other Monoboys slept.'

'And you think that's all right, sir? You're worrying about bad language, but what about that?'

'Well, you'll have to discuss that matter with her, I'm afraid.'

'Don't worry, I will.'

The boss came into the kitchen after midday, suitably sprinkled with holy water after coming from Mass in the town. I'm sure she didn't tell Jesus the way she treated her Monoboys. Before she had time to open her mouth I let fly with a double barrel dose of foul language.

'Don't worry, I'm not staying in this place another day. I don't fancy sleeping on a board in a bathroom with no mattress, pillow or blankets. What kind of fool do you take me for?'

I raised my voice so high that other members of staff came running, in case I was going to hit her.

'You might have got away with that old carry on with other Monoboys but you won't with me. Of that you can be sure.'

'Okay, okay, please lower your voice.'

Turning to the porter she told him to put a mattress, blankets, sheets and a pillow in the bathroom. Over the next few weeks she tried to bully me but to no avail. Her pet job for me was to whitewash the hotel walls. I never did it to her satisfaction and, to be honest, I never really tried. To best her I would deliberately wait until I saw her with guests, coming or going from the main entrance of the hotel, before making my grand entrance via the front door.

A Second Opinion

IT WAS A tough regime. I started work at 7 o'clock every morning and finished at six in the evening, with no day off. There was little to do in the evenings. I either went for walks out the Castleisland Road or read a book. More and more I found myself mulling over Father O'Neill's words – that I would never be a priest because I was a bastard. One evening I decided that I needed a second opinion. I went to have a chat with the parish priest. However, when I called at the parochial house, he was out so I went up to St John's Cathedral to wait for him. It was raining heavily. When I got there I found a number of women in the church, waiting for the Thursday evening Mass. I took a seat at the back, just as an elderly priest walked out on to the altar.

After the Mass I asked this priest if he knew when the parish priest would be back.

'I'm the parish priest. Can I help you?'

'Yes, Father, I hope so.'

He invited me back to the parochial house. When we had settled ourselves in the parlour I introduced myself as Michael Clemenger, explaining that I was very interested in becoming a priest.

'Hmm, I don't know the name "Clemenger". Who's your family? I thought I knew all the families in the parish.'

'I don't know my family, Father. I was reared in St Joseph's Industrial School.'

He seemed a little startled.

'I have a problem, Father, and I was wondering if you could help me. Father O'Neill, the school chaplain, told me that I couldn't become a priest because I was a bastard. Is that true, Father?'

He sat back, looking perplexed. I think my use of the word 'bastard' threw him; he scratched his head and shuffled uneasily in his seat.

'Oh, I see. Yes, I know Father O'Neill well; he's a good friend of mine. Well, son, I'm not really sure how to answer that question.'

'But that's all I want to know, Father. Does being a bastard bar me from becoming a priest?'

He tried to sidestep giving an answer by asking me about the Christian Brothers. I think it's safe to say he was in no way prepared for the honesty of my answer.

'Well, Father, I experienced a lot of physical and sexual abuse by the Christian Brothers.'

'How long were you there?'

'From 1959 to just a few weeks ago.'

I could see he was struggling to try to extricate himself from what had to be a bewildering situation.

'And where are you now?'

'I am working at a hotel as a kitchen porter.'

'Do you like it there?'

'No, Father, my employer doesn't treat me very well. I work long hours and have to sleep on a board across a bath.'

'Really?'

'Look, Father, I just want to know if I can become a priest or not.'

'Tell me, son, are you still in touch with St Joseph's?'

'No, Father.'

'That's good. You should forget about all those things that happened and just look to the future.'

He seemed most anxious to end the conversation.

'But what about my wish to be a priest, Father?'

'Leave that to God, son. Leave it all in God's hands and pray. Have you much schooling?'

'Only up to primary, Father.'

'Well, all I can say to you is what I've just said. Just leave things as they are for the moment.'

With that he ushered me towards the front door. It was still raining heavily outside so he gave me a brolly from a rack just inside the door.

'Goodbye, son, and God bless. Take care now.'

The door closed behind me. He wasn't as brutal as Father O'Neill, but I felt that his message was the same. I hung his brolly on the door handle and walked slowly back to the hotel, hardly noticing the awful weather.

Suicidal Thoughts

THE FOLLOWING MONTH I announced that I had had enough of the job and was leaving. The boss begged me to stay, saying that it would be difficult for me to get another job without a reference. She also rang the school to inform them that I was leaving the hotel. I returned to St Joseph's with £8 in my pocket after my month's work. It might seem strange that I would return to the source of all my unhappiness, but where else was I to go? I was glad that she never had the satisfaction of firing me as she had done with the other Monoboys.

Back at St Joseph's Brother Ryan was waiting for me. I expected him to be raging, but he was most polite.

'I'm sorry, Michael, that things didn't work out for you.'

Interrupting him I told him that she treated me like a dog, making me sleep in a bath with a board on top.

'Go and sit in the parlour, please. I've arranged for new employment for you in a hotel in Listowel. But remember, this is your last chance. If it doesn't work out, you're on your own. I wash my hands of you. Do you understand?'

I made no answer. Twenty minutes later I was on my way to Listowel, with my new employer, a pleasant man in his fifties. I was to be the hotel porter and spent the journey listening to a detailed description of my responsibilities.

I quit three days later. One of my jobs entailed my carrying buckets of coal up three flights of stairs before midday. With my groin injury I found it just about impossible. At about 11 o'clock on the morning of my third day, I walked into the boss's office where he was sitting with his wife.

'I'm off. You don't need a worker to carry buckets of coal up the stairs, you need a donkey.'

They stared back in astonishment. I left the hotel and walked up the street to get a look at John B. Keane's pub. I hadn't a clue who he was, but I had heard in the hotel that he was famous. I got back to Tralee at about five that evening, with no prospects, no job and not the foggiest notion of what to do next. I went into a café and had a meal, wondering where I was going to sleep that night.

After I had eaten I went to sit in St John's Church. My misery was only compounded by the sight of mothers bringing their children into the church to light candles. The children were giddy with excitement as their mothers lifted them up to where the candles were. How I envied them the security of their existence, the careful hands that held them in case they should fall, the hugs and the smiles. I felt very alone. Thinking back to my Confirmation, made in this same church, I was convinced that day that I was on my own forever. And it was turning out to be true. I bowed my head to hide my tears as the women and children passed by on their way back down the aisle, listening hungrily until I couldn't hear their laughter anymore.

It must be wonderful to be going home, to have somewhere to belong to, to know that somebody else was concerned about your welfare and was working hard to help you fulfil your dreams. The town children, with their education, could go on to college to become whatever they wanted to be: a priest, a doctor, a teacher or whatever. Meanwhile I knew that I could never become a priest, which had been my only dream. So, really, what was the point of my life? Suddenly gasping for fresh air I went outside the church to the small graveyard where a handful of priests were buried and sat on the grass.

Reading the headstones I envied the occupants. These men had served God as priests, had had their dreams come true, to say Mass and hear confession. After serving God here on earth they were now sitting at His right hand side, enjoying their reward in Heaven. What a rotten deal I had been dealt. Lord, why did You put me on this earth? I didn't ask to be born, nor did I ask to be physically and sexually abused. According to Father O'Neill, You can see everything, so why did You allow them to abuse me and the other boys? Why didn't You strike them down?

I couldn't help thinking that the person who knows what's going on, but says nothing, is even worse than the abuser. Oh, how I hated God at that moment.

I decided that I would end it all in the very place where I had endured my misery, St Joseph's. It's a strange thing when one finally decides to take one's life. A sense of calm descended on me, silencing all the noise in my head. Before going on to the school I decided to walk up the town for a last meal. I had a bit of money left and was still playing with my newfound freedom, being able to go into a café and order a decent plate of food.

The restaurant was quite busy, with lots of rowdy young people, courting couples and giggling gangs of girls. Older people with furrowed brows sat gloomily over cups of tea. I felt relief that I would never be that old and grey, having to wear glasses or hobble about on a crutch. A major advantage of dying young, I thought, was never having to put up with jibes about going bald or having to wear dentures like Brothers Breen and Roberts. But how would I kill myself? *Don't worry*, said the voice in my head, *we'll decide that closer to the time*.

On the way up to the school I remembered the times I had walked these streets, full of dreams for the future, never doubting that I would one day return to St

Joseph's as a priest, to say my first Mass. This last walk was now one of despair and fury. I arrived in the playground in the monastery at about 9 o'clock.

It was strange to be back there among the familiar smells and sounds. The few remaining boys were in the dormitory getting ready for bed. I headed down to the handball alley, feeling very bitter that my eight years of surviving the school had been for nothing. I looked down the avenue to where the Brothers' graves were and felt cold all over. What was the point of my having been born in the first place? The nuns never cared for me, the Brothers never cared for me and now I didn't even care for me. It was almost funny.

Coming into the centre of the playground I had one last look before walking over to a nearby window, breaking it and rubbing my wrist along its jagged edges. The blood flowed and I sat down to wait for death to take me. My life ran like a film in my mind's eye. I saw the faces of Jimmy, the Reverend Mother, and the tall woman with the bun in her hair who took Jimmy away. Brothers Price and Roberts came briefly to stand over me, one after the other. Brothers Lane, Murphy and Z were sneering at me from behind grotesque masks.

'Go on, you cur. You'll never amount to anything.'

The words of Father O'Neill rang out.

'Bastard, product of sin, that's all you are.'

I offered no resistance. I just wanted to sleep.

Glancing at my wrist the blood was still flowing, but not very fast. *Christ, I can't even kill myself. Am I that bloody useless that I can't even kill myself? Maybe the Brothers were right after all*, said the voice in my head.

As I lay there on the cold ground a strange feeling came over me. It was as if the blood flowing out of me took with it some of my rage. I heard another voice in my head: *You don't have to do this, Michael.*

I found myself giving serious thought to what I was doing and, typically, coming up with a lot of questions. Will the Brothers care if I live or die? Does anybody care? What will they think if they find me dead in the play-ground? Will they feel vindicated? Nobody cared when Joseph Pyke died and nobody will care if Michael Clemenger dies.

In the midst of this internal debate I suddenly smelt the smoke of Archibald the caretaker's pipe as he arrived into the yard to begin the night shift. That ordi-nary event decided my fate. I jumped up from the ground and ran into the toilets beside me. He didn't see me as he walked his bike into the shed where he parked it for the night. Checking my wrist to see if it was still bleeding, I tore a strip from the bottom of my white shirt and tied it tightly around the gash. Then I sat down on the steps, safe in the shadows. What was I going to do now? I had maybe £6 in my pocket and a brand new wish to live. It would seem that I would have to live on my wits. For now I could probably steal in order to feed myself. I was too tired to think any further, it had been a long, long day. I crept out of the yard and made my way down the town to find somewhere to sleep on the green.

Resched

A FEW DAYS later I was sitting over a big, dirty fry in a local café on the main street. I noticed this young man looking in the window at me. I didn't take much notice of him and refrained from returning his nervous half smile. He came into the café and sat down in front of me.

'Hello, my name is Andy. Are you a Monoboy?'

I eyed him suspiciously and became defensive.

'What business is it to you?'

'Oh, I'm sorry; I didn't mean to be rude. It's just that I've seen you hanging around the town for the past few days and I was wondering.'

'I have every right to walk the streets of this town. Mind your own business. If you think I'm queer then you're very much mistaken. So get lost!'

'Calm down! It's not what you think. Can I ask you your name?'

'Michael, if you must know.'

'Okay, Michael, I think I can help you, if you like.'

'Why would you want to help me? You don't even know me. Have you met other "Monoboys", as you call us?'

'Yes, I know a few.'

'Do you know what happened to us? Tell me what you've heard.'

'Yes, Michael, I've heard some stories, but I don't know if I believe them all.'

'Listen, whoever you are, if you only knew the half of it.'

He moved about uncomfortably.

'Just wait here for few minutes, Michael; I'll be back with my father.'

Turning to the waitress, Andy informed her that he would take care of the bill. I didn't honestly expect to see him again and was really surprised when he duly reappeared, about ten minutes later, with his father. They both sat down and the father offered me his hand. He had kind eyes and appeared in no way threatening towards me.

'Tell me, Michael, how long have you been out from St Joseph's?'

'About five weeks, sir.'

'There's no need to call me sir. Just call me Tommy. How long were you in St Joseph's?'

'Since 1959.'

'That long? Have you any parents?'

'I don't really know.'

'Okay, that's enough questions for the moment.'

He beckoned the waitress and young Andy paid for my breakfast.

'Will you come with me, Michael? I'll give you a job and a place to stay where you will be safe. We've known about you for about a week. My son spotted you a few times in the church and thought you needed help. I'm prepared to help you if you want it.'

His attitude completely unsettled me. My mind was in freefall. Should I accept this man? Why would he want to help a Monoboy? I'd no experience of kindness from strangers.

'Don't worry, Michael, I've nothing to do with the Brothers in St Joseph's. You'll be safe with me.'

He could see that I was frightened and close to tears.

'Come with us, Michael. I promise you it'll be all right.'

I was finally persuaded because throughout the whole conversation he made no physical contact with me. The three of us walked out of the café together.

In about three minutes I found myself sitting in the parlour of his fine big house where Tommy introduced me to his wife and others in the house.

'Stay with him, Andy, while I make a call.'

Twenty minutes later there was a knock on the door. A tall man of about fifty was introduced to me as Mr Graff. He brought me and Tommy about a mile up the road to a housing estate and stopped in front of a small house. The door was answered by an old woman, Mr Graff's mother. She welcomed us in and made a pot of tea and sandwiches.

While I ate in the kitchen Tommy (Mr O'Brien) and Mr Graff spoke with Mr Graff's mother.

'That's settled, Michael. You can stay here and next Monday morning at 8 o'clock you'll start working as a labourer for me. Mr Graff, who's my foreman, will collect you until you get to know the route. It's only a short walk away.'

With that Mr O'Brien, who was a builder and under-taker, handed me a few pounds and told me to buy new clothes and shoes and that he would see me on Monday. My head was spinning so much that I don't believe I managed to thank Mr O'Brien for his kindness. In truth I was still reeling from the fact that I had almost killed myself and was even feeling a bit guilty about still being alive. Nevertheless, Mr O'Brien had provided me with a chance of a new start. I worked for him for the next eighteen months.

Jayne Mansfield

A COUPLE OF months later, in April 1967, there was great excitement in the town because an American actress, Jayne Mansfield, was coming to Tralee to perform a show. The news caused consternation in the churches throughout Kerry, with the local bishop urging the people not to have anything to do with the upcoming events. For myself I had never heard of Jayne Mansfield but the fact that her presence upset the clergy made me laugh. Journalists, photographers and television cameras invaded the town, all desperate for a picture or an interview. When I saw a picture of the actress I began to understand what all the fuss was about. The men I worked with waxed lyrical about what they liked best about her; the same two attractions came up again and again. Meanwhile the priests and the bishop beseeched us not to set foot anywhere near the Mount Brandon Hotel, where she was staying, lest we lose our immortal souls. Miss Mansfield, it seems, was a danger to the morals of every young man and woman in Tralee.

Increasing pressure was brought to bear on the management of the Mount Brandon Hotel to cancel her show. I couldn't help thinking that only up the road from the hotel was St Joseph's Industrial School, where moral degradation of young innocent boys was being carried out daily by men of the cloth. At the forefront of the vocal uproar against the presence of the Hollywood actress was the same priest I had spoken to weeks earlier, when I described in detail the sexual abuse I had experienced. It was a pity he didn't apply the same effort on my behalf that he was now expending with regard to Jayne Mansfield. After a meeting one evening about the forthcoming visit, I challenged him about this at the door of the parochial house, but he made a hasty retreat inside.

The clergy was eventually successful in getting the show cancelled. There was great disappointment in the town that Miss Mansfield didn't stay longer than a few days, as her presence was great for business. The incident that sticks out in my mind, however, the one I found most galling, was the refusal of the clergy to allow the actress, who was also a devoted mother to her five children, to enter St John's Church to light a candle. Two months later she was dead, as a result of a car crash in America.

There was great shock in Tralee and the stench of hypocrisy rose from the streets as Mass upon Mass was said for the late film star. It has always amazed me how even the most vile of sinners can suddenly gain respectability through the lid of a coffin. The incident, as far I was concerned, demonstrated the powerful grip that the Church held over the people. Such was my outrage I wrote a long letter to the bishop's house in Killarney, expressing my disgust and outrage at the duplicity of both the parish priest of Tralee and the clergy in general. I also provided specific details of everything that had happened to me in St Joseph's Industrial School, the physical and sexual abuse, from 1959 to 1967.

Needless to say, I never received a reply.

*

I spent the next eighteen months working for the builder. It wasn't all plain sailing. In some ways I felt as trapped as I had been in St Joseph's. The problem was my label of 'Monoboy', which seemed to taint my relationship with my fellow workers. They appeared uncomfortable around me and I overheard one of the men saying that Monoboys were useless workers. In my case, I am sorry to say, this was particularly true because the work was very physical and I was extremely slight for my age. My frame wasn't suited to pulling and dragging nine-inch cavity blocks, or six-inch solids, up and down ladders. It was always a bone of contention with the other men that I wasn't pulling my weight. My hernia, which nobody knew about, often flared up so badly that I had to be sent home for the day.

In time I was reassigned to the role of messenger boy. I took the messages from the shop, made the tea and cleaned up after breaks. In short I became the general dogsbody and was at the beck and call of all the other workers. The only man who ever showed me any genuine consideration or kindness was the 'Protestant'. I don't recall his name, but he was a nice man who drove a green car. My favourite job was to wash Tommy O'Brien's hearse, which was his pride and joy. He was also a local undertaker and had a supply of coffins on the premises that were kept next to his main office. Usually he did a funeral once or twice every other week.

Perhaps my least favourite job was the window-cleaning detail, which usually occurred the first week of every month. My major input would be to stand, for what felt like hours, at the end of a ladder outside such hot spots as the local banks, insurance agencies and Benner's Hotel. There sure were a lot of windows to clean. I hated when the townsfolk and their children would pass by and stare at me, as if I was an ornament. Other jobs included going to people's houses to clean out their chimneys. The last week of every month was assigned to cleaning the yard and stacking away any broken blocks, wire or pieces of timber that were lying around. Tommy hated to bring customers into a dirty yard.

As a way of life it proved, with each passing month, to be utterly monotonous. Was this it? Was this to be my lot in life? Then one afternoon, Tommy came into the yard. He seemed very agitated and asked about another employee.

'Where is he?'

The man had apparently gone home sick. Unable to get anyone else he called me.

'Michael, will you go home, dress and wash, and be back here as fast as you can.'

I was back in the yard in about twenty minutes flat.

'Don't worry, Michael, all you have to do is come with me to Killarney to collect a body for burial.'

The drive took us about an hour. Seeing a rainbow in the sky the builder asked me if I knew the significance of it.

'Yes, sir, it's a promise from God that he won't drown the world again after Sodom and Gomorrah.'

'What happened there, Michael?'

'I think they committed many mortal sins of impurity and refused to repent.'

'Who told you that?'

'Father O'Neill, he was always preaching about that sort of thing.'

After a few minutes' silence he asked me about the goings-on in St Joseph's. By the end of my story beads of sweat were pouring down his forehead. He said nothing, but I could see he was affected.

'Your son is very lucky, sir, that he has you for a father. He can be anything that he wants to be.'

With that I shut up and sat back in the seat.

'Hold yourself together, Michael; don't forget where we are going.'

'Don't worry, sir, I'm a good actor. Nobody will know.'

The body of an old woman was waiting in the hospital for us. We lifted the coffin gently into the hearse. She had no family and apparently had been in a mental hospital for many years. We proceeded back to Tralee and put the coffin into St John's Church. There were a few mourners here, but no relatives as far as I could tell. Tommy supplied the flowers that I placed all around the coffin.

I loved wet days as it meant we couldn't do any work. When it rained the labourers usually gathered in the shed to play cards. Since I didn't know the first thing about cards I found other ways to pass the time. One afternoon I slipped into the coffin room. I liked to feel the timber and the luxurious cloth that lined the coffin's interior. I decided this day to get into one of the coffins and have a sleep. It was hugely comfortable and grabbing sneak midday naps like this quickly became a habit.

Unfortunately, during one of these siestas, Tommy came in to show the coffins to a customer. I must have been snoring because she heard me and gave out an almighty roar that woke me up. I immediately sat up, which only made matters worse.

'For God's sake! What's going on here, Michael? Get out of that coffin and go home. I'll deal with you later.'

He hurried the poor woman out of the room and into his office for a cup of tea. When I turned up for work the next morning the story was all around the yard. Several of the men made their feelings known to me.

'You're gone, Monoboy. Bye bye!'

Mr O'Brien called me into his office.

'Don't worry, sir, I'm going anyway.'

Despite this man's initial support of me I knew he had no choice. My colleagues grumbled loudly about my shortcomings, the fact I wasn't able to carry heavy items as fast as they could and struggled when unloading lorries. I knew in my heart that my time was up and wanted to make it easy for him since he had done so much for me.

'No, you're not going like this. You'll stay until I finalise plans to put you in the army.'

'You must be joking if you think I am doing that.'

I didn't know anything about the army, and could only imagine, from all the war films I had seen in St Joseph's that I'd end up having to shoot people with a machine gun.

'What else can you do? It's the best solution, Michael.'

Reluctantly I agreed. A few days later he left me at the railway station to get the train to Ballincollig army barracks, in Co. Cork.

I was there for about three days waiting for my medical examination. I had to be physically cleared before I could officially enlist. Some of the other lads told me that it was common for Monoboys to join the army and that they usually got on very well too. This was probably the case since the army was only another form of institution. Knowing no other way of life, they would feel safe in similar surroundings.

My medical was set for first thing on the Thursday morning. Everything was going well until the doctor asked me to drop my trousers. I was most reluctant.

'Come along, young man, I'm not going to bite you.'

When I eventually complied he seemed to draw back a little.

'Oh, dear me, what have we here then?'

He placed his hand on my genitalia and pressed hard for a second. I cried out in pain.

'All right, son, you can pull up your trousers now.'

After washing his hands he told me to sit at the table with him.

'Tell me, how did you get that injury?'

'From a beating, doctor.'

'A beating? From who?'

'Oh, the Christian Brothers in the Monastery, sir.'

'Do you have a lot of pain down there?'

'Yes, I suppose I do.'

'How long ago did it happen?'

'When I was thirteen years old, over five years ago.'

'You're a brave young man to have endured it for this length of time. Listen, son, at this time, because of that injury, you're physically unfit for the army. More importantly, though, you're in need of an operation to fix that.

The beating displaced your testicle on the right side and it needs to be put back in place as soon as possible. So go and have your dinner in the mess and come back and see me at 2.30.'

I reappeared back at the appointed time.

'Right so, Michael, I've just spoken to Tommy O'Brien. He's going to meet you off the train at seven this evening. You'll be admitted as an emergency to St Catherine's Hospital and will be operated on tomorrow morning. We'll see what happens after that.'

I thanked him and told him that I didn't really want to join the army anyway. He just smiled.

Tommy met me at Tralee station and immediately drove me to St Catherine's where I was operated on the following morning. He called in to see me a few days later. His major concern was that I return to the army, but I told him that I had no intention of doing that.

'I give up on you, Michael; you have to go back to the army or else what?'

'That's okay, sir, I'll take the "or else". Thank you so much for all your help.'

Generous to the end, he let me recuperate for a month, paying me wages for the four weeks. After that I was on my own once more. I found lodgings a few doors up from the sweet shop where I used to collect the newspapers for the Brothers, which lasted as long as my money did. A couple of weeks later I was back on the streets again.

Brushes with the Law

BY NOW I was sleeping rough in the local park with neither money nor prospects. My hunger drove me to taking the next step. I began robbing shops about the town. It wasn't something I enjoyed, but I had to eat. It was relatively easy too. All I had to do was hang around busy shops and wait for the inevitable distracted customer to put her bag down for a minute. I tried to keep the robbing to a minimum: if I took a woman's bag on days that the Children's Allowance or the pension payments were made, then I'd be set up for the week.

There was great excitement when the RTÉ personality, Brendan O'Reilly, came to officially open a new Dunnes Store. In all the rushing about I managed to slip upstairs to the offices above the shop and take a bag full of coins. I couldn't believe how much was in the bag, about £50 in two and sixes. I hid it in the cistern of a toilet in the Wimpy bar across the street. As I needed money I visited the toilet – it was my own private bank.

It was about this time – July 1969 – that I came to the notice of the local Gardaí. They were already suspicious of me and I wondered why they wouldn't arrest me for loitering. It probably helped that I didn't drink or cause any trouble. However, I wanted to be arrested. I knew I couldn't continue sleeping rough for much longer. Eventually I was stopped on the street one evening and brought in for questioning. Relieved, I owned up to a number of robberies and made a statement before being placed in a cell. A few hours later I was visited by the Superintendent. He asked me if I was a Monoboy.

'Yes, sir, that's the problem. Nobody will give me a job because they know I am a Monoboy.'

'Okay, son, I'll tell you what I'll do. I'm going to get you a job and a place to stay.'

Here I was once again, receiving kindness from a stranger, and a policeman too. I must admit, however, that I was slightly wary of him. The police had never believed the stories they heard from the runaways in St Joseph's. Instead of helping the terrified boys they merely returned them to their abusers. Therefore I didn't have a very high opinion of them. However, this man seemed genuine in his wish to help me back onto the straight and narrow.

He was as good as his word. The following morning I started work in the nearby Denny's pork factory. Wearing a brand new white coat, one size too big for me, and armed with a pair of pliers I took my place on the assembly line. Before me on the treadmill were streams of dead pigs. My job was to pull their toe nails off. I lasted seven minutes, much to the amusement of my fellow workers, and was hurriedly reassigned to more mundane tasks, such as hosing down the blood. The smell was dreadful thanks to the poor pigs shitting themselves on their way to slaughter.

Once again the label 'Monoboy' proved my undoing. I was sitting in the staff canteen having a cup of tea, one afternoon, when one of the men came in shouting.

'Where's that fucking Monoboy?'

On spotting me he roared that £20 had been taken from his wallet.

'Where is it, Monoboy, where's my money?'

I stammered out my shocked denials but he refused to believe me.

'It has to be you. Money has never gone missing before. It's a bloody huge coincidence that it suddenly does now that you're here.'

He grabbed at me. There was only one way to prove my innocence.

'Go on then, search my pockets!'

He did and found nothing. Nevertheless he dragged me to the manager's office and told him that he suspected me of taking his money. The police were called and, as far as I know, the money was found. The manager advised me that it would probably be best, under the circumstances, if I left anyway. Knowing that I was so disliked by my colleagues, and probably going to be blamed for anything bad that might happen in the future, I was inclined to agree with him.

I was back to wandering the town, unsure of what to do next. During the Tralee Festival I went much too far when, out of desperation to eat, I raided a bedroom in the Mount Brandon Hotel. Prowling around the crowded reception, in search of unattended handbags, I noticed three American tourists – fancily dressed, with lots of jewellery, and slightly intoxicated – getting into the lift. I watched to see which floor the lift stopped; it went all the way to the top. That must be where they're staying. As soon as the lift came down I got in and pushed the button for the top floor.

When I stepped out of the lift I noticed an opened cupboard filled with linen. I took a sheet and put it over my head, as if I was pretending to be a ghost. Then I walked quickly down the landing wondering where the rich tourists were and decided to take pot luck. Grabbing a handle I pushed open a door. A woman was sitting up in bed, reading a book. She was much older than the other three and looked genuinely petrified. I made a gesture like I had a gun under the sheet and yelled at her.

'This is a stick-up, give me your money.'

'Okay, okay, take it. It's in my bag there. Take it all.'

I grabbed the bag, turned it upside down, took her purse and fled.

I almost got away with it. She never saw my face but I was recognised downstairs by the porter. I had worked in the hotel the previous year while in the employment of Tommy O'Brien. The police picked me up about fifteen minutes later, much to my relief. Frightening an elderly lady in her bed was no way to live.

Perhaps because of this dastardly act, which could have killed the poor woman, the judge threw the book at me.

'Young man, you have been given plenty of chances to make something of yourself but you have refused to avail of such help. Because of your ingratitude you now find yourself before the court on charges of robbery to which you have pleaded guilty. Have you anything to say for yourself before I pass sentence on you?'

I made use of this opportunity, and tried to explain why I was finding life so hard.

'Sir, when people hear I'm a Monoboy they immediately assume that they are better than me, and that I must be stupid, lazy and unable to read or write. What chance have boys like me got, coming out of a place like St Joseph's Industrial School, where we were beaten, starved and sexually abused by the Christian Brothers? The label Monoboy is the reason why I'm here today. I'm not a liar even though I admit to robbing.'

'I hear what you're saying, young man, and your story is a sad one, but I have a duty to protect innocent people and their property. I cannot permit you to go on roaming the streets terrifying the people of this town.'

I had no legal counsel to represent me so I made no response. He sentenced me to six months in St Patrick's Institution for young offenders in Dublin, but also asked for various reports before the execution of his order.

Over the next few days two doctors came to see me in the cell. A couple of weeks later the order was signed; I was taken by train to Dublin on Friday 14 November 1969, chained to a big, burly garda. Naturally people stared. An old woman came over to me with a cup of tea and biscuits and asked the garda to remove the cuffs. However, he became most indignant and threatened to arrest her for interfering with him in the course of his official business. She became indignant in turn.

'Oh, you're very brave when dealing with old ladies and young boys. Why don't you pick on someone your own size, you big bully?'

As she turned away in disgust she wished me well.

'I hope things work out for you, son. God bless.'

The train arrived in Dublin's Heuston Station on a thoroughly wet and windy evening. We were met by a squad car containing no less than three Gardaí. My God, I thought to myself, I must be a very dangerous criminal to require four guards for an escort. It was like an episode from my favourite TV programme, *The Fugitive*.

St Patrick's Institution, Dublin

ST PATRICK'S HELD no terrors for me. I was back in familiar territory, with no decisions to make for myself. There was a structure to my day once more. Others would decide what time I got up in the morning, what chores I would do during the day, what time I had my meals and, finally, what time I went to bed at night. What could be simpler? I had a cell all to myself, number 28, on 'C' wing. It was fairly big, with pipes on the wall above my bed that belched noisily day and night. Over the door were my details: name, date of sentence and date for release. It seemed that if I gave no trouble I would be released at the beginning of April 1970. Once locked in at night, my toilet was a bucket in the corner. I was assigned to the tailor shop with no specific idea what I was meant to be doing there.

Very soon it was obvious that some of the other prisoners fancied me. I would have to be careful. A couple of days later I left the tailor shop to use the bathroom, where a prisoner I didn't know made a grab for me.

'Come here you, I want to fuck you.'

I struggled and screamed as loud as I could. He

landed a few blows on my head and face before prison officers rushed in and separated us.

'Keep your fucking mouth shut, if you know what's good for you.'

Both of us were taken to see the Governor. My attacker didn't help his case by threatening me within earshot of the three prison officers who were guarding us. I was called in first. The Governor was a tall man whom I had never seen before. Beside him sat another prison officer. Neither of them was smiling.

'Perhaps, Michael, you would like to tell me what happened.'

'Sir, the other prisoner, whose name I don't know, grabbed me in the toilets of the workshop and said he wanted to fuck me. When I refused, he started to attack me, sir.'

'Are you sure you didn't encourage him in some way?'

'No, sir. I don't even know him.'

'Is that how you have the swelling over your right eye?'

'Yes, sir.'

'I haven't met you before, have I? Tell me a bit about yourself.'

'There's not much to say, sir. I'm here because I robbed shops in Tralee.'

'You mustn't have been very good at it. Have you any parents?'

'Yes, sir, I think so, but I don't know anything much about them.'

'Where were you raised then?'

'In an industrial school, St Joseph's in Tralee.'

'How long did you spend there?'

'I went there in 1959 and was released early January 1967. I've always been in care, sir. Before St Joseph's I was in St Philomena's in Stillorgan.'

'Can you read and write?'

'Yes, sir.'

'So how did you get on in school?'

'Not very well, sir.'

'What do you mean?'

'Well, the Christian Brothers didn't treat us very well.'

'How so?'

I looked from him to the prison officer. They both waited.

'Sir, a lot of bad stuff went on. The Brothers physically and sexually abused us.'

The two men exchanged a look. The Governor's features relaxed a little and he put down the papers in his hand.

'What would you like to be when you get out of here?'

'Sir, I would've liked to become a priest, but I can't because I'm a bastard.'

'Who said such an awful thing to you?'

'Father O'Neill, in the school, sir.'

'That wasn't a very nice thing to say, was it?'

'No, sir.'

By this stage I had lost it and was crying like a baby.

'Why are you crying?'

'Because things are so bad, sir.'

He came around from behind the table and placed his arm around my shoulder, telling the other officer to go and get us a pot of tea. His touch, made in kindness, unnerved me slightly as he reminded me a little of Brother X.

'Now, now, Michael. There's always light at the end of the tunnel. We'll work something out.'

He went to the door and told the prison officers outside to take my assailant back to his cell, and that he would deal with him later. I never saw that prisoner again.

When the first officer came back with the tea the three of us had a cup. We talked for almost an hour. The Governor was determined to help me. He was the first person in authority to even half-believe me about the abuse.

'Don't worry, Michael. You can stay in your cell. Your meals will be brought to you. And I don't think you need go back to the tailor shop.'

He asked the prison officer to see to it that I didn't have to leave my cell, as he reckoned I wouldn't last a week with the other prisoners. After that all the officers were very kind to me, which overwhelmed me to such an extent that I couldn't stop crying. How ironic that the third time in my life I experienced genuine kindness (after the kindnesses shown to me by Tommy O'Brien and the Superintendent in Tralee Garda Station) should be from the prison officers and the Governor of St Patrick's Institution. I would always be immensely grateful to them.

The Governor came to see me every other day and then gave me the best Christmas present when he informed me that I was being transferred to an open prison, Shanganagh Castle in Bray, on 5 January 1970.

'You'll be much happier and safer there.'

On Christmas Day he called to my cell with a few westerns and detective novels to help me while away the long hours of the holidays. Through these pages I honour the memory of that kind man. Thanks to him, I felt hopeful about my future, for the very first time since leaving St Joseph's.

Shanganagh Castle and Discharge, April 1970

SHANGANAGH CASTLE WAS a very well run and pleasant place. The staff didn't like to use the word 'prison'. We were allowed to wear jeans and sweatshirts and could go to bed whenever we wanted to. The place was clean, spacious and bright. That alone lifted my spirits. Primarily it was a place of reflection where offenders had time and space to contemplate what to do with their lives. The selection procedure was based on the likelihood of not becoming a repeat offender, and the place developed a very good reputation for complete rehabilitation of the vast majority of boys who passed through its doors.

I spent my days reading *The Irish Times* and any books I came across. There was no formal structure to the day. I was treated very kindly by the prison officers who dressed in suits but, as usual, I experienced great difficulty in adjusting to kindness without strings attached. The staff understood my predicament, however, being most considerate of the environment that I had come from. Each officer had four or five boys in their care. My supervisor was very encouraging, and was particularly patient when, in presenting me with a new shirt and matching tie, he found me reluctant to take it because I was scared that I'd have to do something in return. He wasn't in the least offended, but did emphasise that in order for me to heal completely, I would have to start trusting authority figures. He reassured me that I would learn to trust genuine people in time, but I wasn't so sure. How could I trust anyone properly after all I had been through? Despite this man's assurances his present remained in his office until the day I left Shanganagh. 'Trust' was as strange a word to me as 'love'.

A few days before my discharge, the Governor called me to his office.

'Well, Michael, it's time for you to leave. Don't worry though; we've arranged a job for you as well as a place to stay. We've every confidence that you have benefited from your time with us and are unlikely to return to the prison system. So, you'll start working for Lep Travel and you are going to live with a Mrs Sheridan and her family on the North Strand. Your supervisor will take you there and see that you settle in. If there are any problems, please don't hesitate to contact us.'

On the way into the city my supervisor gave me a bit of a pep talk.

'I've watched you very closely for the past few months and I firmly believe that, with the proper direction and a bit of luck, you'll make a success of your life. There is not an ounce of badness in you, Michael. You're quite clever.

If you get the chance you should try and do some sort of study, make something of yourself. Who knows, you might even get to university some day.'

New Beginnings

WE ARRIVED AT the swanky offices of Lep Travel in College Green, where the manager was waiting to meet me. He was a very holy man who was keen on the Legion of Mary and had worked closely with ex-prisoners. The only real question he asked me was whether I could ride a bicycle or not. I lied immediately, saying that I had no problem in this regard. *After all*, I thought, *even children ride bicycles.* We shook hands and he introduced me to the staff, telling them I would be starting work there the following day.

Next it was off to see Mrs Sheridan, my new landlady. What a delightful person she turned out to be. She was to have a major influence on the course of my life. Any success I have had stemmed from the kindness she lavished on me. There were no sides to this wonderful woman. What you saw was what she was. A kind, gentle, caring, sensitive soul, she always saw the good in everyone, never allowing their mistakes to blind her to their possibilities. In that house I got my first real insight into how a typical family operated; Mrs Sheridan was the boss. Her husband was a very quiet, kindly man with a great interest in horses. There were four children, one girl and three boys. I took to Jim, the eldest, quite quickly. We were roughly the same age and shared similar interests. My, how that boy was loved and spoiled by his mother. I was fascinated by how well they interacted with each other. They both seemed to know what the other was thinking. In her eyes Jim could do no wrong. I even imagined he may have got a little extra portion of whatever was going. That's not to say that she in any way neglected the others, of course. Mrs Sheridan was a very good reader of people and if she liked you especially she would fuss over you.

She was the first 'mother type' person I had ever encountered and, consequently, I began to feel more deeply the loss of my own mother. In bed at night I would dream of finding her, or of speaking to her. Drowsily I would examine possible reasons for why she might have abandoned me. I knew there was a connection between her not being married and Father O'Neill's definition of me as being a bastard. For some reason I never felt the slightest inclination to find my father, imagining him as an extension of the Christian Brothers. It was easier to bond to the fanciful notion that some outside agency had intervened to snatch me from my mother despite her heroic efforts to hold onto me. I didn't want to think that anything sordid could be the reason why we were parted.

Meantime, I settled down well in both Lep Travel and

Mrs Sheridan's but, cynic that I was, I knew such contentment would never last. One evening as I was leaving work I took my wages out of my pocket to set aside Mrs Sheridan's rent. A sudden gust of wind took the money clear over Trinity College to God knows where. I certainly wasn't going to follow it into the college, especially as I had heard that one of the professors had hung himself in there. How was I going to face Mrs Sheridan? I needn't have worried. When, with some trepidation, I ventured to tell her, her reaction was completely unexpected. She laughed her head off until tears flowed from her eyes. I fully expected to be thrown out of the house and who would have blamed her?

'Oh, that's the best laugh I've had in a long time. Don't you worry yourself. Sit down and have your dinner. Just don't say anything about it to the rest of the family.'

A few nights later she came into the lounge, where I was watching television as usual.

'Michael, is this all you want to do with your life, sit in front of the TV, watching rubbish? I'll tell you what you'll do. Come with me now to Marino Technical College, I have a plan.'

I was most anxious to please her and went willingly. Before I knew what was happening she had me enrolled in night classes, which she hoped would improve my prospects in life. She paid the monies due, overwhelming me again with her generosity.

'Don't start crying now, Michael, make a success of it and I'll consider it money well spent.'

I never looked back. Everything I achieved academically was started by this wonderful woman who saw my potential and gave me a helping hand along the way. One never knows how simple acts of kindness can influence the course of a life.

Unfortunately I wasn't experiencing such kindness at work. For one thing my manager was too 'religious', in the Church sense. I found him impersonal and cold to deal with. Perhaps it was because he was less effective in imposing his will on me or bending me to his way of thinking. We were both very guarded in our interactions with each other while the rest of the staff were also wary of me, knowing that I was an ex-prisoner. Consequently, I was given the heave-ho at the first opportunity.

I had never learnt to ride a bicycle; therefore, I performed my errands running alongside the bike. This was fine until I was sent to the docks and arrived too late for the order to be placed.

'The bicycle, Michael, did you not tell me that you could ride a bicycle? I cannot abide a liar above all. It says so much about a person. I think it would be best if you found yourself another job in the next two weeks.'

That was the end of me and Lep Travel. Mrs Sheridan came to the rescue, telling me about a vacancy for a messenger boy at Dublin Fabrics in Dame Street. Halfway through the interview the job was mine. I was

much relieved that riding a bicycle was not a requirement of employment plus the wages were higher than in
Lep Travel. Could I start immediately? Lep Travel was
happy to facilitate my early departure, paying me full
wages even though I didn't work out my notice. I took
the opportunity of repaying the lost rent back to Mrs
Sheridan despite her reluctance to take it.

Dublin Fabrics was a small, tightly run establishment
with a staff of four, including myself. The manager was a
kindly man in his early fifties, while his secretary, of
similar age, wore lots of flowery perfume and fancy
jewellery. The deputy manager, however, was a horse of
a different colour. He sweated profusely and was always
finding fault with my work. I had to be very careful
around him as I didn't want to lose this job. I think he
thought I had airs above my messenger boy status. A
particular irritant for him was the fact that I read a
different newspaper, usually *The Irish Times*, while he
enjoyed the tabloids, the 'working man's papers', as he
liked to call them. Over time he became extremely
inquisitive about my origins, asking me lots of questions
of a personal nature. He was particularly persistent on
the subject of my mother. When I confronted him about
his questions he became uncomfortable and backed off,
but there was something about him that made me
suspect he knew something more.

'How would I know anything about your mother?
Sure, I've only just met you.'

A couple of weeks later he called me into his office.

'The boss is going on holidays next week so I need you to man the front counter and deal with any customers that might come in.'

'But I'm only the messenger boy.'

'Do you want to be a messenger boy for the rest of your life?'

'No, I suppose not.'

'Dress smartly tomorrow and we'll see how you get on.'

I showed up for work the next day dressed to the nines. The deputy seemed very nervous and uptight, pacing up and down the floor and fiddling with the cloth, pen in mouth. Then the door opened and in walked two women.

'See to them, Michael. I'll be in the back keeping an eye.'

Anxious not to make any mistakes, I turned to face the customers. The taller of the two women seemed to be crying, wiping away her tears with a soft yellow handkerchief. The smaller one had a cold determination about her and her fingers were brown from continuous smoking. I didn't think I'd like her one bit. The way they were tensely handling the drab material made me think that a relative had died and that they were buying a burial suit for him. After about ten minutes they turned to leave the shop.

Suddenly, the taller lady grasped my hand very tightly for a moment, sobbing uncontrollably. Her companion told her sharply to pull herself together as they went through the door. *She must have loved her husband very much to be crying like that in front of a complete stranger*, I thought. The deputy manager rushed towards me.

'Well, Michael, did they buy anything?'

'No, they didn't. What a strange pair they were, the tall one couldn't stop crying.'

'Will you mind the shop? I'll go after them to see if everything is okay.'

'Don't blame me; I did nothing to upset them. She came into the shop crying. It's not my fault.'

He was gone for about half an hour. When he came back he said nothing to me. Instead, he disappeared into the office.

Shortly after this incident I decided to finally start the search for my mother. The church where I had been baptised, St Nicholas of Myra Church, in Francis Street, was the obvious starting place. After asking the manager for directions I made my way to Francis Street during my lunch hour and rang the doorbell of the parochial house. It was answered by a priest in his early fifties.

'Father, I think I was baptised here in November 1950 and I was wondering …'

'Come in, come in and let's see.'

He brought me into a sitting room.

'Sit down, son.'

He went to another room and returned with a big, long green book.

'Okay now. What's your full name?'

'Michael Clemenger, Father.'

'That's an unusual name. I don't think I've ever heard it before.'

Stopping on a particular page he began to scroll down using his index finger; just then the phone rang.

'Excuse me for a second, I'll just go and answer that.'

Instinctively I turned the book around as soon as he left and there in front of me was all the information I needed.

Mary Clemenger: Unmarried

Address: —, Crumlin, Dublin 8

Father: Unknown

Son born: 1 November 1950, Michael Francis
     Clemenger

Baptised: 6 November 1950

My God, what a shock to see it all written down in black and white. I was somebody's son after all, not a nobody 'unfit to breathe the air of decent people', as Brother Lane had been fond of saying. So my mother really hadn't been married to my father. Father O'Neill's description of me as a 'bastard' now made sense. Was that the reason I was sent away? I had brought shame on the family, but what family? My confused thoughts were interrupted by the priest.

'Sorry about that, I was waiting on that call. Oh yes,

you were enquiring whether you had been baptised in this church.'

'Yes, Father.'

'What year did you say?'

'November 1950, Father.'

'Yes, I can see that you were baptised here on 6 November 1950, but that's all the information I'm prepared to give you.'

'Why, Father?'

'Well, it's a bit complicated.'

He was clearly embarrassed by what he was reading.

'Could I not get a copy from you, Father, or something?'

'No, that's not possible, I'm afraid. Right, I have to go and visit someone, so we'll have to end this conversation now.'

He wished me luck as he closed the door behind me.

Jim Sheridan

I HADN'T HAD a best friend since Jimmy, at St Philomena's, but once I moved in with the Sheridans, I quickly became very close to Jim Sheridan. As I said we were around the same age and got excited over the same things. Furthermore he treated me like a mate. He involved me in discussions around the dinner table. We both shared a love for debate and opinions. He ran a little drama workshop in the evenings. While he was clearly the leader he gave the others the energy to move forward. His attitude was simple – anything can be done if you have a mind to do it. It was through this group that I began to explore the possibility of one day going to university. Jim thought it was a brilliant idea. One Saturday morning he brought me to a student meeting place that was behind the Department of Foreign Affairs on Stephen's Green. Once inside the building I got such a buzz that I knew then that I wanted to pursue the life of an academic. Banging the table with his usual intensity Jim would bark out defiantly that I could be anything that I wanted to be. I hadn't the heart to tell him otherwise, especially about my now-long-gone desire to be a priest.

One evening he confronted me with something that had been on his mind.

'Michael, you should get yourself a girlfriend.'

He caught me by surprise. To that point, I was fairly unsure of my sexuality and fretted that I might be homosexual, thanks to my experiences with the Christian Brothers. There was some reassurance on that point, however, when I watched Dana singing 'All Kinds of Everything' on the TV. I was aware of a stirring down below, along with bad thoughts that would excite me whenever I saw pictures of her.

Jim invited me to Galway where he was taking a play to Eyre Square. I ended up in bed with one of the actresses, and to this day I'm convinced that Jim had something to do with this. She was a lovely girl, in looks and personality, with thick locks of long, red hair. Naturally I was very nervous but she soon put me at ease. I don't think that she appreciated that I was a virgin. Eventually after much fumbling in the dark, the bits fitted together in the right order and, upon gyrating for a short but intense period, the act was finally performed. The noise the poor girl made I feared would bring the whole troupe to our door.

Long after she was asleep I lay there in bewilderment. Is that all there is to this mystery of lovemaking? I reached the conclusion that it was highly overrated.

Going up and down with one's bare bottom saying hello to the moon was not very romantic. The next morning at breakfast Jim beamed at me, almost as if proud of both me and himself. Mission accomplished.

PART THREE

Family?

Meeting the Clemenger Family

ABOUT THREE MONTHS later, as I was coming out of Clery's Department Store on O'Connell Street, I decided out of the blue to get a bus to Crumlin. A bus conductor told me which bus would leave me just outside the house. Without thinking about what I was doing I jumped on the first one I saw. My mouth was dry and my heart was racing as I looked out the window. Would my mother want to know me? Would she be very old? It never once entered my head before now that she might be married with other children. If so, did she tell her husband about me? My head was filled with questions.

My legs shook a little as I got off at the bus stop. There, in front of me, was my mother's house. I felt dizzy. There was no sign of any movement, though the curtains were drawn back and a small window was open in the front room. I must have walked up and down the path in front for about ten minutes or more, in utter dismay. My nerve failed me and I found that I simply couldn't knock on the door. The house looked very clean from the outside and a little green mini car stood in the driveway. Suddenly the front door opened and a middle-aged man stepped out.

'Are you lost? You seem to be looking for someone. Can I help you?'

In for a penny, in for a pound. It was now or never.

'My name is Michael Clemenger. I'm looking for Mary Clemenger; I think she's my mother. Does she live here?'

The poor man stared at me. For a second I thought I had killed him, the colour drained so fast from his face. I grabbed him, thinking he was going to collapse.

'Are you okay, sir? I'm sorry; I didn't mean to frighten you.'

Quickly regaining his composure he seized control of the situation.

'I'm okay. You just gave me a bit of a shock, that's all. Come into the house for a minute.'

I followed him inside. The front room was clean with a few photographs hanging on the wall. A young girl of about eighteen looked up as I came in the door.

'Oh no! Not you!'

She knew immediately who I was. How, I don't know. It was utterly bewildering.

'I don't mean any harm; I'm just looking for Mary Clemenger, who I think is my mother.'

The pair of them looked at one another.

'Just give me a pen and paper please and I'll write down my address. Perhaps she could get in contact with me.'

They remained motionless as if struck by lightning. Just then I heard the door open behind me and in walked another young girl. I dreaded more shocked reactions, but I needn't have worried. She also seemed to know who I was and addressed me calmly.

'I'm Catherine. Would you like a cup of tea?'

'No, thanks. I think I've caused enough trouble already.'

The first girl came back into the sitting room with paper and pen. I sat on a chair and wrote out my name and the address of Mrs Sheridan's house and handed it to Catherine. She asked me again if I wanted a cup of tea, but I told her that I thought I should get going. She led me to the door.

'How did you get here?'

'On the bus.'

'Well, you can get the bus back into town a few doors down.'

I thanked her and she closed the door behind me. I was glad to escape to the bus stop and be alone with my thoughts. I was struck by the fact that Catherine had shown no surprise at my visit, and wondered would I ever hear from them again.

That evening I was having a bath when there was a loud bang on the door.

'Michael, are you in there?'

'Yes, Mrs Sheridan.'

'You better get dressed quickly; I want a word with you.'

When Mrs Sheridan wanted a word with you she

means to lay down the law. *Bloody hell, what had I done?* I hated to upset her because she was so good to me. I was in the bedroom dressing when she rushed in, all excited.

'Michael, come here to me now, did you not tell me that you were an orphan and that you were reared in an industrial school?'

'Yes.'

'Well then, you better prepare yourself for a big surprise. Tidy yourself up and comb your hair, you've visitors in the parlour.'

I never had a visitor in my entire life. Suddenly though, I knew who it was, or might be. In a panic I blurted out to Mrs Sheridan where I had been that morning, adding that I was sorry. In fact I felt like climbing into bed and pulling the blankets over my head.

'Well son, it's too bloody late to change that, you'll have to face them now.'

I walked down the stairs, my legs shaking and my heart beating very fast. Mrs Sheridan opened the parlour door and I saw three women sitting on the settee. I recognised the young girl immediately, but couldn't place the other two in my nervousness. They all stood up to greet me. The smaller woman spoke first.

'Hello, Michael, I'm your Aunt Josie. This is your Godmother, Kate, and Miriam, your younger sister, who you've already met. The man you met was my brother, your Uncle Paddy.'

For a second I thought maybe she had said that Kate was my mother. I wasn't sure what a 'Godmother' was, though my heart certainly leapt at the second part of the word. I stared at her incredulously.

'Are you my mother?'

'Oh no, love. I only stood for you at your baptism. That's what a Godmother does.'

I was speechless. Everybody in the room was crying including Mrs Sheridan. Miriam sat beside me and gave me a box of chocolates. I still couldn't speak and just sat there dumbfounded. Five minutes ago I was an orphan and now I had an aunt, an uncle, a Godmother and a baby sister. Mrs Sheridan was clearly glad for me and expressed great admiration for what I had endured in my life. Because, I suppose, nobody else was able to make conversation she began to tell the women how great she thought I was, especially after all the hardship I had endured at St Joseph's. Noticing that Miriam, *my sister*, was getting very upset about what she was hearing I quickly changed the subject. Mrs Sheridan understood immediately, and stopped talking.

'Did we not meet some time ago?' I asked Josie.

Josie denied it, but I was most insistent.

'Yes, we did. I met you when you came to buy cloth in Dublin Fabrics.'

My Godmother spoke up.

'Yes, Michael, we did come to visit you. You see, your

supervisor is married to a relative of yours and we knew all about you within a short time.'

I couldn't believe it, that man knew everything and kept it from me. Wait until I see him Monday. The women stayed about an hour. Aunt Josie did most of the talking. My two sisters lived with her and Uncle Paddy in Crumlin while there were various other relatives in the area. It seemed my mother lived elsewhere, which I thought was a bit strange. Nobody mentioned my meeting her and I felt I shouldn't try to push it just yet. For the moment I had plenty of others to be introduced to.

Josie made arrangements for her other brother, my Uncle Michael, to collect me at midday the following day for Sunday lunch. With that they said their good-byes. Aunt Kate took a tight hold of me.

'There, Michael, that's the hug I wanted to give you in Dublin Fabrics that day. You seemed settled and I thought it was better to let things lie as they were.'

'Do you mean, Aunt Kate, not to look for my mother?'

'Yes, I suppose so.'

'But why?'

'Sometimes these things don't always work out because of the passage of time.'

Aunt Josie remained silent throughout and betrayed no emotions, unlike my Godmother.

'Just look at you now. I last held you in my arms when you were five days old.'

'But Aunt Kate, I would like to find my mother some day. Surely you wouldn't deny me that, would you?'

'No, Michael, of course not, but everything in its own good time. Anyway we'll talk about it again. Sure we'll see you tomorrow.'

Miriam said goodbye. I could see that she was very confused about the whole situation and was bent on seeking answers when she got home. Mrs Sheridan let out a huge sigh after they left.

'Oh, Michael, I don't ever want to go through that again. I just don't know what to say. Come on, let's have a good fry-up, just the two of us. Then you go straight up to bed after tea. I'm sure you have a lot of thinking to do about tomorrow. Try to get some sleep.'

Sleep was impossible. It was extremely difficult to get my head around the fact that I had a large extended family. All along I had only thought about a mother, but now I had aunts, uncles and two sisters. It was shocking in a way. Did this mean I wasn't a bastard anymore? I wondered what Uncle Michael looked like, and how soon it would be before I could meet my mother.

After a restless night I got up early the next morning. Mrs Sheridan did her best to calm me down. After breakfast I walked into town for my newspaper, like I always did on a Sunday morning. The rest of the morning dragged. At 11.30 Mrs Sheridan told me to go and tidy myself up. The house was quiet, since everyone else was still in bed. Then, at ten minutes before midday, the door bell went. Mrs Sheridan answered it and I heard a man's voice saying that he had come to collect his nephew, Michael. She invited him in, but he declined, saying we had to be in Crumlin for dinner at 1 o'clock.

'Come along, Michael, and meet your uncle.'

I could see that he was flustered by the whole situation, but was trying to give the impression of being in control. Nevertheless he looked as nervous as I was. I glanced at Mrs Sheridan who nudged me out the door.

'Go on then, Michael. I'll see you later. All the best, love.'

My uncle and I walked in silence to the car. As soon as we got in he put on the radio, the silence having grown uncomfortable. After a while he eventually managed to say something.

'You know, Michael, don't you, that you can't marry your sisters.'

'Fecking hell, I only just met them. I have no intention of falling in love with them that way,' I replied angrily.

'How were you treated there by the Brothers?' he asked me.

'Apart from being half starved, physically and sexually abused, what do you think?' I answered.

'What sexual abuse?' he asked.

Halfway through the details he cried out,

'Enough, Michael, enough. I don't want to hear any more!'

I felt that he was physically disgusted by the details, but disinclined to believe me.

When I arrived in Crumlin I expected to see my mother. There were a lot of family members there, Aunt Josie, Uncle Paddy, my two sisters, my oldest sister's boyfriend, Uncle Michael's wife, Aunt Kate and her husband, but not my mother. I also spoke to my Uncle Tim on the phone for the very first time; he lived in Wembley in England. I wondered why my sisters didn't live with our mother.

Later that afternoon, sitting in Aunt Josie's house, I was confused by the variety of emotions I was experiencing, ranging from anger to despair. Foremost in my mind was the belief that I should have been allowed to grow up here with the comfort of a normal family environment. My dream of priesthood would surely have been realised then. In fact my future would have been wide open. I might have changed my mind about becoming a priest and replaced it with wanting to be a teacher, doctor or solicitor – or God only knows what. The tears welled up at the thought of all those lost possibilities. Looking at the framed photographs on the walls I felt an actual ache that there was none of me as a chubby toddler or precocious four-year-old. It struck me that my entire life had gone undocumented. That's what not having any family meant, no one else is interested enough to take photographs. Again, when out in the small backyard, I couldn't help thinking that should have been my first playground, free from bullies and ever watchful Brothers.

And then there were my sisters. It had never once entered my head that I might have had siblings. I felt so envious of them. They seemed to have been well looked after, secure in love and constant affection which, I fervently believed, cannot but result in the sort of confidence that I profoundly lacked. Thanks to the likes of Aunt Josie and Uncle Paddy they knew who they were and where they had come from. Not knowing who you really are is a strange thing and a difficult situation to live with. The questions regarding the missing chapters of a childhood just get louder and louder week by week, month by month.

Later that night, back in Mrs Sheridan's, overcome with the emptiness of my life when compared to my sisters growing up within the bosom of a family, my family, I cried myself to sleep. I couldn't help it, I felt very bitter.

My sisters were very different in both looks and personality. Catherine was two years older than me, having been born in 1948. She was primarily raised by Aunt Josie who had never married. They had a very strong bond. When speaking to Catherine, Josie always dropped that 'mask of invincibility' that she wore with everyone else. Catherine seemed to be the child she wanted, but never had. Their relationship, as far as I could see, was very different from the relationship that

Mrs Sheridan had with her son Jim. In their frequent battles of wills Catherine usually won through, though Aunt Josie always liked to string Catherine along before finally saying 'yes'.

I don't think that Catherine and I would have got on well together. Our personalities were completely different; she liked to get her own way too often and would have never settled for second place, not even in the playground. I would have been more than a match for her. Perhaps Catherine knew that too. We would have killed each other. Just like her aunt she quickly formed the opinion that I was too much like our mother for her liking.

My little sister Miriam was born in 1952. She was more like me in temperament and we looked very similar; Mammy always said that we shared the same father. Much quieter than Catherine, she preferred to stay in the background and was never less than deferential to Aunt Josie; generally Josie spoke while Miriam listened. She was gentle and kind to everyone, and could light up a room with her smile. As I got to know her I regretted that I wasn't there for her in the playground. We would have easily handled Aunt Josie and Catherine together. Of that I am sure. I fancied that she wasn't privy to the same level of affection and love that her big sister enjoyed. Catherine seemed to suck all the attention of Aunt Josie so that there was little left for Miriam – or perhaps I was just attempting to create more similarities between us, to make up for all those years when neither of us knew the other existed.

Over the next few months I spent my Sunday afternoons in the family house in Crumlin. These afternoons were infinitely more relaxing when it was just me, Miriam and Uncle Paddy. The three of us would settle down together, with mugs of tea and plates of biscuits, in front of the television to watch an old black and white film. The only light was the flickering screen as we let ourselves get hopelessly lost in the story. We shared a love for sentimentality and cried easily at sad or romantic films.

One evening Catherine came in unexpectedly and turned on the overhead light. She didn't try to hide her disgust.

'Fecking eejits, crying in front of the TV like babies and in front of *him* too.'

This made Paddy angry and he exploded.

'"Him?" That's your brother you're talking about. Call Michael by his name.'

Miriam ran out of the room crying. There was not much said at the supper table that evening. When Josie heard about the incident she wasn't pleased, but she said nothing.

I was finding being part of a family more complicated than I'd thought it would be.

*

One Sunday Paddy invited me into his bedroom, which surprised Miriam.

'Bloody hell, he never likes anybody to go in there.'

He took out an old shoe box from under the bed.

'You've no photographs of your sisters, Michael, would you like a couple?'

'Oh yes, please. And can I have one of you too?

He seemed surprised and pleased.

'Sit down there on the bed for a minute. I want to tell you a bit about our family – yours and mine.'

What a lovely feeling of inclusiveness. It was very deliberate on his part. I thought to myself that it was a pity he wasn't my father. A deep bond was developing between us and I think both of us knew it.

'Right so, my father, that is, your grandfather, was married twice and had eight children in all. Your Aunt Frances, the eldest of his children, was born in 1916. However, her mother, your grandmother, died while giving birth to her. A sad, but common occurrence in those days. So your grandfather married again and had seven more children. That's your uncles – me, Michael, John and Tim who lives in England; your mother, Mary, and your aunties Josie and Kate.'

I couldn't remember all the names. It seemed like such a crowd after being an orphan for the last twenty years. The whole thing threatened to overwhelm me. If I had so many aunts and uncles and sisters why was no attempt ever made to find me? After all it couldn't have been that hard. At least they could have tried.

'What happened to my grandparents?'

'Well, your grandfather fought in North Africa, during the Second World War, and died of his injuries in January 1946. He's buried across the water in England.'

This surprised me.

'Why wasn't he buried here in Ireland?'

'The cost, Michael. We couldn't afford to bring him home. Remember these were the war years. Nobody had any money.'

His voice shook a little and he looked out the window for a few seconds before gathering himself together again.

'On the other hand, your grandmother lived to a ripe old age and only died a few years ago.'

'Can you tell me about my mother?'

He now became alert and more careful in his response.

'Well, Michael, I have to say your mother is not an easy woman to get on with. She's highly strung and suffers with her nerves. It goes back to the time that she fell off the back of a lorry and hit her head on the road. She was never right after that.'

He showed me a black and white photograph of her. There was a marked resemblance between us. I greedily took in every detail. She was sitting alone in a garden and looked quite small, with short hair. Instead of smiling for the photographer she looked morose and sad.

'Now, unfortunately I can't let you keep this picture, in case Josie sees you with it. Anyway you'll be seeing

Mary soon enough. There's no love lost between your mother and Aunt Josie, I can tell you that much.'

'What about my father?'

'Ach, Michael, Michael, you ask far too many questions. Take your time. Don't be in so much of a rush. All I can tell you for now is that he was a nice enough fella.'

'Okay. Do I look like him?'

'No, you definitely don't. Can you not tell from that photograph that you're the spit of your mother?'

'I guess so. Would you have any photos of him?'

'No, there are none at all. To be honest, we haven't seen him in years. He could be dead now, for all we know. But don't worry; you'll get to see your mother real soon. All in good time. After all I'm still getting over the shock you gave me when I first went out that morning to ask you if you were lost. Remember?'

'Did you know who I was?'

'There you go again; questions, questions, questions.'

The Big Debate

ABOUT SIX MONTHS later, thanks to my persistence, Aunt Josie and Uncle Michael called a family gathering, about my wanting to see my mother, which allowed me to meet my mother's brother John and his wife Sarah for the first time. Uncle John greeted me with a big bear-hug.

'How are you son? Keeping the best? Bloody hell, you look like your mother.'

Once the discussion got under way it appeared that both Aunt Josie and Uncle Michael were dead against the idea. This seemed to infuriate Uncles Paddy and John. Paddy spoke up immediately.

'Why do you pair always try to make things complicated?'

Uncle Michael started saying things aren't that simple and what do we know about the boy when John interrupted him.

'Bloody hell! Why can't you call the boy by his name? Is it because it's the same as your own?'

Josie stepped in to try and control the situation.

'Please, there's no need to adopt that tone of voice. It's not helpful to anyone.'

Uncle John, however, was having none of it.

'Michael just wants to meet his mother. What's wrong with that?'

'Well, for a start Michael has recently been in prison.'

My face dropped, especially with my sisters sitting there. There was a pause as everyone looked at me, in spite of themselves. I felt so embarrassed and studied the faded carpet until Uncle John suggested that we all took a break. He asked me to come out to the backyard for a cigarette. I followed him, grateful to get out of the crowded room.

'Okay, Michael, I want you to tell me as best you can where you have been all these years.'

I quickly told him about the physical abuse in St Joseph's, and about the hard time I had trying to keep a job since leaving the school. I also explained how I ended up in prison. Within a few minutes he had a much clearer picture of my situation.

'Well now, you haven't had it easy, have you?'

'No, no. I suppose not.'

I felt my eyes welling up with tears.

He pulled hard on the remains of his Woodbine.

'Your sisters have been very lucky then. Right, let's go back in and face them.'

Back in the house, I think Uncle Michael and Aunt Josie expected John to have changed his mind about me, but they were mistaken.

'Okay, I've heard what Michael has to say. His sisters

were very, very lucky that they didn't have to go through what he did. And now I'm more convinced that he should see his mother. Anyway, if she finds out that her son is back and you didn't tell her, then God help us all. She'll be back here throwing bricks through the windows and frightening the neighbours. Do you really want everyone to see her getting arrested again?'

Christ! What? Mammy arrested? What was this all about? I wondered.

I turned to Josie.

'She's in jail?'

Instead of answering my question she turned on John and roared at him.

'See what you've done now, you've only gone and upset the child.'

With that my uncle lost his head.

'Child? What child? Would you look at him for Christ's sake! He's twenty years of age. He's no longer a bloody child.'

I sensed that a bigger row was about to erupt that had nothing to do with me. I was quickly learning that families can contain a lot of anger, so I decided to make a stand and remind them why we were all here.

'Aunt Josie, I really want to meet my mother. Please.'

After that the battle was lost, though Uncle Michael still attempted to counsel caution. His irate brother bellowed at him.

'You can shut your mouth and all.'

Uncle Michael quickly sat back in his chair. I stared in wonder at John. What a champion to have in my corner. I took the opportunity to hit back at Uncle Michael saying innocently that he hadn't been very nice to me when we first met. John nodded violently at him. Of course, I was repeating a pattern of behaviour I'd learned as a child; this was how I'd learned to protect myself in St Joseph's. I had learned that it was important to have someone on my side, fighting for my cause. One way of forging a bond with this 'someone' was to report to them how I had been mistreated by someone else. Thus I burst into tears in front of Brother Price in full view of Brother Lane as he was leaving the yard, all those years ago.

'Now, why is that not a surprise?' said John.

Emboldened by his support I continued.

'He told me I couldn't marry my sisters. He seems to think that I am a bloody fool or something.'

This sparked Paddy who hadn't said anything in a while.

'Always trying to lay down the law. Bloody idiot!'

Nobody knew what to do next, such was the level of hostility in the room. My sister Catherine seemed upset that Uncle John was picking on Aunt Josie while Miriam was upset that Uncle Paddy was getting upset. I must admit to finding it all fascinating.

So this is family life, I thought. *Is this what was going on inside everyone's house?*

All those walks down the streets of Tralee, when I used to wish I belonged to one of those houses, was this sort of warfare going on behind all those rows of curtained windows? It seemed to me that there wasn't much difference between my relatives' warring factions and the constant edginess and suspicion that existed between Brothers Roberts and Price. And it was impossible for me not to take sides. Of course I sided naturally with Uncles John and Paddy against Aunt Josie and Uncle Michael. Meanwhile my sister Miriam and Aunt Sarah busied themselves making tea and sandwiches for the opposing teams.

After two more hours of conflict, with neither side prepared to compromise, I suggested a possible solution.

'Why not give me her address and I'll just go knock on her door myself?'

Both sides finally agreed on something – that this wasn't a good idea at all.

Uncle Paddy was concerned about my mother, how she might react to me and the possible effect it could have on her nerves. When I asked about the exact state of her nerves everyone remained vague. My sisters expressed concern about how I would cope if things got out of hand with Mammy. Later on, in the kitchen, my Aunt Sarah, whom I had taken to immediately, put her arms around me and urged caution in a knowing way.

Were the circumstances of why I had been put away related to Mammy's suffering with the nerves? All along

I had nurtured the romantic notion that I had been taken away from her against her will. Was I in some way responsible for her suffering? Could that have been the reason I was sent away and not my sisters? Nobody wanted to tell me anything more about Mammy's personality. The only information I had was the brick-throwing and her subsequent arrest. Could her behaviour be connected to me?

Eventually it was suggested that both Uncles Michael and John would introduce me to my mother. John baulked immediately.

'Ah, no way! I'm not going anywhere with that shite!'

So then it was just me and Uncle Michael. We would go visit my mother this coming week. John caught me by the arm and made me promise that I would tell him if Uncle Michael upset me in any way ever again. With that the meeting, or battle, was over. This was it, after twenty years of missing her, I was about to meet my mother for the very first time.

Mammy

UNCLE MICHAEL ARRANGED to meet me outside Kevin Street Garda station on Friday evening. The whole week went by in a blur. As I walked to the station I was giddy with excitement. My uncle was there, waiting for me, stiff as a board.

'Do you see that building across the road? That's where your mother lives.'

Just looking at the building gave me the creeps. It lacked any kind of colour and looked for all the world like an old workhouse. When we stepped inside, the ugly, drab interior reminded me of St Joseph's. I asked Michael why she lived here and not in Crumlin, but he just stared ahead and kept walking. We passed by a number of blocks before stopping at a block at the end of a row.

'This is where she lives.'

What a kip! There was a strong smell of urine in the hallway while the stairs were dimly lit. Halfway up the steps Michael stopped suddenly.

'Are you sure you want to do this? Once I knock on that door there's no turning back. You understand?'

'Yes, yes I want to see her, no matter what.'

He sighed heavily and continued up the steps.

'Well, then, it's your funeral.'

I was mystified by this. Could he not be just a little bit happy for me? What was wrong with him?

He plodded up the rest of the stairs like a man on the way to his own execution. I skipped hurriedly along trying to reach the top of the stairs before him, such was my excitement.

'What do you mean by "funeral"?'

'Son, I did say it would be complicated.'

When we got to her door I made to knock on it.

'Don't go near the door, Michael, I'll do it.'

Once again he asked me was I completely sure about this, only now he was whispering. In fact he seemed a little frightened. This was getting ridiculous.

'For God's sake, Uncle Michael.'

'Yes, okay, okay. Just keep your voice down.'

He actually took a deep breath before knocking on the door. There was no answer. I feared that she wasn't in. He tried again, a little louder this time. A voice – my mother's voice – called out, asking who was there.

'Mary, it's your brother Michael.'

'What do you want?'

'I just want to talk to you for a minute, please.'

There was a second of silence before she replied, 'okay'. When the door was finally opened to us we were enveloped in a cloud of smoke that appeared to be fleeing from the room. My uncle whispered at me out the side of his mouth.

'I hate bloody cigarette smoke.'

When the fog lifted I was almost sorry. I guess I must have been expecting someone else, perhaps someone like the tall woman with the bun in her hair who used to visit Jimmy. She was nothing like the old photo that Uncle Paddy had shown me. Instead, before me was a small, thin, emaciated woman with no hair and not one tooth in her head. All her fingers were copper brown from smoking too many cigarettes and she was badly in need of a bath. Was this really my mother? And what on earth had happened to her that could have reduced her to these pitiful circumstances? I felt so utterly, utterly sad for her.

Uncle Michael and Mammy glanced awkwardly at each other. It was probably obvious to her that he wanted at that moment to be anywhere else except standing here at her door. Nervously he cleared his throat.

'Mary, do you know this boy?'

She stared at me with her full attention for a minute. When I met her gaze she suddenly turned away and shouted at her brother.

'No! I never saw him before in my life.'

'Are you sure?'

I felt like a parcel somebody had lost and might not want to reclaim.

'Look at him again, Mary. Take a closer look.'

Please, Mammy, I prayed silently, *recognise me and claim me*.

This time she took her time, even walking around me so that she could see me in profile. She began to nod her head.

'Yes, I could have seen him before, somewhere.'

'Where do you think you saw him, Mary?'

'I don't know, maybe I saw him on the street.'

I wanted to scream with the suspense.

'Who is he then?'

Slowly Michael put his hand on my shoulder.

'It's your son, Mary. It's Michael, your son. He wanted to meet you.'

She stared at me in silence, for maybe ten seconds. I was rooted to the floor, unable to move, and desperately afraid that she wouldn't believe her brother. Then a shout rose from deep inside her and she put her hand to her mouth.

'Oh my God! Oh my God! Is this really my son? Is he really my son?'

I foolishly stood there, forgetting that I had a part to play. Michael prodded me.

'Answer your mother.'

'Yes, mother. I'm Michael Clemenger.'

'There's no mistake, is there?'

'No, Mary, there's no mistake. It's definitely him.'

Nobody seemed to know what to do, until Mammy

swept past Uncle Michael and threw her arms around my neck, hugging me, kissing me and rubbing her fingers through my hair.

'He really does look like you, Mary. Wouldn't you say?'

She didn't answer him, just kept embracing me.

'My son, my son.'

She had a mighty grip for such a small woman. The first thing I could think to ask her was what happened to her hair.

'Oh, that. It fell out.'

She laughed nervously to reveal a toothless mouth.

'My son, I knew that you would come back some day. I knew it!'

She flung a look of defiance at her brother.

'None of you in Crumlin believed me, not one. What have you got to say for yourself now? Oh, my son is back. Thank God. Michael, my own little boy!'

We were still in the hall. She clung to me as if afraid I might fly away or she would wake up from a dream. Michael glanced around him warily.

'Let's go into the room, Mary. The noise will upset your neighbours.'

'Pah! My son Michael is back. I don't need them.'

'Perhaps, mother, it would be better if we went into your room.'

I led her gently inside.

The room itself was chaotic. Things were scattered

everywhere, with an impressive amount of boxes of cigarettes and matches lying all over the floor, fireplace and
bed. It looked like a bombsite, much worse than Father
O'Neill's and Brother Burke's rooms combined. There
was a small table and a single chair by the window. Near
the door, in the corner, was an old TV with rabbit ears
sticking out of it. There were neither pictures nor photographs on the walls. A small china cabinet was beside the
TV containing dainty little ornaments of various kinds,
her only luxuries. A large coal bunker and sink sat behind
Mammy's bed. It certainly was no castle. Something
serious must have happened to Mammy to have reduced
her to this sorry state of affairs.

She tried to make tea but in all the excitement she
couldn't hold anything still in her trembling hands.
Uncle Michael sat rigid on the bed, afraid to move.

'It's all right, mother. I'll make the tea.'

'Good boy, son.'

She showed me where everything was. I moved about
the room with a confidence that belied my nervousness.
I was determined not to give my uncle the impression
that meeting my mother had overwhelmed or upset me.
I sensed that she didn't like her brother and that boosted
my confidence enormously, especially when the old shite
wouldn't take the tea that I had made. Her dislike of him
was one thing we automatically had in common.

'When did you come back, son?'

Instinctively I was vague. Even at that early stage I

didn't want to give Mammy the impression that I had been back in the bosom of her family for the past six months.

'What did you make of Aunt Josie?'

Over her shoulder I could see the fear in my uncle's eyes.

Be careful now, I thought to myself, *don't give the impression that you like Aunt Josie very much.*

Shades of Brothers Price and Roberts! God only knows what Mammy would do had I given the 'wrong answer'. The windows in Crumlin would probably be in mortal danger. Uncle Michael visibly relaxed when he understood his nephew wasn't a total idiot and could read the danger signs.

'It's nearly time to go, Michael.'

'Go where? Where are you taking him?'

Mammy practically snarled.

'It's okay, mother. What Uncle Michael means is that it's time for us, including you, to go to Crumlin. There's a party on for me and you're invited. So go on and get ready now.'

The room was very crowded with the three of us in it. It would have made a good confession box. She looked so much better a few minutes later, when she reappeared from behind the bed.

'Bloody hell, mother, where did you get the hair?'

'That's my wig, son. I'm just putting in my teeth now and I'm ready to go.'

Mother looked years younger and even quite attractive when she was made up. I could see that Uncle Michael was mighty relieved to leave her building at last and get back to civilisation. My mother beamed as she walked through the corridors with her son on her arm and her brother walking sheepishly behind.

When we got back to Crumlin everyone was waiting for us: Aunt Josie, my sisters, Uncles John and Paddy, Aunts Kate and Sarah and a few of the cousins. Aunt Josie looked fairly terrified and I had to park myself beside mother when she expressed a desire, several times, to slap her sister. Every so often she would content herself by shouting at the family.

'You see, all you gobshites! I always told you that my son would come back one day. None of you ever believed me. You believe me now though, don't you?'

'Mother, please be nice. Everything is okay now. I'm here to stay.'

The family were surprised and relieved that I didn't act like Mammy, shouting abuse and using bad language over the past. Now and again I brought a drink over to Josie, trying not to play favourites. She didn't know what to make of me. It seemed to me that she felt trapped, like her brother Michael, when she was in a situation that she couldn't control. Neither would be much use in a crisis. Nevertheless I had a great night with Paddy, John, Sarah and Aunt Kate. My poor sisters seemed lost. They clung to Aunt Josie like frightened chicks to a mother hen. Neither of them was anxious to be in Mammy's company. Catherine, in particular, it seemed to me, was on guard duty protecting Josie from her erratic mother.

It dawned on me that while Josie and Uncle Michael generally ruled the roost, they were both reduced to blobs of wobbling jelly when my mother was around. Something must have happened in the past and it must have involved me. Over the course of the evening I heard how I had ended up with the nuns.

It seemed that following Catherine's birth the family, in the shape of Aunt Josie and Uncle Michael, decided – albeit reluctantly – to keep her. In that era having a child out of wedlock was a shameful matter for any family. The view of the Church prevailed so that these 'products of sin' were usually hidden away from decent people. Therefore Catherine was very lucky. Then, when Mammy became pregnant again for the second time, the family, unfortunately for me, sought the advice of the local parish priest. There was a great fear that the home would become a house full of 'bastards'. So, I was taken away by the Church authorities after first making sure that I was baptised into the Catholic Church. After that the family just hoped that Mammy would not become pregnant again. But she did, and eighteen months later a second girl arrived. The reasons why they decided to keep Miriam remain unclear to me; perhaps they decided that Catherine needed a companion. Why they let me go so easily was never explained to me. What's worse is that Mammy told me she offered me back to the family. I don't know if this is true, but I wish that I had been reunited with my two sisters as a child.

*

They all warned me against doing it.

'You'll live to regret it. Nobody can live with your mother. She suffers with the nerves. That means she's likely to fly off the handle at any moment and God only knows what she'll do then.'

But I was having none of it.

'Look at her, for Christ's sake; she's only a small woman. Surely she couldn't hurt a fly.'

I was torn between the advice I was being given by my aunts, uncles and sister Catherine, while, on the other hand, I felt a profound sense of sadness regarding the conditions my poor mother was living in.

Of course, I allowed my heart to rule my mind, and besides she was my mother and I felt a sense of responsibility towards her. Why, I don't know. After all I had only just met her but she was my mother nevertheless, and I was her son. Perhaps too, in the final analysis, I made my decision based just a little on the coldness of Aunt Josie and Uncle Michael. Their open hostility towards her, their air of superiority and condescension and their belief that I was a bit too sentimental towards Mammy infuriated me. Like my Uncle John I thought who are they to sit in judgement on *my* mother? So I felt protective towards her.

I gave up the job in Dublin Fabrics. It was a hard place to be once I found out my supervisor was married to my relative and had said nothing to me for over a year. However, I didn't leave without giving him a piece of my mind. Neither the manager nor his secretary was very impressed by his behaviour. They both wished me good luck. Also I decided to say goodbye to Mrs Sheridan. This was a much more difficult decision because she had given me the first taste of a mother's love and I was extremely fond of her. She advised me to stay with her a while more and visit my mother at weekends to see how I got on. It was she who spoke freely to me about what my family only hinted at.

'You know, Michael, your mother isn't right in the head. She's highly strung and quite impulsive. That means she could do anything, anything at all.'

Aunt Josie must have spoken to Mrs Sheridan. I explained that my mind was made up and that I just felt my mother needed me. I thanked her for all she had done for me, including putting me into night classes. She knew she couldn't stop me.

'Okay then. If you must go, so be it. Just promise me one thing though, that you'll be very careful, you could be in great danger.'

She gave me a great big hug and I closed the red front door behind me for the last time. It would also be the last time that I ever saw Mrs Sheridan, but I would never forget her generosity, including the life-changing opportunity of an education.

Mammy was very excited about me moving in with her. I had to be quiet as she wasn't allowed to have anybody staying with her. She bought me a mattress and blankets and I usually slept on the floor. I got a job close by as a cleaner in the Meath Hospital. I would like to write that everything worked out just fine and we were very happy together. But I can't. It was a complete disaster.

Perhaps the first problem was that the room was so small that there was little privacy for either of us. The second problem was that Mammy didn't fully understand that I was twenty years old. I think she wanted me to act like a baby so that she could relive babying me once again. Apparently she had kept me for a while after I was born. We lived near Stephen's Green with the nuns while she worked in their laundry. One evening she came home and found me scalded on the bottom. Apparently, Mammy assaulted the Reverend Mother, then she was arrested and I was sent away. That was the last she saw of me – until now. The third problem was that we had absolutely nothing in common. I liked to read a lot while she just sat and knitted God knows what. She never finished anything, always preferring to start something new instead. So, what with the lack of living space, the fact I was a grown man and the reality that we were, in truth, total strangers to one another quickly combined to make our situation a stressful one. It was only then I learned what happens to Mammy when she gets stressed. The paranoia started in earnest.

She became suspicious whenever I said hallo to anybody on the street, especially to girls. Often she would wander onto the wards where I was working and make a holy show of me. When I came home she would go through my pockets searching for drugs. No amount of argument would diminish her obsession about my being hooked on drugs.

'Admit it, Michael, you're a drug addict.'

My denials only made things worse. She collected dust particles in envelopes as evidence and sent them over to Kevin Street Garda station for analysis. When the results came back negative she was always disappointed. I reckoned she was well known in Kevin Street and the guards just humoured her by sending a note back about the 'test' results.

'Don't worry, Michael, you can't fool me. I'll get you.'

The tension was building steadily until I actually became too afraid to go to sleep at night. Her frequent rages were terrifying. That was when she was at her most unpredictable. She even tried to set my hair on fire by pushing a firelighter and paper under my pillow. Eventually things reached such a point that I told her that I was leaving.

'Oh no, you're not. I'm calling the guards; you're a drug addict and a drug dealer.'

When I made to leave she stood in my way, wielding the bread knife. Then she lunged at me.

'Michael, you'd be better off dead because you're a drug addict.'

I managed to push her away but she fell, hitting her head on the fireplace with a sickening thud. Blood flowed from the wound and there was no movement from her on the ground. Christ almighty, I've killed her. I rushed to the next-door neighbour who called the guards. They arrived within minutes, by which time she had come round. When she saw them she exploded.

'Arrest him, he's a drug addict and he tried to kill me.'

With that a Garda with huge hands, and built like a rugby player, lifted me clean off my feet and threw me on the bed. He landed a couple of blows on my chest and lower back.

'So, you like to hit women? You like to hit your mother? Well, boyo, by the time I'm finished with you, you'll be sorry.'

He threw me over his shoulder and walked to the stairs. Mammy followed, grinning.

'That's it, Garda. Give him a good hiding. He's a drug addict.'

'That I will, Mrs Clemenger. Don't you worry; he won't be back here again to cause you any trouble. I'll see to that.'

As I was being unceremoniously carted off to the police station the irony of it all wasn't lost on me. After all it was only a few months ago that I rushed up the same steps with a giddy delight at the prospect of seeing my mother for the first time. Uncle Michael's words of caution were ringing in my ears: *Are you sure, Michael? Once I knock on this door there is no going back. Well, son, I did tell you it's complicated.*

In Court

THE GARDA WHO arrested me was huge. I imagine he used his size to instil the fear of God in prisoners and make them shite in their underpants. However, with me he did neither. I had survived Brother Lane. Surely he couldn't be any worse?

'What's your name?'

'Michael Clemenger, sir.'

'What relation are you to Mrs Clemenger?'

'Her son, sir.'

'Indeed. So you like to hit your mother, do you?'

'No, sir. I only hit out at her when she lunged towards me with a knife.'

'Likely story. Don't give me any more of your lies. She says you're a drug addict, is this true?'

'No, sir.'

'How old are you?'

'Twenty, sir.'

'That's it, my boyo, come with me to the cells. Don't worry; I'll be back later to deal with you.'

He slammed the door behind me and I listened to the sound of his heavy footsteps disappear into the distance. The cell contained one solitary item of furniture, an iron bed without so much as a sheet on it. There was a lot of pain in my lower back so I lay down on the floor. It was 4.30 and I was exhausted from all the upset. Also I couldn't remember the last time that I had enjoyed a good night's sleep. Somehow I nodded off and slept until I heard the key turn in the lock about four hours later. It was the Garda making good on his promise. Briefly I wondered when I'd get something to eat.

He was alone and closed the door behind him with a sense of purpose. Instinctively I knew what was going to happen next. He gave me a hiding that the Christian Brothers would have been proud of.

'You like to hit your mother, do you? You little bastard!'

All the punches were aimed at my back, lower body and legs. He was most careful not to hit me in the face. I ended up flat out on the floor, just as I had with Brother Lane all those years ago. As he slammed out of my cell, he informed me that I was going up before the judge the next morning.

'It's jail for you, my boy.'

Needless to say I was given no food or drink before appearing in the dock.

The next morning I duly appeared before the judge, without any representation.

'Stand up, please, you in the dock. I can't see you.'

'But sir, I am standing.'

'Oh. Could someone get him a box so that I can see him? Thank you. Ah, that's better. Now, what is your name?'

'Michael Clemenger, sir.'

'How old are you?'

'Twenty years old, sir.'

'And do you understand why you are here?'

'Yes, sir.'

'All right then, let's proceed.'

With that the Garda got into the box and treated the court to a litany of charges that he read out from his black notebook. Of course, he made no mention of having beaten the shite out of me. He sounded very convincing as he detailed his heroic efforts to apprehend a hardened, violent and dangerous criminal. However, he seemed less than confident when the judge asked him for clarification on certain points regarding my arrest. When he was finished the judge looked at me intently. Did he actually believe that I was a hardened criminal, a menace to society, and a danger to all women and children of Ireland? I sensed he didn't because of the way he kept looking from me to the Garda. He seemed slightly amused if anything. Sensing his dilemma I decided to make use of this opportunity.

'Sir, I would like to say something. Please, sir.'

There was something in his demeanour that gave me the impression that he, however slightly, doubted the policeman's words. Perhaps it was my size, all five foot, three inches of me.

'Can I move out of the box, sir?'

'Why?'

'Because I want to show you something, sir.'

One of the guards moved towards me.

'Leave him. Look at the size of him; he's not likely to attack me from there, now, is he?'

'No, sir, I have no intention of doing that.'

I pulled up my shirt and dropped my trousers.

'What happened to you, son?'

I pointed at the Garda.

'Him, sir. That Garda beat me in the cells. Plus I've had nothing to eat since my arrest yesterday afternoon.'

The entire court looked in my accuser's direction. The blood drained from his face and he put his hands on the bench in front of him for support.

He began to stutter half explanations for the violence he had inflicted on my body.

'But he was resisting arrest and trying to escape.'

'That's a lie, sir.'

'I had to restrain the prisoner forcefully.'

The judge looked disgusted.

'Enough! Enough of this.'

But the Garda persisted. He was in a hole and he just kept digging. I looked around the court and felt a groundswell of sympathy for me and, more importantly, that not even the judge believed the Garda by this stage.

'Look at the prisoner, guard. Do you really expect me to believe that he would put up much resistance to you?'

'But he hit his mother.'

'That's quite enough. Son, put your clothes back on and come up here.

'Young man, I'm not going to send you to prison but I cannot set you free under the circumstances. Therefore, you are to be held over for two weeks pending an evaluation. Will you do something for me? I want you to go to St Brendan's Hospital for those two weeks.'

'Yes, sir.'

'Very well, then.'

He turned to the Garda.

'See to it that this boy has a good breakfast immediately.'

And that was that.

St Brendan's, Grangegorman, 1971

I HAD NO idea that St Brendan's was a psychiatric hospital until I arrived there that Wednesday evening. Perhaps I assumed that I was going to hospital pursuant to the injuries I had received from the Garda. Upon arrival I heard a bunch of keys been rattled as the door was unlocked. Once inside it quickly became obvious that all the patients in Ward 10 were suffering from various types of mental illnesses. There were between twenty and thirty patients on the ward. Mammy, I couldn't help thinking, would have fitted in here very well. The nursing staff, who were mostly male, wore white coats.

'Sit in that chair and don't move.'

That was the only conversation I had with the nurses. I could see that they meant business. There was a TV on the wall in front of me and I was happy to sit there because I knew that *Hall's Pictorial Weekly* would be on at 8.30. Just then one of the nurses came up behind me.

'Here, drink this now.'

I offered no resistance. He had a menacing look about him, plus he was huge.

After that I have no memory of time until I woke up at 8.10 on Friday morning. There was a clock on the wall opposite my bed. A nurse, or so I thought, was hovering over me, holding my hand somewhat nervously. Once I opened my eyes I was suddenly overwhelmed by a ravenous hunger.

'I'm very hungry. Can I have a piece of bread, please?'

The man who I thought was a nurse turned out to be a doctor. He was much older than the nurses I had seen and spoke in quiet, gentle tones. Letting go of my hand he beckoned to one of the nurses to bring me some breakfast. It must have been the medicine that made me so hungry.

'My name is Dr Noel Browne. You can call me Doctor.'

'I'm telling you now, Doctor, I'm not mad. I shouldn't be here. It seems that this hospital is for mad people, so what am I doing here?'

He made no reply to this, only asking if I needed anything else.

'No thanks, Doctor, but you could get me out of this locked ward.'

'Okay, I'll do that. I'll see you later and perhaps we could have a chat then.'

'Thank you, Doctor.'

About midday on the Friday I was moved to an open ward, which was a bit more pleasant and – more importantly – wasn't locked. Also, the nurses on that ward didn't seem quite so fierce nor did they wear white coats. I didn't see Doctor Browne again until Monday evening, when a nurse brought me to his office at his request. As she was leaving he asked her to bring a pot of tea and some biscuits.

'Michael and I will be a while. Okay, thank you, nurse.'

She stared at me, suddenly curious. Dr Browne knew my name. I must be important if he wanted to see me without a nurse present. Surely, at least, he must believe that I'm not dangerous. As it turned out he had a lot of questions he wanted to ask me.

'Do you know what kind of doctor I am?'

'No, sir, not really.'

'Well, I'm a psychiatrist. I specialise in treating people with mental problems.'

'You mean like me, Doctor?'

'Perhaps.'

He pulled out a sheet of paper from his desk drawer and took up his pen.

'Well now, Michael, you don't seem afraid of me, are you?'

'No, Doctor, I'm not. Why should I be?'

'Very well then, tell me about yourself. Start from the very beginning.'

And so I did. Initially he just listened, but soon he began writing furiously.

'You certainly have been through a lot. I would like to concentrate particularly on your time in St Joseph's Industrial School in Kerry. You say you were sexually abused by a number of Brothers?'

I interrupted him.

'Dr Browne, I don't just "say" I was abused, I was abused. Why would I lie about such a thing?'

'Did you ever report these incidents to the police or other authorities like the Church?'

'Yes, I did, but no one believed me.'

'How did you feel about that?'

'Very angry and frustrated. Do you believe me, Doctor?'

'I don't know, really.'

'You see, Doctor, it doesn't matter what authority I report sexual abuse to, nobody will believe me anyway. That's the problem. It's hard to understand why people think I am lying. Why would I make all this up? Why?'

I continued with my narration as the tears ran down my cheeks. Dr Browne's interest in the topic diminished as I provided him with more and more details. In fact he seemed to recoil from me.

He never discussed the topic with me again; he placed me under the care of another doctor; I'll call him 'Dr Zavier'. I had no idea at the time that Dr Noel Browne was so well known throughout the country. As far as I can prove, he never made any entries in my case notes regarding the sexual abuse; this has always been a source of sadness to me. Strangely he made only a passing reference to the incident with my mother that landed me in St Brendan's in the first place, which surprised me even then.

Dr Zavier certainly had none of his colleague's gentleness. Maybe he had conferred with Dr Noel Browne and their conversation might have coloured his reaction to me. I found him very formal, rigid in his manner and somewhat distant. Because of what I felt to be his air of superiority and condescension whenever he spoke to me, I initially refused to co-operate with him. However, he may have found me interesting and something of a challenge.

'You have read my notes from Dr Noel Browne, I suppose. So why are you asking me the same questions about my mother? You know the answers already. Go and ask her yourself then.'

'Oh but, Michael, I have, and she paints a very different picture from what you have told us.'

Raging at his attitude I grew vocal in my defiance.

'She's the one that's mad, not me!'

'That may well be the case but she isn't here, Michael, you are. You were sent here for a psychiatric evaluation.'

'What's that, Doctor? Do you mean I am mad?'

'No, not necessarily.'

'Tell me, Doctor, do you think I'm mad?'

'Well, I haven't made a final determination on the matter.'

'I am sorry, Doctor, but I don't understand what that means.'

'What means?'

'Final determination.'

'Well, it just means that I haven't made up my mind yet.'

'And when, Doctor, will you make up your mind?'

The man seemed frustrated by the way I was able to stand up for myself.

(I only learned afterwards that Dr Zavier made the determination that I wasn't mad that very morning.)

'Tell you what, Michael, will you do something for me? Will you attend a meeting on Friday morning at 10 o'clock? It's an important meeting; there'll be a lot of people there.'

'Do you mean other doctors?'

'Yes, mostly, but there will be some psychologists too.'

'Psychologists? What do they do?'

'A psychologist is somebody that studies the mind.'

'What's the difference between a psychologist and a psychiatrist?'

'Well, essentially a psychiatrist is a medical doctor while a psychologist generally isn't. You ask a lot of questions, Michael, that's good. Don't be afraid to ask as many questions as you like at the meeting.'

On that Friday morning I was led into a room full of doctors and psychologists, male and female. The room was somewhat intimate, small and cosy. There were maybe thirty people in attendance. I only knew the two doctors, Noel Browne and Zavier. It would have been natural to have been completely intimidated by my auspicious surroundings and the amount of clever people in the room. I reckoned I needed all my wits about me to survive this lot of intellectuals. As far as I could make out Dr Noel Browne was acting as if he had never laid eyes on me before. I was on my own and I knew it. The atmosphere was very formal.

Dr Zavier opened the proceedings, welcoming everyone and thanking me for agreeing to be present. Turning to me suddenly he asked me to leave for a few minutes.

'I want to talk to the team alone.'

I looked around the room. They looked fierce enough to take the head off someone and I was going to make sure that it wasn't my head they took, psychiatrist or psychologist or whatever they were. I was less than impressed and did my best to listen to the pep talk through the keyhole, as presumably it was all about me. Alas, I could hear nothing.

After about seven minutes or so Dr Zavier invited me back into the room and told me to sit on the chair that was placed in front of the blackboard, facing the audience.

While I certainly felt nervous I was more than used to being stared at as if I was some kind of freak. It was just like taking a stroll through the streets of Tralee.

'Well, Michael, I've just filled in everybody about you. Would you like to say anything further?'

'I'm sorry, Doctor, but I don't know what you have told them about me.'

'Well, indeed. Then perhaps we'll just take some questions from the floor.'

From the floor? I wanted to giggle. *Wouldn't it be funny if the floorboards could talk?*

A voice called out from the back.

'Michael, why did you hit your mother?'

'Because she was coming at me with a knife.'

'But why did she come at you with a knife?'

'Because she thinks I'm a drug addict.'

Another voice rang out.

'Michael, how do you feel about your mother now?'

'Feel? I don't know what you mean by that.'

'Well, do you want to harm her in any way?'

'No, I don't want to harm her.'

'Are you sure? Judging by the tone of your voice you sound pretty angry to me.'

'That's your opinion, whoever asked that question, but it's not what I feel.'

By this stage I was beginning to warm to the task.

'Perhaps I could make a comment please, Doctor.'

'By all means do, Michael.'

'Why is every question about my mother? Why has nobody asked me a single question about the physical and sexual abuse that I suffered in St Joseph's Industrial School at the hands of the Christian Brothers?'

I rose from the chair and started to pace across the floor. You could have heard a pin drop. I turned to meet the uncertain gaze of Dr Noel. He knew what was coming and tried to make himself as inconspicuous as possible.

'Surely, Doctor Browne, you have a question you would like to ask.'

No response.

'Very well then, I'll ask all of you a few questions. How would you feel if you were taken from your bed in the middle of the night and brought to a Brother's room to have sex with him? How would you feel if you were beaten by an older boy because your bottom was too small for his penis? What about having a Brother's tongue shoved so far down your throat that it almost comes out your ears?'

I looked around for answers, for some kind of understanding or acknowledgement that they even half believed what I was saying. They all appeared uncomfortable and started to shuffle papers around.

'Well, any more questions? Surely someone must have a question they would like to ask.'

I could hardly contain my anger. They didn't believe me. Dr Zavier addressed me.

'Do you intend to go back to your mother if released?'

'Doctor, I have no problem answering that question, but could I stick to discussing sexual and physical abuse that I have just mentioned, please. Why is it that you and Dr Noel Browne don't want to talk about this subject? After all I only lived with my mother for a few months whereas the abuse in St Joseph's went on until I was sixteen years old.'

'Well, well Michael …'

'I'll tell you why, it's because none of you believe me.'

A voice called out from the audience.

'Why is it important that we believe you, Michael?'

'Because it *happened* and nobody seems to want to know anything about it. People think I'm telling lies, but I'm not. Everything I have said is the absolute truth and that's why it is important to me to be believed.'

'What do you want to do with the rest of your life?'

'I would have liked to be a priest, but I can't because, as I was told by Father O'Neill, the school chaplain, I'm a bastard.'

'But you could become something else.'

'Like what?'

There was silence.

'It's easy for you to say "something else".'

'Have you ever tried to kill yourself, Michael?'

'Yes.'

'What happened?'

I didn't answer. It seemed to me that they just wanted to ask me about everything except the sexual abuse.

'Yes, I tried to kill myself because I thought the world didn't care if I lived or died.'

'But you're still alive. Why?'

'I don't know. Doctor, you asked me earlier if I was going to go back and live with my mother. Would you want to go back and live with your mother if she tried to stab you?'

'I suppose not.'

'And you can be sure that I won't either.'

With that the meeting came to an end. Dr Zavier told me afterwards that the meeting had overrun by half an hour. I could've gone on for another two hours. I experienced a certain satisfaction in being the sole focus of their attention. I was also pleased by the way I had acquitted myself in front of the high calibre audience. At the same time, however, I was sad that they hadn't believed me about the abuse.

'You handled yourself well today, Michael. To answer your question from earlier in the week, no, I don't think you are mad and that will be my recommendation.'

Pointedly he made no reference to my allegations of physical and sexual abuse. I was discharged a couple of days later and never saw either of the doctors again.

PART FOUR

A New Life

Discharge to Nowhere

SOCIAL SERVICES TOOK over my case and I was released to a night shelter in the centre of Dublin. What a place of utter desolation, isolation and sadness. Hundreds of men, many well past their prime, lay huddled together in cramped quarters. The noise was constant: the raucous spitting, farting, shouting and cries of despair that echoed through its long corridors.

My cubicle had '44' on the door. There was no privacy of any kind, with thieving and fighting going on throughout the entire night. It was no place to send a young fella, likely to fall prey to the wiles of older, heartless and cruel men who had long since lost any concept of right or wrong. All their yesterdays, dreams and hopes were gone.

Determined to prevent myself from drowning in their brand of hopelessness I swapped the shelter for Stephen's Green, preferring to sleep out under the stars, comforting myself with the belief – however delusional – that better days lay ahead of me. It was becoming harder and harder to maintain this belief.

After all that had happened, and the disastrous end to

my moving in with Mammy, against all my relatives' advice, and Mrs Sheridan's, I just couldn't bring myself to go back to Crumlin or the North Strand. I would die before I'd let Aunt Josie and Uncle Michael know that they had been absolutely right. I was determined to stand on my own two feet for once in my life.

After a few nights, sleeping rough soon lost any romance it ever had for me and I was glad to accept an offer of a bed in a Salvation Army Hostel that was right across the road from the College of Surgeons. I watched a lot of foreigners, black men in particular, coming and going from that building. Quite unexpectedly the 'Captain', the man who was in charge of the hostel, asked me one morning if I would like to work on the staff there: free board and lodging, as much food as I could eat, and a few pounds in my pocket at the end of the week. How could I refuse? Initially, however, I was reluctant. Most of the staff were ex-down-and-outs and as a result were perfectly content now to stay in the hostel. I was afraid I'd end up the same way and lose any remaining ambition for a much better life. The Captain's wife, a kind and gentle lady, persuaded me to take the job, at least until something better came along. Something worse came along instead, in the form of my mother. She turned up one day and told the Captain that I was a druggie and had tried to kill her. Upping her increasingly melodramatic visits to three times a day, disrupting both staff and residents, she made it impossible for me to stay. I didn't want to be around her anymore. She was trouble, and she could land me back in prison if I wasn't careful. I no longer had any hope of building a relationship with her. I went back to living on the streets. A few days later I was approached at the top of Grafton Street by a young couple.

'We love you and we have been sent by Jesus to help you.'

Bloody hell, I thought, *they're mad*.

'How can you love me when I've only just met you?'

'Jesus commands us to love everybody and that includes you. By the way, what's your name?'

'Michael.'

'We've noticed you around for the past few days, Michael. We know that you're sleeping rough.'

'How?'

'By the state of your clothes and, well, you need a shave. … You're very suspicious, aren't you? Why do you keep looking around? We don't want to hurt you, only to help you. You do believe that, don't you?'

'Look, I believe there's nothing for nothing in this world. So what is it I have to do for you to help me?'

'We act for Jesus; it's He who wants something from you. He loves you very much and just wants you to love Him back as much.'

'Huh! If Jesus loves me, He has a funny way of showing it.'

'You're angry, Michael. Why?'

'I don't want to talk about it.'

'Okay, do you know Jesus?'

'Of course I do. Who doesn't?'

'But that's where you're wrong. A lot of people have heard of Jesus, but not many "know" Him. Do you "know" Him, Michael?'

They were talking in riddles and were on a roll so I let them rant on.

'To know Jesus, *really* know Him, Michael, you must acknowledge your nothingness. Cast yourself at the foot of the cross, confess sincerely to all your sins and fully accept Him as your Lord and personal saviour. It's almost like being born again.'

It was too much for me.

'Well, I'm afraid that the Jesus I know hasn't been very kind to me. I find it difficult to believe that He ever loved me. Why else would He have given me such a hard life?'

'Give Jesus a chance, Michael.'

I found myself liking their sincerity, in spite of myself, and was even a little envious of their certitude.

'I tell you what, explain what you meant by "love".'

By this stage I was fully engaged and interested in how they would answer that question. They answered it with a question of their own.

'Don't you know what love is? Didn't your parents love you?'

'Ah, indeed. That's the problem, see. Your Jesus never

gave me proper parents. Now why do you think that was?' Boiling inside with my usual rage I grew sarcastic. 'Is it because I was a bad person in a previous life and have been sent back to pay for my sins? Well?'

They declined to answer, but they knew they had me because of my apparent willingness to engage with them.

'Michael, if you come with us we can show you a new way of life. It'll get you off the streets and you'll have three square meals a day. Would you like that? Put your trust in Jesus. Jesus is love.'

'Trust and love Jesus? No, I don't think so.'

'Just come with us, Michael, and give it a try. That's all we're asking.'

It was the three square meals a day that finally persuaded me. I certainly wasn't buying any of that Jesus crap. I had Jesus fatigue. All my life I had placed my faith in Jesus and look where it got me. Plus there was the fact that the people who claimed to be working for Him, that is, the priests, Brothers and nuns, rarely turned out to be nice, in my experience.

People down in their luck are always very vulnerable to 'Jesus people'. Sometimes it's easier not to resist. They can be very persuasive when they think they are working for Jesus/God. The young couple were convinced that they had won me for Jesus as we left Grafton Street to get the bus that took us to Rathmines. I let them believe they had me. It was easier to play the Jesus game. I was down on my luck, and besides it wasn't likely that Mammy would ever dream of looking for me in a 'Jesus people' compound.

The irony of my situation appealed to me – I was moving into a religious community to get away from the mother I had spent years hoping to find, and it was a religious community that had separated us in the first place. The romantic fantasy that I had harboured about my mother, her trying to hold onto her baby against the mighty forces of others, had been dismantled and replaced by my sordid reality. Somewhere in the back of my mind, thanks to Brother Price's hints, I had suspected that there was something squalid about my begetting. Father O'Neill was still right, I was a bastard. There was no getting away from it, my unstable mother had never been married.

When I thought back over my discovery of my family, and my problems with my mother, I realised that it was something I was still having difficulty with. It wasn't that I regretted finding her – I didn't – but I was taken aback to find she had two other children. I was glad for them that they hadn't had to endure what I had. While I didn't know exactly if I was stronger from my life experiences I certainly felt that I had coped better than either of my sisters would have. It was hard to deal with the fact that I had a whole family to identify with after being reared for sixteen years as an orphan. Their subtle rejection of me, after I moved in with Mammy, was quite understandable. My arrival had turned the family upside down and my sisters, especially, were as ill-equipped to deal with me as I was to deal with them. The situation was nobody's fault. I simply went back to being an orphan again. At least I had accomplished something, I had wanted to find my mother and so I did. That little feat contented me. I had a clearer idea of where I came from. Now it was time to move on again.

The 'Jesus people' brought me to a large rambling building that had lots and lots of rooms. There were about fifty people living there already. I slept in a sort of dormitory with fourteen others, in bunk beds. It wasn't always easy to sleep because more than likely, on any given night, one of the men would jump out of his bed anxious to share a 'vision of Jesus' that he had just experienced. Some of these guys would give Brother Murphy a run for his money, such were their theatrics. Almost immediately on entering the house I came into the presence of the Leader, 'the great one'. What a chancer he was. If he was God's chosen one to convert sinners around Dublin then I feared all was lost. He was a cute hoor with eyes that could take out your appendix while you slept. The recommended treatment for new converts was to treat us with kid gloves in case we ran away, overwhelmed by all the praying and chanting. Jesus loves you. Having come from the Christian Brothers I was used to all that old shite. It didn't bother me, I hardly believed in God anymore. My desire to become a priest had completely left me, and I had no interest in religion.

Whenever the Leader made a grand entrance to the main hall he was always accompanied by his adoring wife. They had their own family, which made me think that the Leader might be half normal. But he wasn't. Instead he was every bit as mad as Brother Murphy had been in St Joseph's. Thankfully, though, he was just as entertaining. He walked around the house in a slow procession with his loving wife in tow, until suddenly he would stop and go into a trance, whereupon he would start to see visions. As if on cue everybody gathered round him. Then, when he had a full audience, he would start speaking very fast in a language I didn't recognise. I did think he was good enough to be an actor. His wife would be furiously writing down his pearls of wisdom as fast as she could. It was hard not to laugh.

After his ecstatic visions the 'great one', as I liked to call him, fell down on the ground, with beads of sweat rolling down his face while chanting over and over again that he wasn't worthy. I hated this in particular because it usually meant that there was at least an hour of chanting 'Jesus, Jesus is coming' to be endured. It was hard going. If you weren't into this Jesus game, every minute felt like an hour.

We seemed to live off about thirty members of the community who had normal jobs and handed their entire wages over to the Leader. This they were glad to do without question. The evenings were the worst. There was no television allowed; only a tape recorder that played some kind of religious music. Everything was constantly aimed at reminding us of the transience of human existence and that we should expect the second coming at any moment. Most evenings we sat about on the floor, in our bare feet, chanting the mantra 'Jesus loves', while reading passages from the Bible. I dreaded anybody going into ecstasy and having visions because it meant a long night on the hard floor. The prayer meetings started at 8 o'clock, but it was a rare night that I'd get to bed before 2am, such was the level of ecstasy and praying.

There were no Catholic rituals like Mass or confession; if we had any problems it was expected that we would seek the counsel of the Leader. Needless to say, I was always engaged elsewhere rather than availing of his services. If someone displayed any kind of internal conflict with God, the whole community met together to pray over the unfortunate one.

There was the belief always that the devil hated this community because we were working for Jesus. The devil must have finally succeeded because a few months after I moved in, 'the great schism' erupted. The 'schism', as the Leader liked to call it, arose from a misinterpretation of a piece of scripture between himself and another senior member of the community. It seemed to me that they didn't like each other anyway and that their row had more to do with who would continue as leader. We were in session for a few days praying, arguing and struggling to try to make sense of the scriptural reading. It was open to interpretation but my reading of the entire situation was, don't get involved. I knew by now that about half the members would eventually leave and form their own community. So I had a choice, do I stay or do I go?

Both men were determined to gather their own followers. Accordingly the 'alternative leader' laid his hands on my head one evening and started chanting. Word spread and the 'great one' came running to my 'rescue'.

'Leave him alone! I claim him for Christ Jesus. Satan has no control over him.'

Then he too placed his hands on my head and started praying. It was comical. Every few minutes the 'great one' fell to the floor, shouting his explanation up at me.

'Michael, it's the devil pushing me down. He's trying to claim you for his own, but just like Jesus, I'll get up again in your defence.'

This madness went on for about three quarters of an hour.

Both of them, I thought, *are chancers!*

'Do you feel the spirit of the Lord moving through you, Michael? If you do, then push forward towards me. I won't let you fall. I promise.'

Bloody hell, where were Dr Noel Browne and Dr Zavier when I needed them? Who would save me now from all this nonsense? I thought.

When the 'alternative leader' left with his posse I stayed on in Rathmines. I preferred 'the great one' to his mutineer who gave me the creeps. As a reward for staying put I was given possibly the most important job in the community. The house was plagued daily by relatives and friends of members looking to speak to them. The Leader strongly discouraged anyone from meeting their families. I didn't agree with this. The families were really concerned about them. In the early seventies, dear reader, there was a glut of religious sects sprouting up all over Dublin, exploiting the confusion of young people. Leaders of these Sects had no conscience about exploiting their vulnerability.

Because I could articulate well, it became my job to answer the door and be economical with the truth. I felt extremely uncomfortable about this since I had been fobbed off many times in my own search for answers. I found it impossible to ignore the pain on the relatives' faces. For that reason I was the worst person 'the great one' could have chosen for this job. I wanted to help the callers and discreetly arranged meetings between families and members. Had I been caught I would have been out on my ear. Then, one Tuesday evening, at about 8.15, the doorbell rang. Before me stood an attractive young woman, of about twenty years of age.

'Hallo, my name is Mary. I'm looking for the brother of my friend who is living here. Can you give me any information?'

Normally I answered all queries at the door or in the hallway. Never before had I invited visitors any further into the house in case they would create a scene and try to grab their loved one. Why I broke that rule on this occasion I have no idea. Neither can I explain why I brought her down to the kitchen for a cup of tea. Before long she was enquiring more about me than her friend's brother. Then she startled me with the simple truth.

'You don't belong in this place.'

I was speechless. She suggested that we go for a walk there and then. It felt so natural that once we got down the road we started holding hands. We talked for hours, discovering that we shared a love for the music of Bob Dylan and Leonard Cohen, had much the same view regarding ambition and a desire to improve ourselves and enjoyed a good debate on religion and the meaning of life. Before we parted I had pretty much told her everything and started to fall in love. The feeling was mutual.

She came back for me the following morning. The Leader followed us down the street in his car. He pulled down the car window and started shouting at me.

'Come back, Michael, she works for the devil. It's a trap.'

It's strange how instantly protective towards Mary I became at that very moment. I had never experienced such naturalness in my feelings for another person, not since Jimmy.

'Fuck off, you old hypocrite!'

We made good our escape on a bus into O'Connell Street. I had no idea where the relationship was heading, but it could be no worse than where I was living now. Mary was working as a nurse and sharing a big house with four or five other girls. I moved in that day and a few weeks later we got our own flat down the road.

She took a massive chance on me and the fact that our relationship has endured has always been something of a wonder to me. Through her efforts my talents, such as they were, got to shine in the warmth of the midday sun. What a glorious pathway she opened before me, never flinching in spite of opposition from those she loved. She picked me up from nothing and nursed, with heroic fortitude, that potential she saw in me even when I myself faltered. I shudder when I think of what would have become of me had she not knocked on the front door on that cold Tuesday night in April 1973.

Anything I have achieved in my life thereafter came through her. Mary believed me about the abuse I had endured. From the first time I told her, in April 1973, long before the sexual abuse of children in institutions became well known, she believed what I told her. We went to Tralee, in 1975, so that she could walk the grounds of St Joseph's, drinking in fully my dreadful memories of that place. It was this total belief in my story that caused me, initially, to hold on to her for dear life. I never thought, for one moment, that she might share the rest of her life with me or want to invest her love in one deficient in both the ability to love or trust at such an intimate and emotional level. Over time, however, I grew in confidence and shed many of the hang-ups that had threatened to bring me down. Mary was like Mrs Sheridan who believed in the possibilities of tomorrow, and also like her son Jim who believes that anything is possible if you put your mind to it.

I became so confident that years later many of our friends are dumbfounded that I could have come through my childhood apparently unscathed. Only Mary knows the high price that I paid and am still paying. The tyranny of my memories hasn't gone away.

Education At Last

AND SO IT was that I pursued, with Mary's full support, the educational pathway to freedom. We lived in a flat off the South Circular Road, while I enrolled for a two year Leaving Certificate course at Ardscoil Eanna in Crumlin. Mary was working full-time as a nurse. At twenty-three, I was the eldest in my class by a good five years, but it didn't bother me. Besides, it took Mary a couple of years to put a bit of weight on me, so I probably looked a lot younger than I was. Thanks to a dedicated teaching staff, and some hard work on my part, I passed the Leaving Certificate, getting into Arts in Trinity College in 1975–76. Third-level education had been my dream since the time I first got to know Jim Sheridan. He had told me I could do anything I wanted and now I had. The high point of my time in Ardscoil Eanna was watching an obviously reluctant teacher, Mr Gabriel Byrne, who taught Spanish. It seemed to me that he disliked teaching, and I always felt that he would rather be anywhere else than standing in a classroom. I'm glad that he found his true vocation in acting, becoming a major movie star.

I was in Germany, on holidays with Mary, when I got

news that I had secured a place in Trinity College in 1975 to study History, Economics and Psychology. Thanks to a grant and the fact that Mary was working full-time I could now make up for all those lost years by throwing myself into study. Such was my excitement that I didn't look at the traffic, stepped out into the road and was bounced off a moving car. Mary got an awful fright.

'It would be just like you, love, to get killed after you have worked so hard to achieve this.'

Trinity College was my first choice. The ban on Catholics attending the college had only recently been lifted and I think the church's suspiciousness of the place was the reason for my attraction.

I sat on the grass on the first day of term crying. No one saw me. How could this be? Why couldn't I just accept this and move on? My head was full of the taunting echoes of my teachers in St Joseph's, telling me that I would never amount to anything. What about all those other boys who should be where I was now? I felt guilty at their loss. Why had I survived? I had been given the chance of college, the promised land, something I had only ever dreamt about as I looked out the top window of Lep Travel over at Trinity College. And here I was, an actual undergraduate now, and yet I never felt as miserable as I did on that first day. I passed my first year examinations in June 1976, but I never really settled into college. I didn't bother making many friends; after all I had Mary to go home to. I did join a couple of societies and attended a few debates, though. I discovered a love for studying and could spend hours on end poring over my books in the library. Nevertheless, over the course of the year, I found that I wanted to do something else, something I hadn't even told Mary. By the time I completed my first year exams I had made up my mind. Mary was surprised when I told her – I wanted to become a doctor.

The subject Biology was the initial spark for me; I loved studying the organs of the human body and the pathophysiology that followed their breakdown, from the effects of disease and so on. During the summer months I had worked as a nursing assistant and found that I thoroughly enjoyed looking after people. I wanted to be able to alleviate pain and suffering. Of course Mary was immediately supportive, as I knew she would be.

'Why not, if that's what you want to be? Although you mightn't like the night duty and the weekend work!'

So I didn't return to Trinity for a second year. Instead I looked into what I needed to get into medical school. Science was the primary requirement, Biology, Chemistry and Physics. I had never heard of Chemistry or Physics, but I had done Biology for my Leaving Certificate. The only place on offer was the Institute of Education in Leeson Street, just off Stephen's Green. They had an advertisement in *The Irish Times*, stating that anyone interested in attending should contact the principal, Raymond Kearns. It cost a lot for tuition there so we weren't sure if we could afford the fees. But it didn't cost anything to go along and ask.

So I took myself off to the Institute and met a man on my way into the building.

'Excuse me, sir, would you know where I could find Mr Raymond Kearns?'

He smiled at me.

'I am he. How can I help?'

He brought me into his office and we had a chat.

'You're certainly not typical of the students we get here. Tell me a bit more about yourself.'

I gave him a summary of my background, telling him I had been reared in an industrial school, but I didn't mention the abuse. Instead I told him I had ended up in prison, but had been fortunate enough to meet a woman, Mary, whose belief in me had helped me do the Leaving Certificate and obtain a place in Trinity College. He marvelled at my resolve and the journey I had made academically.

'Tell you what, Michael, you can start at the beginning of September and what's more I'm going to suspend any payment of fees for the duration. Gosh, wouldn't it be wonderful if you did become a doctor?'

I didn't let him down and, in June, achieved very high marks in my exams, making me eligible for an interview for Medical School. Neither Mary nor I could contain our excitement at the prospect. I can never thank Mr Kearns enough for the chance that he gave me.

Marriage, 1980

AFTER SEVEN YEARS of living together we decided to get married. I had been somewhat reluctant, being afraid of commitment. At the back of my mind I feared that tying the knot might change things between me and Mary, but I needn't have worried. We decided that we'd rather get married in the registry office in Kildare Street. Mary's side of the family would be well represented, but what about mine? Mary suggested that I go to Crumlin and invite my mother. I hadn't had any contact with any of the family since 1973 and wasn't that keen on reopening old wounds. Mary was insistent, however, so I agreed, but insisted in turn that she come with me.

So we knocked on the door of the house in Crumlin. The door was opened by Aunt Josie who was surprised to see me. I introduced her to Mary and she invited us in. Uncle Paddy took a great shine to my Mary and seemed pleased that I had found someone who could make me happy. All my relatives were invited to the wedding. When I asked about inviting my mother, Miriam told me not to worry.

'Me and Catherine will look after her. It'll be fine.'

Mammy no longer lived in Kevin Street; she had moved to a three-roomed flat in York Street. I rang to ask if we could visit and she was delighted. When we arrived I was relieved to find her looking well, she had put on weight and was sporting new teeth and wig. The flat was spotless. She took great pride in the fact it was so bright and spacious, showing off how she had her own bathroom and slept in a big double bed. Her pride and joy was the colour television that stood in the corner of her living room. She had prepared a lovely tea for us and proved herself a friendly, chatty hostess. I was surprised to notice a few holy pictures around the flat, plus a set of white rosary beads sitting on her bedside table. She had never struck me as a religious person. All her fire and awkward behaviour must have faded away with the years. I sensed some sadness under her chattiness; I suppose she was just getting old.

My family were not particularly happy that the wedding ceremony was taking place in a registry office. They would have preferred if it was in a church, but we did not want that. Josie, Paddy and my Aunt Kate chose not to attend the short ceremony in Kildare Street; instead they met us afterwards at the wedding reception in the Clarence Hotel on the quays.

We hired a pony and trap to bring Mary to the registry office. She looked beautiful on the day and I had no second thoughts despite the knots in my stomach. We drove down Grafton Street in the horse-drawn trap with people waving at us. My only concern was how often the horse might shit on its way to the reception. Both my sisters kept a close eye on Mammy and she behaved very well. We danced together a few times in the course of the evening, but I knew things would never be the same between us and I think she felt it herself. She tried to rake up the incident where she had me arrested, but I just whispered in her ear that after the honeymoon I would come and see her. I think that meant a lot to her. Perhaps, I felt, I owed her that much. Nevertheless I made sure that I never visited her on my own. We took a lot of pictures that day and the one Mammy liked best was a picture taken in Stephen's Green – her with her three children and her new daughter-in-law.

Applying to Medical School

THE TIME HAD come to have my big interview for medical school. I waited nervously outside the interviewer's office, surprised to discover that I was the only candidate that morning. When I was called in there was only one gentleman sitting at a desk; he didn't bother to shake hands with me. I immediately felt this was a bad sign. He remained seated behind his desk, made little eye contact and seemed uncomfortable as he played with the papers in his hand.

'Well, Mr Clemenger, I'm just going through your application. You seemed to have done well in your Leaving Certificate, particularly getting an A in honours Chemistry.'

Somehow I just knew there was a 'but' coming.

'But you haven't given us much information about your background, have you?'

Before I could answer he came out with what was really on his mind.

'Tell me, Mr Clemenger, who is your father?'

The question threw me completely and my mind started to race.

Should I tell him the truth or lie? After all, my father could be dead. No, why should I lie? I have nothing to be ashamed about.

'Well, sir, I don't know the answer to that question.'

'What? Surely it's a simple enough question to answer?'

'That's just it, sir, it's not. I can't say who my father is because I never met him.'

He sighed heavily.

'So, you have no father?'

'No, sir.'

'Hmm. Tell me then, Mr Clemenger, why do you want to become a doctor?'

'I would like to help people, sir.'

'But surely you could help people by being a bus conductor.'

I think I knew then that it was all over for me.

'You know, Mr Clemenger, our students usually have some member of their family – for example, their father or uncle – who is already in medicine. Do you have any such family member?'

'No, sir, I don't. Why should I have to have such a family member? Does that mean only sons of doctors can become doctors?'

'Not necessarily, but it helps enormously.'

There was no denying it; my dream of becoming a doctor was dead. Struggling to control my growing distress I wondered if I should just leave. There seemed

339

little point in staying. Sensing that I wanted to go, the man leant towards me and uttered the words that continue to haunt me to this day:

'Young man, you were born on the wrong side of the tracks, don't aspire above your station in life.'

My old rage erupted instantly, out of nowhere. Without thinking I stretched across his desk and gave him a slap across the face. He fell back into the chair while I jumped up and started calling him the worst things I could think of.

Hearing the commotion his secretary ran in.

'Shall I call the guards?'

I answered her.

'Please do, I'll be more than happy to tell them what this man has just said to me. So, yes, by all means call them.'

'No! No! Don't call them.'

He was still slumped in his chair. My rage gone, I collected myself together and stood up.

'I'm sure that this isn't the first time you've said something like this to an applicant. You should be ashamed of yourself.'

With that I left. It was a long time before I admitted to Mary that I hit the man. I did science in Trinity College, but I didn't finish out the year. My heart just wasn't in it and by now my mind was consumed by the meaning behind the man's words. They echoed Father O'Neill's when he told me I could never be a priest. That was back in 1966, and I was still hearing them all these years later. My background still mattered after all.

Being rejected for medicine in the 1980s was every bit as devastating as being found unsuitable for the priesthood back in the 1960s. Both decisions were based on prejudice. Being a 'bastard' and being 'born on the wrong side of the tracks' seemed to me to be the two sides of the same coin of prejudice. I seemed to attract labels whose weight seemed at times to suck the fight out of me. Perhaps that is why they were applied in the first place. Typical labels included 'orphan', 'Monoboy', 'bastard' and – the newest one – being 'born on the wrong side of the tracks'; labels were used to denigrate me and keep me from aspiring above my 'station' in life.

But I was a fighter and I resolved to find a way out of the oppressiveness and disappointment. I refused to see myself as a victim, nor did I feel sorry for myself.

Initially, I withdrew into myself and sought comfort from my closest friends – books. Mary kept my spirits up. Her view was that holidays were a great way of getting over disappointment. She made sure that we went on holidays regularly to such places as the USA, Germany, France, Spain and so on. She was fond of saying, 'Travel broadens the mind and lifts the spirit.'

I had gathered a large volume of books for my library. The lives of world leaders such as Richard Nixon, Chairman Mao, Gandhi, Hitler and Stalin fascinated me. The lives of Hitler and Stalin in particular intrigued me.

I read and reread many times studies of these infamous murderers and the path they took in the destruction of whole classes of people. It was not lost on me that Hitler had actually been born a Catholic and that Stalin as a younger man wanted to be a priest. Sigmund Freud became my other great hero and I wondered what kind of psychoanalytic sessions he would have had with these gentlemen.

All the while I worked as a nursing assistant in Dublin Hospitals. I only went through the motions of work at one level while always observing my 'betters'.

A Career At Last

IN THE EARLY eighties I came to the realisation that if I was to survive we would have to emigrate to England. This presented no problem to Mary.

Friends of ours at a party, in – of all places – Grangegorman, first suggested that I would make a fine psychiatric nurse. I had a reputation for being a very good listener and people frequently sought me out to discuss their problems. The idea appealed to me. Following a successful interview I was accepted for training as a psychiatric nurse in Surrey. England was good to me and I will always be grateful to her. In its vast population of 56 million, there was none of the prejudice that I had encountered at home. One's background was less of an issue. What contribution you could make to the country was far more important. I enjoyed the freedom to think, to want to aspire and to achieve. If you had the ability you could go as far as you liked. The dominance of a Catholic perspective on life and its rigidity in terms of a sexual moral code was completely absent. There were no restrictions on the right to think agnostically and I was free to indulge in the process of intellectualisation. Over the next three years I passed my examinations, eventually graduating, in November 1989. During the graduation ceremony I couldn't help thinking that this would never have happened in the Ireland of this time.

I always endeavoured to treat every patient as a reflection of myself. How would I like to be treated? This was my motto. I was a fierce defender of the rights of patients and many a time my views ran counter to the stridency of psychiatrists that I had to deal with. However, I found that through persuasive argument it was possible to ease the misery of those that I came into contact with.

I also had the opportunity, from time to time, to be involved in cases of sexual abuse and attempted suicide. Tactfully I used my own experiences to help alleviate the 'psychic pain' of patients entrusted to my care. It was this ability, to be able to compartmentalise my own pain and rejection, which enabled me to become part of a specialist team that dealt primarily with these types of patients. Some of them were from Ireland but the majority were English. It was depressing to discover that 'child abuse' was a worldwide phenomenon.

One of the psychiatrists I worked with actually specialised primarily in this field. He liked to have me sit in on some of his sessions. I never ever gave him a hint that I had any personal experience of abuse and whether he ever suspected I had, I never knew. Yet he did comment on occasion that I had an uncanny insight of always asking the right question or making the appropriate response when patients were in deep psychological distress. What I learned from these sessions was the limitations of the counselling process. The patients came in with an imaginary black bag over their shoulder. When sitting comfortably they would reach into the bag and take out the topic 'sexual abuse'. For the next forty-five minutes they could give free rein to their emotions, which ranged from anger, helplessness and rage – along with utter despair over the fact that people didn't believe them. Some days I found it hard to hold it together, such was the degree of similarity of their cases to mine.

The patient experienced a degree of relief in being able to relate his or her experience in a safe therapeutic environment and be fortified by the reassurance, comfort and belief on the part of the team. The problem that arose for me was that there was no 'closure' for them. Once the session was over the patient would put their problem topic, 'child abuse', back into the imaginary black bag, place it over their shoulder and leave. Every session began and ended in the same way. The patient wasn't healed and therefore could never be free of the psychiatric manifestations that necessitated their hospitalisation, often for many years.

It was this inability to 'let go' of their memories that was the problem. 'Letting go' requires that something else fills the void in their lives. I believe it's this tyranny of memories in the dead of night that ultimately triggers acute breakdowns. How can one control the intrusive thoughts, the constant replaying of the savagery of the violation? That was the real reason why I never availed of this service myself. I had to find my own way to peace of mind. I devised my own way for coping with my abuse experience.

Certain factors had to be faced before I could get a handle on my emotions:

I refused to see myself as a victim,

I avoided too much introspection and analysis,

I refused to believe it was something I had done that caused the sexual abuse to occur in the first place,

I refused to feel sorry for myself,

I refused to be bound by other people's opinion of me,

I refused to hide behind the mask of depression or other labels,

I refused to let my past dominate my horizon,

I refused to entertain ideas of revenge or apologise for my existence,

I refused to allow other people to place limitations on my dreams.

Rather:

I saw myself as a survivor,

I developed hobbies and interests, which meant less time for navel gazing,

I would come to terms with events outside my control and concentrate instead on those things that would make life better,

I would accept that there would be bad days,

I would educate my way to freedom,

I would plug into the generosity of those who wanted to help me along the way,

I would invest myself in my emotional life with my wife and become less occupied with 'if only',

I would try my utmost to be optimistic,

I would always, *always* try to follow my dreams.

However, I do accept that many have found counselling beneficial. Everybody's experience of violation of their person is different. For me scabs that are continually picked at never heal. Healing would only come through forgiveness. Unfortunately many victims of child abuse lack the ability to forgive their abusers and so the tears flow on.

Mammy Once More

IN 1992, I had exchanged psychiatric nursing for a four-year course in Applied Human Physiology, which is the study of how the human body functions. My interest in medicine had not waned in the intervening years. I completed the honours degree in 1996, by which time Mary and I longed to come home to Ireland. We had only planned to stay in England for five years, but had been delayed by my completing my degree. So we returned to Ireland, quickly found work and settled down to enjoy our middle years. We had no children of our own and so took great delight in the growing families of Mary's sisters and later her brother.

A couple of years later I answered the phone one night, in the first week of November. It was a relative of my sister-in-law enquiring if I knew a Mary Clemenger who had died on 1 November 2001 – which was my birthday – and if she was related to me. She had read the death notice in that evening's *Evening Herald*. The shock of that enquiry lives with me still.

Luckily I had Mary to comfort and support me. She took immediate control of the situation and gathered her sisters and brother in force to support me for the funeral that was to take place the following morning. On the journey to Crumlin I couldn't get over the fact that Mammy had died on my birthday. I held tightly onto Mary's hand as we walked towards St Bernard's Church. We met Aunt Kate who seemed very surprised to see us.

'My God, Michael, I didn't know that you were back in Ireland.'

With tears flowing down her cheeks she told me that Aunt Josie, Uncles Michael, John and Paddy had all died over the last few years. Uncle Tim came to give us both a hug, expressing his sadness at Mammy's death. I really appreciated that.

Bracing myself I entered the church, hand in hand with Mary. There was an air of unreality about the whole situation. A magnificent brown coffin sat in front of the altar, with a photograph of Mammy on top. There were a few people in the Church; some smiled at me as I made my way to the seats beside the coffin, on the left side of the church. It took a few moments for me to realise that my two sisters were sitting on the opposite side, in the front pews. They were both crying and being consoled by my two nephews, who wouldn't have known who I was. *Should I go over to them, or not?* I wondered. I decided not to, as they looked far too upset to talk.

Then the bell rang to announce the commencement

of the Mass. The priest asked for prayers for the deceased, imploring that God would give both daughters of Mrs Clemenger the strength and fortitude to cope with their sad loss at this most difficult time. Mary grasped my hand tightly. Perhaps it was understandable that I had been forgotten. Aunt Kate beckoned to me to join my sisters, but I feared that it was too late to move, once the Mass had started. Besides, when all was said and done, I was with my real family now. Mary had been by my side through the long lonely years when there was nobody else around and a funeral couldn't change that now.

The priest gave a moving homily about Mammy. I couldn't help thinking of the parish priest who took me away from Crumlin in November 1950. Would he be aghast at the lovely words being said by his colleague over the remains of my mother. It always amazes me how people, no matter how bad a life they lead, in the eye of others, are lavished with respectability through the lid of their coffin.

During the communion my sister Miriam's eyes met mine for a moment. She looked so sad and I could see that she wanted to come over to me, but found that she just couldn't. My sister Catherine was too overcome with grief to know where she was and needed the constant support of her sons to keep her upright. I waited my turn before I made my way towards the priest with Mary close in attendance. When I faltered

Mary touched my shoulder, giving me the strength that I needed. As I received the Holy Communion the tears flowed down my cheeks, which seemed to surprise the priest.

When the prayers for the dead were being said, at the end of the Mass, a loud wailing came from the direction of my sisters. They were crying for their mother but what they didn't realise was that I had been crying for her all my life. I felt their pain but I don't think they had, or could have had, any appreciation of mine. In their misery they were unable to share their mother with me. When the coffin was being wheeled out of the church both of them were in such a state of emotional turmoil that they had to be helped down the aisle. Feeling the outsider I stayed in my seat until nearly all the congregation had left.

Instinctively I approached the priest and thanked him for his wonderful homily.

'Oh, but I didn't know that Mary had a son. As far as I knew she only had two daughters. Why didn't I know?'

He was embarrassed and confused.

'That's all right, Father, perhaps it was less complicated this way.'

'I'm sure you're right.'

When Mary and I stepped outside, strangers came over to commiserate with me on the death of my mother. It was very gratifying that people recognised that Mary Clemenger was my mother.

At the very last minute I decided against going to the graveyard for the burial. I think I felt that my sisters would prefer me not to be there. I guess it was understandable, under the circumstances. There was nobody near the hearse. It started to rain heavily as I walked over to it. I saw my sisters in a car to my right. Once again I wondered should I go over to them. Instead I went to the back of the hearse to say a little prayer and give Mammy one last symbolic hug. So much sadness in her life, and for what? To have it all end in this way.

How I would have loved the opportunity to touch her face somehow, to let her know that I was there for her in death. Perhaps if there really was a Heaven, she already knew. It was calming to just lean there against the glass, with the rain tapping against us. At that moment I very much wanted to believe in a God, if only to make sense of the sadness that she must have endured in the stillness of the night.

Good night, dear mother, take care, love from your son, Michael.

The touch of my wife's hand on my arm brought me back to myself; she was holding an umbrella over me.

'Come away, love, you'll get wet.'

Going towards my car we passed Aunt Kate who asked if I was going to the graveyard.

'No, I don't think so; I've said my goodbyes to her. I just don't think it would be right.'

'Perhaps not, son. That's it then, Michael.'

'I guess so.'

'At least you got to say goodbye. That's something. God bless, Michael. Stay in touch.'

I got into my car with Mary, tears streaming down my cheeks. We passed the hearse as we moved out of the church grounds. I dared not look back.

Images of my uncles Paddy and John flashed through my mind, and I said a silent prayer for them. Their support, warm embrace and absolute acceptance of me had touched me more than they could know.

The rain crashed down hard against the roof of the car as we drove through what should have been the familiar streets of my childhood.

I stared out the car window, remembering all those cold, wet nights I had been obliged to spend outside, in a park or in a doorway. I was alone then, but not anymore. I was suddenly overwhelmed with a new appreciation for the role that Mary had played in my life. I would never have made it through the long and difficult years without her. She is the real hero of this book. She dragged me through the low points and celebrated all my successes with gusto. She kept me focussed on the here and now, refusing to let me dwell in the past. Jim Sheridan was right after all – you could go a long way with just a positive attitude. Learning about the deaths of my uncles and Aunt Josie reminded me that I too was getting old. Therefore I intended to enjoy and always remember to appreciate what I had with Mary. As the traffic lights changed from red to green I sent up a little word of thanks for the life I was leading now, against all those odds.

Afterword

THIS BOOK WAS never intended to be written. But then everything changed in 1996, when my wife and I returned from the UK, to live in Ireland.

Gradually I began to notice small items in the Irish media about the widespread sexual abuse of children by priests and Christian Brothers. Resolutely I blocked my eyes and ears, doing my best to ignore them. Then, in April 1999, I opened the newspaper to see a photograph of St Joseph's Industrial School, in Tralee, alongside a small photo of what looked to me to be 'the murderer', as we had called him, Brother Lane. It stopped me full in my tracks. It couldn't really be him, could it? It was. I studied the face for a long time in my back garden and as I did my repressed memories began to rise slowly, from wherever I had put them. My hands shook as I continued to read the article. Brother Z was also in the dock with Lane, on charges of physical and sexual abuse.

What upset me most, however, was the jeering of the angry mob that stood outside the court. Where were these brave men and women back in the fifties and sixties, when their voices would have made a big difference? How many of them, if any at all, were past pupils?

In May 1999, the then Taoiseach, Bertie Ahern, made a fulsome apology to all abuse victims, including the pupils of all the industrial schools in Ireland. This public apology began to stir up resentment in me. I found myself vividly reliving the memories long since hidden behind a mask of respectability and normality. They gave me no peace, holding me prisoner to the past.

Matters came to a head when I read a series of books by other men detailing their sexual and physical abuse. Their stories contained many similarities to mine.

- *Fear of the Collar* by Patrick Touher
- *Founded on Fear* by Peter Tyrrell
- *In Harm's Way* by Sean Hogan

These three books made a deep impression on me and drove me almost to breaking point. The memories which I had spent over forty-five years suppressing, into the deepest recesses of my mind, broke free of their chains and began to torture me night and day. After watching Mary Raftery's RTÉ documentary on industrial schools (*States of Fear*, 2003) I became dependent on anti-depressants. I had gone from a happy-go-lucky, optimistic person to the simmering volcano that had first come to light in Father O'Neill's room on 1 November 1966. How I hated not being in control. I realised I had been living a lie to myself for years, silently enduring the pain that I had internalised and couldn't speak about. Compartmentalising painful memories works only for a while. This means that one is always at the mercy of events. Accordingly I felt exposed by the number of cases that were being reported daily. Eventually I reached a point where I was afraid to sleep at night because I would be transported back in time, via my dreams, to relive all the fear and pain again.

I found it difficult to listen to well-meaning people ringing into the likes of Joe Duffy's *Liveline* radio show and going on and on and on about *their* shock, *their* disgust, *their* opinion. In fact it sickened me and did absolutely nothing to alleviate the torturous re-runs of the memories that I fought so hard to keep at bay. A turning point was overhearing a work colleague furiously exclaim that all these child abuse stories were just an attempt by communist agitators and agnostics to tear down the Catholic Church. I was shocked to the core.

'Have you ever met any victims?'

'No, of course not, and I'm sure that there aren't as many as we're being led to believe.'

'Well, today is your lucky day because you're looking at one.'

Her face fell.

'But how, Michael? You look so normal.'

Over the while I began to tell one or two friends my story. It's funny how people react. There is this sense of belief that a victim of child abuse must be very different from the rest of the human race.

I became convinced that I should write this book not only as a cathartic process, but also to honour all those boys who had passed through the gates of St Joseph's Industrial School in Tralee. Many of them, I am sure, were unfit for the vicissitudes of life outside those walls, slipping quietly into lonely mediocrity never to be heard of again. Many died filled with rage, unable to form close physical relationships with the opposite sex, have families of their own or find fulfilment in their lives.

As I began to write it all down I came to realise that St Joseph's was only half my story. I was also compelled to describe the search for and subsequent discovery of my mother and her family, and the unexpected after-math. This notion had always lurked in the back of my mind. And though it was to prove a chaotic relationship I don't have any regrets about it. Consequently I was able to discard the label 'orphan' that had consigned me to the dark shadows as something bad or a product of sin. Now I was a 'somebody' with origins. This was a source of great comfort to me.

The fact that I was born 'on the wrong side of the tracks' shouldn't have barred me from reaching for the stars. I belonged to this world. I had the right to form and pursue my dreams. The fact that I didn't attain them is a testimony to the short-sightedness of those who should have known better. Let history be their judge.

However, I did manage to educate myself to third-level, practise as a psychiatric nurse and later as a lecturer in biological sciences. I am now retired and enjoy golf, reading and world travel with my wife, Mary.

Finally, I take full responsibility for the opinions I express in this book. It reflects events as I experienced them. I am sure there are many other views of these events and people I describe. It's for them to write their own story.

'You Were Not Destined To Grow Old'

By Michael Clemenger

I pass your picture on the wall
Your eyes that showed promise,
Your jaw bestowed with firmness
And yet your flowering was cut down by a weed
Uncalled for brutality took you
And instilled in me a fear of the dark

You had no time to say goodbye
I had no time to weep
You lie forever young in the cold clay
I sit awhile beside your grave
And ponder the possibilities

Fifty years have since gone by and still I see your
    picture on the wall
You are caught forever, young full of promise
I don't think you would mind at all
Full turn the circle of time
Sleep well friend
Away from the crown of thorns

I never got to say hello, but I honour you in saying
    goodbye
Old age would not have suited you
With all its pains and disappointments
Sleep well, comrade on the wall
You were too good a flower struck down by a weed

*In memory of Joseph Pyke, 1941–1958, who met his death in
St Joseph's Industrial School, Tralee, Co. Kerry in 1958*

Appendices

My Thoughts On The Redress Board

IN MY VIEW, the Redress Board was one of the greatest disappointments for the victims of child sexual abuse. Following an apology in May 1999 by the then Taoiseach Mr Bertie Ahern, the Redress Board was set up by the Government to help redress the injustices inflicted upon the thousands of victims of child abuse. It was generally acknowledged that both physical and sexual abuse had occurred to children while in the care of various religious orders that had been financed by the state.

The impression was given that – at long, long last – victims could go before the Redress Board, tell their stories and be believed. There would be no adversarial system as would be expected in a criminal court case, and after careful consideration of the extent of pain suffered, victims would be somewhat compensated financially. For many victims, however, it was never about the money. Their consolation would be derived from the outing of the gruesome details of their abuse.

It soon emerged that the victims were deceived. The

reality bore no relationship to the pious platitudes that heralded the introduction of the Redress Board. It seemed to some victims that the Redress Board itself was the new abuser, with little empathy for the broken men and women that appeared in front of them. Victims felt that they were perceived in terms of percentages. The impersonal style of the interviews caused a great deal more pain that only compounded the victim's sense of utter betrayal. The Redress Board tried to justify their stance, saying that it was the only way they could operate in such a sea of misery: they had to remain aloof and think in terms of percentages primarily and just get through as many cases presenting to them.

The vast sums of money made by the lawyers representing the victims were conveniently ignored. Politicians of all persuasions kept quiet throughout this whole savage process of degradation, salvaging their collective conscience with the delusional belief that the Redress Board would do right by the victims. They conveniently allowed themselves to be fooled while ignoring the protests by victims that were ongoing outside Dáil Éireann. Most particularly they studiously ignored the repeated rape of the minds of victims forced to remember, relive and prove the gruesome details, which, after all these years, were locked deep within the recesses of their minds. Though they wanted and needed to tell their stories, the way in which they had to tell them, and the need to provide minute details, often proved difficult and traumatic. Into such infested waters I tentatively dipped my toe when I applied to that august body for Redress, in 2002.

From the first moment I made contact with the Christian Brothers, via my solicitor Mr Harry Hunt, who tirelessly helped me prepare for the Redress Board meeting, I experienced the full onslaught of their attacks. They rubbished my allegations of physical or sexual abuse as bizarre fabrications, unworthy of credence. Vehemently they repudiated all allegations of sexual abuse by Christian Brothers as lies, claiming that all abusers I named, in my statements, had either died in good standing or had left the order with the highest commendations. In fact one Christian Brother, in his written response to the Board, accused me of being an abuser myself.

One evening, a few days prior to my appearance before the Redress Board, I was reading my newspaper. A man who had been in Artane Industrial School in the 1950s was currently on hunger strike outside Dáil Éireann. It sent shivers through me when I read that he was protesting, not about his experience in the school, but about how he was treated by the Redress Board. I went to see him outside Dáil Éireann and was moved by his resolve to die outside the Dáil so as to alert the public about what was really going on. With my background in healthcare and science I was concerned that this man, who hadn't eaten since the previous week, would do serious damage to his health. I told him that I was going before the Redress Board the following Friday.

'Be careful with that lot. It's all a publicity stunt by the Government to get the people off their backs.'

At that moment I was fearful about the Redress Board because I knew that I had the resolve to join the hunger striker if push came to shove. I first met my barrister, who accompanied my solicitor, an hour before the formal meeting with the Redress Board the following Friday. He commented that I looked nervous. He also made it clear to me that I was in for a hard time if I went before the Board in the adjoining room. The questioning would be hostile and there would be nothing he could do to protect me. By way of illustration he spent the next half hour going through the details of my story with a degree of hostility, as if he didn't believe one word of the charges I had made against my abusers.

'I must warn you, Mr Clemenger, I've only given you a taste of what to expect. There is an alternative solution; the Board have all your details and supportive evidence to enable them to reach a financial settlement without you having to meet them face to face.'

My wife Mary encouraged me to settle as she believed facing the Redress Board would be too upsetting for me. I never argued when Mary made up her mind. So, with some reluctance, I agreed to settle.

There was a Report prepared for the Minister for Education and Science in January 2002 called 'Towards

Redress and Recovery'. On page 63 of this report was the following statement:

First the 'injuries' received by a number of victims are among the most serious kinds of personal injury known to the law: many survivors not only 'lost' their childhood, but much of their adulthood as well.

To cut a long report short, after reviewing a load of research on the topic around the world, the injuries were categorised. These categories included sexual abuse, physical abuse, emotional abuse and neglect. Each injury was then accorded a numbered weighting and matched to a sum of money, up an absolute maximum of €300,000.

Back and forth the parties haggled about percentages in the room next door. The conversation was conducted clinically; 40 per cent to 43 per cent was the percentage category margin that my years of physical and sexual abuse fell into. The bargaining was like something out of a horse fair. Trading my entire childhood for percentages was most distasteful, but it was the only realistic option on the table that day.

I had to waive my right to take an action against any public body within the meaning of the Redress Board Act or against any person who had made a contribution under the said Act. Mary and I left the Redress Board with mixed feelings. She persuaded me that I had done the right thing in settling, while I felt that I had been robbed of the chance to tell my story. Mary acts from the head while I act from the heart. In this situation she was probably right.

I visited the hunger striker over the next few days. As his health deteriorated further some kind of accommodation was reached with the Redress Board, much to the relief, I'm sure, of all the politicians in Leinster House. Consequently he discontinued his fast. The brave man had made his point emphasising that it was never about the money, it was the fact that the paltry payment confirmed his belief that the Redress Board didn't believe the extent of his physical and sexual abuse.

The Ryan Report

THE EASTER RISING of 1916 paved the way for the overthrow of the British presence in Ireland. However, it was soon replaced by a home-grown, secretive and repressive regime called the Irish Catholic Church. Under Eamon de Valera's 1937 constitution, the special position of the Catholic Church was enshrined in law. Over the subsequent half century the Catholic Church hierarchy, with the passive connivance of successive governments, presided over the most shameful chapter in the history of the state.

The Ryan Report of May 2009 exposed the dark, pitiless side of the Catholic Church. Its unbridled corruption stemmed from the exercise of absolute power by an institution so arrogant that it believed that it was answerable only to God. The manifestation of their conceit was vividly displayed in the row over the 'Mother and Child Scheme', in 1951, between the then Minister for Health Dr Noel Browne and the most feared member of Ireland's Catholic hierarchy, Dr John Charles McQuaid. Dr Noel Browne had tried to improve social services for the people but McQuaid, mistrustful of the

Minister's motives, intervened. This bloody-minded interference, coupled with appropriate pressure applied to political parties, Fianna Fáil and Fine Gael, ensured the bill's defeat. And so ended the political career of one of the foremost political talents of his generation.

Consequently, social development in Ireland lagged behind the rest of Europe for many years. From the 1920s to the 1970s this country was one of the most conservative in Western Europe, taking instruction from Rome via the Irish Bishops.

When we speak about education today, there is still a widely held view that we owe a profound debt of gratitude to the religious orders involved. Singled out for particular praise in many quarters are the Christian Brothers. However, the lack of a secular education system led to the Church being responsible for the education, and at times the welfare, of the nation's children. These children came from disparate backgrounds, but it's unlikely that the children of the middle classes ever set foot inside the Church's grim industrial schools or orphanages.

Many of the inmates of these institutions found themselves incarcerated through no fault of their own. Some had been born illegitimate, while others were products of broken homes. There were also problem children, those who 'mitched' from school, or who were obliged to resort to crime in order to survive and feed their family after the death of a parent. What all these children had in common, however, was that they represented the seedier side of life, and if left to roam wild they could disrupt the tranquillity of middle-class suburbia. The middle classes were thus more than happy to see these children taken off the streets and placed in institutions of relative safety. The religious would take care of them and in time reintegrate them back into a society as useful productive members.

Instead these children became lost from society. Being out of sight and mind they became vulnerable to unscrupulous religious men and women. With the tacit approval of the Church and State there began a reign of unbridled terror against thousands of these defenceless unfortunates. Meanwhile, beyond the walls of these institutions, the rest of Ireland behaved like the three monkeys, in that they saw no evil, heard no evil and spoke no evil. Like Pontius Pilate they washed their hands of any responsibility, oblivious to the rumours of physical and sexual abuse. Subsequently there was no one to rescue the children from the individual sadistic savages who hid behind the respectable guise of religion.

The Ryan Report's greatest contribution to these lost children is to validate their stories about the years of horrific abuse, the cold and hunger and the lack of education that had to be endured in silence. Furthermore, the Ryan Report described the ritualistic humiliation and repression of the human spirit, in children already handicapped by their low social status. The report also highlights and emphasises what society knew, but studiously avoided – the systematic, secretive system of human degradation, misery and the stripping of humanity on a scale hardly imaginable. All sectors of society are condemned for closing their eyes to the evidence paraded before them – the government, the police, the judges, the doctors and the teachers. Had they listened, had they cared at all, much misery could have been avoided. Our greatest sin, in Ireland, was possibly the degree of deference given to the Catholic Church. The professional classes had all benefited and owed their place in society to the education they had received from religious orders.

A major question posed by the Ryan Report relates to the Department of Education regarding their inaction during these years. It would seem that the school inspectors, sent out by the Department, never ventured beyond the fine parlours of the religious houses where they were entertained to high tea and cake. There is little evidence that school inspectors ever spoke to the children. Furthermore, the nuns, Brothers and priests always knew about a visit well in advance, giving them plenty of time to make their preparations. The fact that many of the school inspectors didn't ask the right questions, nor express a desire to see and talk to individual children, is a terrible shame.

According to the Ryan Report, more complaints were received against the Christian Brothers than any other named religious institution. The Brothers were cited as being most reluctant to co-operate and resisted the Commission to iÉnquire into child abuse at every turn, in order to protect its members – whether they were former, still living in their community or deceased – despite the mounting accusations made against them. They endeavoured to delay the work of the Commission by taking judicial proceedings, claiming that criminal action against named members shouldn't proceed due to the lapse of time.

Allegations of physical violence in Artane Industrial School were known to the Department of Education and the Catholic hierarchy as early as the 1950s. The Micky Martin case is a fine example. During his residence in Artane, in 1953, Mr Martin, now deceased, had his arm broken by a Christian Brother. His father reported the incident to the Department of Education and his case was discussed in Dáil Éireann. Nevertheless, despite calls for a public enquiry, no action was taken. In 1961 the Archbishop of Dublin, Dr John Charles McQuaid, asked the resident chaplain of Artane's industrial school, Father Henry Moore, to furnish a report on conditions in Artane. Because the findings were so damaging, however, the report was withheld. Its contents were only disclosed in August 2007, by the present Archbishop of Dublin, Dr Diarmuid Martin, much to the consternation of the Christian Brothers, who expressed outrage at its publication.

In October 1996, both Church and State were well represented at ceremonies in the Vatican, for the beatification of Edmund Ignatius Rice, the founder of the Christian Brothers. During his homily Dr Cathal B. Daly was profuse in his praise for the Brothers and their heroic efforts regarding the education of several generations of children in Ireland. Dr Daly criticised the media's distortion of the image of the Christian Brothers. The media, he contended, were trying to smear a fine religious order while conveniently ignoring their valiant contribution to the Irish educational system. Not surprisingly, no reference was made to any impropriety on the part of that august body towards children.

As a result of their dealings with the Commission to inquire into child abuse, the Ryan Report is emphatic that the Christian Brothers made false, misleading statements and callously challenged the accusations of abuse, thereby increasing the victims' pain. The biggest regret of their victims was the order's victory in the courts, which prevented the disclosure of the names of the abusers, living or dead, and whether they had been previously convicted of sexual abuse against children in the criminal courts. Having taken this self-serving stance the Christian Brothers' subsequent profuse apologies, in my opinion, are not worth the paper they are written on.

The Ryan Report of 2009 has exposed the Catholic Church in Ireland; I wonder now, in light of these revelations, would one million people make their way to the

Phoenix Park if Pope Benedict XVI came to visit Ireland today?

Even as the numbers of religious dwindle and the seminaries close, the Catholic hierarchy has not come to terms with the reality of the inevitable. They issue apologies through gritted teeth, but survivors like me believe this has come far too late. There doesn't seem to be any real understanding of the extent of the damage done to the lives of many children. With their lack of education and inability to fit into the norms of society, many of these victims succumbed. Many lost the will to live, while thousands left Ireland never to return. As far as the thousands were concerned the crimes of the religious orders went unchecked by the Catholic hierarchy; they knew and said nothing. The Ryan Report condemns them. The survivors of child abuse condemn them. If they were honourable men and women they would dissolve themselves.

The midnight choir is gathered, the pall bearers are assembled, the candles are lit, the prayers for the dying are being said though the corpse is still resisting. The game is up, and it's time to leave the stage with as much dignity as possible. All that remains is for the survivors to turn out the lights. Cause of death in the pages of the Ryan Report is overdose of conceit and arrogance complicated by excessive abuse of power.

RIP.

Acknowledgements

I would like to thank the following people for their help and advice in the writing of this book:

Mary Clemenger, my wife, who encouraged me to write the book in the first place and for typing up the entire manuscript. I am grateful to Sean Conaty, my brother-in-law; to Michael O'Brien of The O'Brien Press for encouraging me to complete my story; to Nicola Pierce, my editor, for weeks of fine tuning my text; to Emma Byrne; to Ivan O'Brien and Helen Carr for their help; to Danny O'Brien for recent photographs; to the Clemenger, Conaty and Sheridan families, for sharing aspects of family life with me over the years; to Raymond Kearns for providing me with the opportunity to further my education; to the Governor of St Patrick's Institution (1969) for the considerable kindness shown to me while I was there, and to Dr T. Ryle Dwyer, journalist and historian, for all his help. Finally, I would like to thank Charlotte Cole and Susan Pegg from Ebury Press for their helpful advice on the new 2012 edition titled *Everybody Knew*.

About the Author

MICHAEL CLEMENGER was born in Dublin in 1950 and raised in orphanages, spending eight years in an industrial school in Tralee, Co. Kerry, where he was subjected to physical and sexual abuse. He has had a successful career, both as a psychiatric nurse and as a lecturer in biological sciences. He is now retired and enjoys golf, reading and world travel with his wife, Mary. This is his first book.